King of Ranleigh

F. S. Brereton

[ZHINGOORA BOOKS]

"CLIVE WAS DASHED BACKWARD WITH TERRIFIC VIOLENCE."

CONTENTS

CHAPTER I

THE CONSPIRATORS

Clive Darrell took from the pocket of a somewhat tattered coat, which bore many a stain and many a sign of hard wear, a filbert of good size, and having admired it in silence cracked the same by placing it upon a miniature anvil and giving it an adroit blow with a hammer. There was a precision about his movements and his action which spoke of practice. Clive was inordinately fond of nuts. His pockets bulged widely with them. As he ate he extracted a handful and presented some to each of his two comrades.

"Here, have a go. I've heaps to draw from. Well?"

"Well?" came from Hugh Seymour, a boy of his own age, just a little more than thirteen.

But Bert Seymour, brother to Hugh, made no answer. Taller than the other two, a year older than his brother, he was a weedy, lanky youth, running to height rather than to breadth. He had tossed his cap on to the bench, so that he presented a tousled head of hair, above a face thin like his frame, but ruddy enough, with keen penetrating eyes which wore a curiously dreamy aspect for such a youngster. He was cogitating deeply. That was evident. But being the prince of good fellows, one who made a point of returning hospitality, he rummaged also in his pocket, producing a medley of articles to be found nowhere else save in the case of a schoolboy. A piece of tangled string, half a broken hinge, a knife, a second knife, somewhat bigger and distinctly rusty, a length of galvanised wire which made one wonder if he were a jack-of-all-trades, three handkerchiefs, each more terrible in appearance than the last, a number of air-gun slugs, a broken box for the same, now empty and severely damaged, and lastly, that for which he searched, a respectably sized piece of toffee in a wrapping of paper which was broken at one corner, and through which a half-dozen slugs had contrived to insert themselves and were now nicely imbedded in the sweetmeat.

"Have some," he said laconically, handing over the packet to Clive.

"Fair does then. Thanks."

There was a strange taciturnity about these three lads. A silence and absence of words to which they were unaccustomed. But then, great events bring about equally great changes on occasion, and this day saw the trio face to face with a circumstance which baffled them, rendered them almost inarticulate, when they were accustomed to chatter, not seldom either in the lowest tones, and made of them a somewhat morose gathering.

Clive split the toffee into three equal-sized pieces with the aid of a huge pair of metal shears, distributed two of the pieces, and thrust the third into his mouth.

"Well?" he asked again, almost inarticulate since the sticky piece held his jaws so firmly. "We've got to move."

"Or funk."

"Or go on getting kicked."

"Not if I know it!" ejaculated Clive, with a distinct effort, tearing his two rows of shining teeth asunder. "Who's he? We've been here ages, and he has the cheek to order us about."

"Suppose he imagines we're going to fag for him," exclaimed Hugh, pulling his piece of toffee into the light of day as speech was otherwise almost out of the question. "He's a cad, this Rawlings. Vote we go for him."

"How?"

It was almost the first word which Bert had uttered. A keen glance shot from those dreamy eyes, searching the faces of his two comrades. He borrowed Clive's hammer and mechanically cracked the handful of nuts presented to him, preparing a store for consumption after the sweetmeat was finished. His dreamy eyes slowly travelled round his immediate surroundings, noting without enthusiasm the many tools and appliances which to boys as a general rule are the greatest of attractions. For Bert was no mechanic. At the precise period of which we write he was immersed in the intricacies of a calculation having for its object the purchase of sundry cricket stumps, bats and a ball with a sum raked together after noble self-sacrifice and still all too small for the purpose. He was, in fact, keen on cricket, and no dull hand at the game. Fair at the wicket, he could send down a ball at any time the varying length of which might be expected to baffle one who had not stood up to his bowling before. While at "point" he had already gathered laurels in the village matches, to which residence in the depths of the country confined him.

Mechanics distinctly bored Bert. He had no use for hammers, other than that of cracking nuts, and even then he managed to hammer his fingers fairly often. And there he differed from his brother, just as the latter differed from him in appearance. For Hugh was a rosy-cheeked fellow, short and active and strong, quick and brisk in his actions, and with eyes which sparkled and could never be accused of presenting a dreamy appearance. Always ready for cricket or football or any other game that might be suggested, and shining particularly in the gymnasium, there were two hobbies which absorbed his every waking thought, and contrived to make him Clive Darrell's boon companion. For both loved the wild things they saw about them. They were the terror of gamekeepers in all directions, and there was not a copse nor a cover for miles around which they had not visited in their search for nests. And the winter season found them both for hours together in this workshop, once the happy rendezvous of Clive's father. What wonder if they were enchanted with the place? Imagine a large room, with steeply sloping roof, in which were a couple of lights. A range of shelves down one side, each carrying planes or cramps or wood tools of some description. While against the farther wall stood a cabinet, glazed at the top, and presenting a range of calipers, micrometers, drills, gauges, taps and dies and what-not; while nests of drawers beneath contained every tool necessary for both wood and metal turning. That was the triumph of this workshop. A five-inch lathe stood against the far wall, the floor beneath stained with many a splotch of oil. A belt ran to it from a shaft overhead which travelled the length of the shop and was there fitted with a wheel of large diameter to which a second belt was attached. This latter travelled to the fast and loose pulleys of a second shaft, and thence to a petrol engine, which puffed and rattled at the moment.

Clive toyed with the lever which operated his pet lathe. As he and his comrades cogitated, he pushed the lever over, setting the shaft above in motion and the spindle of the lathe revolving. A chunk of brass bolted to the face-plate of this latter spun round at speed, while the tool he had fixed in position shaved a neat ribbon of metal from it. Then the lever swung back, the spindle of the lathe came to a rest, while the shaft above ceased to rotate, leaving the engine still running.

"I know. We'll make a trap for the ass. Catch him as they catch elephant and rhinoceros in Africa," he suddenly blurted out as he turned from the lathe. As for his hearers, they received his suggestion with scant sympathy.

"Trap! How? Where? Rot!" ejaculated Bert. "What's the good of trapping an idiot?—unless, of course, you mean setting a thing like a rabbit-trap. That'd fix him. Imagine the great and noble Rawlings, fresh from a public school, lord of all he beholds, caught by the toe and left singing!"

A wan smile wreathed his lips. Hugh giggled, and then looked serious. "A precious row we'd get into, too," he cried. "Try again, Clive. Don't talk rot; we're serious."

"So am I; we'll fix a trap for this bounder, a trap that'll not hurt him, you understand, but one that'll make him look a fool and an ass, and'll teach him not to interfere with his betters."

"Meaning us," grinned Bert.

"Of course! Who else? You don't imagine that an ass like that's on the same plane, do you?" demanded Clive loftily. "Now I'll tell you how we'll do it. There's the path down the spinney."

"Ah!" A frown crossed Bert's face. Hugh's ruddy cheeks grew redder. For that path happened to be the bone of contention which had brought about this meeting. But for that, Clive and Hugh and Bert would not have been gathered in the workshop on this fine morning, cracking sundry nuts upon a miniature anvil, and sucking sticky toffee. Bert, for instance, would have been down at the one single store which Potters Camp, their local village, boasted, where he would have painfully haggled for the stumps and other goods he coveted. Then Clive and Hugh would have been otherwise occupied. They had a big mechanical scheme on foot, no less an undertaking than the manufacture of a motor-car, a real motor-car to run upon the high-road. Morning and afternoon and evening they had been at it through these holidays. And the scheme was so very simple, and promised such certain success! To begin with, there was the petrol engine at that moment puffing and rumbling in the shop. The framework they had made was the precise thing for it. They had only to erect a species of crane above the engine and they could lift it into the frame and bolt it down. That was childishly easy. The rest was a triumph, or almost so, inasmuch as it was on the high-road to completion. For the front axle was already fitted. True, it was not quite up to modern form, since stub axles at either end were missing. But then necessity is the mother of invention, as Clive had told his chum often and often. That axle was bored at the very centre and swivelled about a pin bolted to the framework. As for springs, who wanted any!

"Tosh!" declared Clive.

"Meant for ladies and kids and invalids," said Hugh, equally emphatic.

"It'll shake about a bit, of course," admitted the former grudgingly. "I reckon she'll do a good twenty miles an hour, and on the awful apologies for roads round about here, why, naturally, she'll hop and bump no end. But who cares so long as she goes? Not me. Only those wheels look a bit rocky, eh?"

Hugh must have been an enthusiast, or else he would not have denied the obvious fact to which his fellow inventor had drawn his attention. For the wheels of this car-in-making were decidedly groggy, to use an expression common to this mechanical couple. But then again, necessity was here the mother of much inventive genius. Lack of funds could not cripple the enthusiasm and ambition of our two mechanics. Wheels they must have if they wished their car to run upon the road, while cash was decidedly lacking. But both had a bicycle the back wheel of each of which fitted with commendable niceness upon the spindle ends of the steel bar which Clive had used for a front axle, while the back axle and its wheels were supplied from the stable of no less a person than the Rev. James Seymour, the respected parent of Bert and Hugh, Rector of the parish, and owner of a tricycle.

"Fits rippingly! Just the thing!" commented Hugh, when he produced the article for Clive's approval. "Only it'd be a bit unlucky if the Governor wanted to trike just at this moment. Of course, he can't. Dare say he'd be ratty, but then, think of how he's helping. It's just the thing."

"Just!" Clive whetted his lips at the sight. The one great difficulty of this ambitious undertaking was conquered, and, of course, they were only borrowing the axle and wheels for a time. They'd have a run on the road and then bolt them back into position. No one'd be the wiser, certainly not Hugh's Governor. "But—just a trifle light for the job," he added. "Still, you never can tell till you try. But it'd be mighty awkward if there was a bust up. There'd be a ruction then."

Hugh had agreed to that point, and for a moment had repented his action. But then, think of being beaten just for the want of a little courage! After all, the wheels and axle of the tricycle might be the very thing. They certainly looked it. And the Rector had not ridden his machine for a month at least, and for all he knew might have discarded it altogether. In any case, the parts had been borrowed, and as the trio stood about the lathe Hugh's admiring eyes were upon it.

"Pity this cad's come along just now," he grumbled. "Everything's ready and fitted. A morning's work would drop the engine in and connect up the levers and the chain. That steering gear ain't too magnificent. But then, if one manages the engine and the other steers her, it'll be as right as anything. Hang this Rawlings!"

Others echoed the same malediction. For the Rawlings family were not popular in the neighbourhood of Potters Camp. In the first place, they were new-comers, and in the depths of the country that is sometimes a sufficient offence. Then they were purse-proud and apparently rich, and apt to patronise their country cousins. Mr. Rawlings was of decidedly pompous appearance. Very stout and heavy, he had a way of lifting a condescending stick when greeted by neighbours. And Albert, his son, was a shining copy. He looked down upon the village youths from a lofty pinnacle. He nodded, when he remembered to, to Hugh and Bert and Clive, though to the latter he was not always so gracious. For Clive had once been master where the pompous Rawlings now stepped. Once he and his people had lived in the big house at the top of the hill, with its acres of park land about it. But times had changed sadly. Perhaps his father had been too immersed in his workshop, and had given little attention to the more serious affairs of life. Whatever the reason, his riches had left him, and here was his widow, with her only son, living in a small house at the far corner of the park, and once occupied by a bailiff. From the said house a path led through a long spinney to the high-road, and made a short-cut for its inhabitants. Otherwise they must needs go a long way round to get to the village.

"And the cad forbids us to use it!" ejaculated Clive, as he recollected the occurrence. "Of course, the father's behind the business. He must be. But the son does the talking. A precious nice business."

"Here, you get off! This isn't yours. Just cut it!" Hugh deliberately mimicked the youth of whom they were talking. "A fine sort of fellow," he exclaimed. "So you'll set a trap for him, Clive?"

"Now. Without waiting. I'd fifty times rather stay along here and finish this job. Just think, this evening we'd be ready for running. We'd have a trial spin on our car, for there's certain to be things to adjust. But we'd have her running top hole before it got dark. Then we'd make a trip to London."

Hugh's eyes opened wide at the statement.

"It's seventy miles if it's an inch."

"Who cares? We can do it. But——"

"Eh?" asked Hugh, scenting another difficulty just at the moment when he felt confident that all were overcome successfully.

"How long would it take? Let's see. We do twenty miles an hour."

"Hardly that all the way."

"Why not?" demanded Clive, in whose fertile brain the whole scheme had originated, and who panted to be testing his first attempt at road locomotion. "Why not?"

"Well, there's punctures," said Hugh lamely, and without thought of grammar.

"Yes; possible."

"Then there's traffic. Besides, we've got to eat."

Yes, they had to do that, without a shadow of doubt. Seventy miles, with sundry delays—which, however, were not likely, oh, certainly not!—meant four hours on the road. A fellow couldn't hold out all that time. Impossible!

"We'd have a blow-out before starting," declared Clive, his eyes on the machine he and his chum had been so diligently building. "Then we'd be off before nine. We'd get a real good feed at one. By then we'd be in London. That means we'd have to go to rather a swagger sort of place. I say, that's a bit awkward. How's the cash-box going?"

There wasn't a cash-box. Hugh was the treasurer, and he slowly and somewhat sadly counted out three shillings and fourpence halfpenny. Not a big sum, perhaps, but nearing the end of the holidays, and after considerable expenditure already on their ambitious project it was certainly a triumph of management.

"Bit short," said Hugh. "But it'll do. We must fill up well before we start, and take things in our pockets. I dare say we'll be able to find a place where you can get a feed for a shilling. Perhaps they'd take two for less. Things like that are easy to arrange in London."

"Easy. But I was thinking of the return journey. There's a lamp wanted."

"And numbers, and a licence," said Hugh, aghast at the thought which had never previously occurred to either of them. "My eye, that's a deuce of a job. The police would be on to us."

Clive's was one of those jovial, optimistic natures which overrides all difficulties. "Hang the police! We'll chance it. We'll stick up a number of some sort. I'll ink one out on cardboard this evening. As for a lamp, there's the gardener's. I'll borrow it. It'll do, hanging on in front. It'll make us go slow, of course, but all the better. It'll be a joke to be kept late on the road and have everyone in fits about us. But we can't move to-morrow. It'll have to be the next day."

Ruefully Hugh agreed to the plan, for he would have loved to proceed with the finishing of the car now so nearly ready. He sighed as he looked at the framework at the end of the shop, with its somewhat flimsy front axle and bicycle wheels, its borrowed back axle, its steering gear, a complication of steel wires about a drum mounted on a raked tubing, and surmounted by a cast-iron wheel at one time adorning the overhead shaft which drove the lathe. What thought that gear had cost them! What a triumph its construction had been, and how well it seemed to act now that it was duly assembled and mounted on the wooden chassis of the car! Only the engine needed now to be lifted into position, a chain run from it to the sprocket on the back axle till a few days ago part and parcel of his father's tricycle. There was the mere matter of a lever or two to control the engine, that strip of cardboard, with a number inked upon it, and they would be off. His imagination whirled him to the giddy heights of enjoyment as he thought of the trip before them.

"But that cad's got to be dealt with," he agreed. "Right! What's the particular movement?"

"A trap," interjected Bert. "A man-catcher. Go easy with the saw-edge of the concern and the spring, or you'll break his legs. We don't want that, even if he is a bounder. You'd have thought, considering Clive was the owner of the spinney only a year ago, a fellow would have been ashamed to order him off what had been his own property. But there's no counting on what cads'll do, or won't do. He threatened to throw us out. He's big, though only fifteen, they say. But if we tackled him together we'd make mincemeat of him."

"Better make a fool of him, though," said Clive. "You come along with me now to the spinney. We'll fix the thing so as to make as big an ass of this Rawlings as possible. We'll rig a trap that'll hold him tight, and yet not hurt him. It's near twelve now. By two hours after lunch we'll have it finished. It'll be ready and working by to-morrow morning."

They shut off the engine destined on the morrow to be lifted into their motor-car and provide the propelling force, and shutting the shop went on their way to the spinney. And the same hour found them hard at work upon another contrivance, conceived by Clive's inventive brain, and prepared for the purpose of lowering the pride and dignity of one who had given them mortal offence. Rawlings, the fifteen-year-old son of the pompous new-comer to the parish of Potters Camp, little dreamed of the consequences of his loftiness and of his churlish treatment of Clive Darrell.

CHAPTER II

A BOOBY TRAP

"Five feet and a bit," announced Bert Seymour with gusto, measuring the depth of the pit which he and Hugh and Clive had been digging in the centre of the path leading down the much-discussed spinney. "Two feet either way, and a precious job to dig it on that account. Jolly well too narrow."

"For working in, rather," agreed his brother. "But about right size for a trap. A bit big, if anything. Top edges nicely sloped off, so as to give nothing for a fellow to cling on to."

"And a good foot of sticky clay pudding at the bottom," grinned Clive. "That'll hold him like bird-lime. It'll be bad for his boots and his pants. But, then, it can't be helped. He shouldn't be such a cad. It'll help to teach him manners. I say, do you think a foot of pudding's enough? Suppose we make it two. It'd make things certain."

A second foot of the sticky puddled clay was therefore added, and Hugh tested its adhesiveness with a long stake he had discovered in the forest.

"It'll hold him like wax, till he hollers for someone to help him," he announced, with radiant face. "Of course, we ain't likely to hear him for a goodish time, are we? and there's no one else who'll be about. Old Tom knows what we're up to, of course, but he's a clever bird. He'll be out of the way, or deaf or something. Tom don't like the Rawlings."

That was true enough. If Clive and his chums had suffered from the loftiness and condescension of the new-comers to Potters Camp, Old Tom, Mrs. Darrell's gardener, had likewise suffered. He'd been used to quality.

"The folks up at the house was different to that," he had assured his cronies in the village. "The old master'd never have thought of passing without a nod and a smile, and most like he'd have pulled up his hoss and had a chat about things in general. As for being proud, why he'd have his hand out to shake whenever he came back home after a holiday; while he'd come to the wedding of his gardener's daughter, and it was a five-pound note, all clean and crisp, that he'd slipped into her fingers. He was quality. These here Rawlings ain't the same product. They're jest commoners. And I'll tell yer more," observed Tom, dragging his clay from between a pair of fangless gums and looking round at the company slyly and cautiously.

"More?" ejaculated one of his cronies, encouragingly. "More, Tom? Then let's have it. We don't hold by new-comers."

"Then here it is. But no splitting, mind you. No going about and telling others. Else the whole of Potters Camp and the neighbourhood'll have it before evening."

He lifted an admonitory finger, and glanced sternly at his audience, a collection of village gossips of the type usually to be met with. There was Tom himself, tanned by exposure, his rugged face wreathed by a pair of white whiskers of antique fashion. A bent but powerful figure was his, while in spite of his stooping shoulders he stood half a head above his companions. Then there was the publican himself, rubicund and round and prosperous, his teeth gripping the stem of a favourite pipe. Mrs. Piper also, the said publican's helpful wife, ensconced behind the bar, clattering glasses and bottles and yet managing to hear all that was of interest. Joe Swingler, groom at the Rectory, fondly imagined by his employer never to frequent such a place as a public-house, was in a corner, jauntily dressed, the fit of his gaiters being the despair of Jack Plant, the bailiff's son. But the latter could at least display a suit to attract the fancy of all in the village. There was enough material in his riding-breeches to accommodate two of his size, while the cut of his jacket was ultra-fashionable. The slit at the back extended so high, and the tails were so long, that one wondered whether the garment were actually divided into two portions. For the rest of the audience, they were shepherds, pig men—for Potters Camp prided itself on its pigs, while there was even a small bacon factory—cattle men, carters and agricultural labourers, and all, without exception, agog to hear news of the Rawlings. That caution which Old Tom had given was as certain to have its effect as if he had gone upon the house-tops and called therefrom the news he was about to give to his audience on the promise of their secrecy. It was certain, in fact, that within a short hour every inhabitant of Potters Camp of adult age would be possessed of the information.

"It ain't to go further, mind that!" repeated Tom, wrinkling his face and glaring round. "It's a secret; but it's got truth behind it, so I tell ye. I ain't so sure that these here Rawlings come by the house and the park in a square sort of way. You take it from me, I ain't so sure. There was queer doings afore the old master died. He got to runnin' up to Lunnon, which ain't no good for anyone, least of all for a squire as has things to see to in the country. There was letters to this man Rawlings. I knows that, 'cos I posted 'em, as I always posted all the letters from the house. Then the master dies, and this here Rawlings come down and takes the place and starts ordering people about."

"And he ain't got it fair?" asked one of the hearers.

15

"I ain't a-going to say that," nodded Tom cautiously. "But I kin think as I like. You can't go and stop a man thinking, can yer? No. I thought not. You can't. So I thinks what I like, and thinkin' with me's precious nigh knowing."

The old fellow gave the company generally the benefit of a knowing wink, and lapsed into silence. But from that moment all who had heard him speaking thought as he thought, and were as equally certain. Such is the unstable foundation of tales which at times go the round of the country. Not that Tom was altogether wrong. There were others who might have said more, others in the city of London. But Tom did not know that, nor any of his audience. But the conversation at least gives one the impression that if Clive and his chums were not enamoured of the new-comers, Tom was even less so.

"It'll come to blows atween that ere son of Rawlings and Master Clive and his friends," he observed to the company present. "There's been words already, and ef Master Clive's like his father—which he is—why, it's 'look out' fer this here Albert Rawlings."

That pit so craftily constructed would have made Tom even more emphatic. For when all was ready, and Clive and his accomplices had completed their work to their own satisfaction, even they could hardly say where the pit existed.

"Of course," observed Hugh, with that grin to which his friends were accustomed—"of course, if we were actually setting the proper sort of trap we'd have to bait it, eh, and put sharpened stakes in it to kill the game. But it isn't necessary here, eh?"

"To bait?—not a bit. This is a booby trap," laughed Bert. "It's meant for an ass, and an ass is the one that'll fall into it."

It came as a shock, rather, to this lanky young hero that he himself was trapped within the minute. For Bert was not too observant. That dreamy eye was not meant for close watching, while here it wanted the eye of a hawk to detect the presence of a pit. For Clive had been very thorough. To the covering of reeds and light sticks laid across the pit mouth had been added a thick sprinkling of leaves which were most bewildering. Bert's description of the trap as a booby one carried him away into a whirl of delight, during which he strutted aimlessly along the path. And in an instant he was immersed. There was the sound of rending reeds, his lanky figure disappeared as if by magic, and only the top of his cap remained in view, frantically bobbing.

"Hi! Here! What's this?" he shouted, roused to a pitch of indignation.

"Booby trap. Well caught!" cried Clive, dancing with delight at this unexpected demonstration of the successful working of his invention.

"And done without baiting," gibed Hugh, shaking with laughter. "Now, Bert, you've spoiled the thing. Come along out. Don't stop hiding in there."

That was an impossibility. Two feet of glutinous clay adhered to the boy's boots and trousers and refused to be shaken off. He raised one leg with an effort, gripped the sloping side of his prison, and endeavoured to raise the other limb. The result was that he was dragged back into the depths promptly.

"Well, it's a beauty," he grinned at last, beginning to relish the fun of the scene himself. "Regularly tested the trap, eh? and been badly had myself. But lend a hand. This stuff'd stick old Rawlings himself, let alone his son. And it's beautifully hidden. I was never more surprised in my life."

"Then it'll be ten times more of a jar to the fellow we're after," gurgled Clive. "My! You do look a beauty! And what a mess you've got into!"

Bert was smothered in sticky clay from the knees downward, and had need to stand in the stream adjacent and wash his boots and clothing. Meanwhile Clive and Hugh completed their repairs to the covering of the pit, scattered leaves about till the surroundings looked quite natural, and having concluded matters to their satisfaction passed out of the spinney.

To-morrow, they promised themselves retaliation. "And it's not been such a long job as I thought," said Clive, as he put Old Tom's garden tools back into the shed from which they had been taken. "Supposing we tackle the car again. She'd be ready, perhaps, by the morning."

But tea was of almost equal importance. Hugh and his brother therefore partook of Mrs. Darrell's hospitality, the state of Bert's trousers and boots being skilfully concealed by that young gentleman by the simple expedient of standing well in the background. But he left a stain here and there. Peering through her spectacles on the following morning, Clive's mother was astonished to find red lines of clay on the chintz cover of one of her chairs.

And then the workshop claimed the three young fellows.

"Ready for dropping the engine in," declared Clive, surveying the skeleton of his motor. "By the way, we've forgotten seats, haven't we?"

"That's a nuisance!" admitted Hugh. "But we'll not let that bother us. We'll fix it by nailing boards across. I know. We'll get a box and make that fast. That's what all the garage people do. A shop body, you know. Smart! Eh? I rather think so."

Behold them, then, struggling with the sheer legs erected over the petrol engine so nicely fitted in the workshop. Watch the pulley contrivance secured to those legs above and the rope passing about it. The slipping of the legs of this improvised crane was a distinct nuisance at first, and made the lifting of the engine difficult, if not impossible. But an iron peg driven in between the tiles of the floor put an end to the trouble, while, once the bolts of the engine had been freed, Bert and Hugh were easily able to haul the engine clear of its foundation.

"Hoist!" shouted Clive, "and stand clear. I'll shove the chassis beneath the engine. Then lower gently. I don't want to have my fingers pinched off, remember that; so slack an inch at a time, and be ready to haul again."

Oh, the triumph of this final achievement! That engine went into position with the docility of a lamb. The chassis framework might have been its intended resting-place from the very commencement. It bedded down on the wooden frame snugly, hugging the timber. The bolt holes matched beautifully with those bored by Clive perhaps a week before, calling shouts of approval from his comrades. And when the hoisting rope was thrown off, and the sheer legs removed, there the engine was in position.

"And the wheels don't even feel the weight. Look. See if they do," cried Clive.

"A bit wobbly, eh?" suggested Hugh grudgingly, pushing the chassis from side to side, when it certainly had what might be described as freedom of movement. "Just a bit, eh? Still, that don't matter. Make her run all the better. But I'm glad she hasn't springs. She'd fairly roll herself over if she had them."

"But the back part's as steady as a rock," reported Clive enthusiastically. "Don't rock. Not a bit. Anyway, she runs forward and backward easily. By George! That's a bother!"

"What? You make a fellow ask such heaps of questions," grumbled Hugh, dismayed himself at the sudden fall in Clive's features.

"We've forgotten something else, and the bally thing's frightfully important."

Hugh gaped; Bert looked somewhat amused. To tell the truth, though glad always to lend a helping hand, he looked upon all this unnecessary work as a species of madness.

"You'll have to sweat at things like this when you're older," he declared. "No one's going to let you live at home and walk about doing nothing. You won't have time for games, and this sort of thing'll keep you from morning to evening—that is, if you take up engineering. Then why not make use of the good times and freedom now and play cricket?"

That had led to a somewhat animated discussion on the subject and seriousness of games as compared with mechanics till Hugh and Bert were within an inch of a struggle. But that was in the past. The plot they had so recently discussed, and the pit they had dug for the downfall of young Rawlings, had drawn the bonds of friendship more closely together. So Bert changed his expression of amusement to one of concern.

"What's the jolly thing?" he asked. "It looks complete—in fact, ripping. There's an engine and wheels and steering gear and frame. What more do you want? Ah! Got it! There's nothing there with which to cool the engine. Well, you two are precious mugs! Just fancy, taking all the sweat to mount an engine and then forgetting such an important matter!"

Clive's eye kindled, while his cheeks reddened. He could afford to pity a chap who showed such tremendous ignorance; only, coming as it did at a moment when he himself was distinctly distressed, the idiotic suggestions of this ignoramus made him angry.

"Hang it!" he growled. "Don't talk such rot! Cooling indeed! Why, even—even Rawlings could tell you that the engine's air-cooled. There's the fan, stupid! staring you right in the face. The thing that's worrying me is the lever for chucking the concern out of gear."

Hugh gripped the side of the chassis as the secret was mentioned. It made him shiver to think that just as every difficulty that could be foreseen had been surmounted another had cropped up.

"And it's a beast," he groaned.

"A teaser," admitted Clive desperately.

"What's a gear lever?" asked Bert, with aggravating coolness and flippancy.

"What's a gear lever!" growled Clive, regarding him with an eye that positively glared.

"What's a mug?" shouted Hugh, ready almost to strike him.

"Someone who forgets that there is such a thing as a gear lever, and then can't or won't explain," came the irritating, maddening answer.

"Look here," began Clive, flushing hotly, and stepping nearer to Bert, "I've troubles enough already. I'll trouble you to——"

"He's punning," shouted Bert, seizing the angry Clive by the shoulders and shaking him. And then, careless of the anger he had aroused, for that was the way with him, he began to cross-examine the two mechanics on the uses and abuses of every class of lever. The meeting, in fact, was in grave danger of a sudden break-up. But a shout from Hugh helped matters wonderfully.

"I've got it!" he bellowed.

"What? The lever or the measles?" asked Bert, still amused and facetious.

"Shut up, you ass! The measles indeed! No, the bally difficulty. I've a way in which to work it."

Clive agreed with the suggestion when it came to be put to him, agreed with ungrudging enthusiasm. "It'll be as easy as walking," he said.

"Or falling," suggested Bert.

"You'll get your head punched yet," growled Clive. "But it's fine, this idea. You see, we start our engine. That's easy enough."

"Well, it may be," from Bert. "I'll believe you."

"Then we take our seats."

"Don't see 'em," came from the critic.

"Ass! You've heard of the box we're going to fix."

"But that's a box. It's not a seat."

"Go on with it, Clive," urged Hugh, looking as if he would willingly slay his brother. "Take no notice of the ass. We start her up, and then get seated."

"On a box."

"Yes," agreed Clive, glaring at Bert, who had again interrupted. "The engine's going. The chain's free-wheeling. We have a lever somewhere."

Hugh pointed out its position with triumph, and the two promptly proceeded to fit the contrivance. But levers are not made in a moment. It was, in fact, noon of the following day before they were ready for an outing.

"You manage the steering, that's agreed?" asked Clive, when the amateur-constructed motor-car had been pushed as far as the road.

"That's it. You control the engine. Don't let her race too much at first. Remember I ain't used to steering. Besides, those front wheels are frightfully groggy. She'll sway at corners, and if we put on the pace I shall be piling the whole bag of tricks up on one of the banks. Bert'll keep cave. There's no police about here to matter. Jimmy, the local constable, 's a real good fellow. He'll see the thing from the right point of view. He knows we're experimenting and'll sympathise."

"Particularly if he's called in at the inquest," gurgled Bert, irrepressible when his chums desired to be so serious.

"Inquest. Eh?" asked Hugh. "What's that?"

"Enquiry held on the bodies of Clive Darrell and Hugh Seymour, late of this parish, killed on the high-road. Died in the execution of their duty'll be the verdict. Great inventors cut off in their prime!"

Bert had to run an instant later. For Clive came at him with a hammer, while Hugh looked distinctly furious. However, the incident quieted down, the inventors took their seats on this chassis of their own making, while Bert, having seen that the coast was clear, listened to the puff of the engine. Hugh gripped the steering gear. True, it was somewhat flimsy, and bent easily from side to side. But nothing can be perfected in a moment, he told himself. It would do for this first experimental run, at any rate.

"Ready?" asked Clive deliberately.

"Let her go."

Clive did. There was a painful clattering of gears. The lever jerked violently, while the engine almost came to a stop. However, a touch of the throttle and ignition levers put that right, while the gear lever behaved itself of a sudden. The chassis bounded forward, very nearly hurling the box which acted as a seat from it. But for the steering wheel Hugh would have been deposited in the gutter. But he clung manfully to the frame, and in a moment was hurtling forward.

"Steady!" he called. "She don't steer so nicely."

She didn't. She—that is, the car—swerved frightfully. Those front wheels had rather the appearance of wheels trying to twist round to look at one another. Then the swivelling axle wasn't altogether a brilliant success. It refused to swivel at inconvenient moments. The heroes of this expedition were within an inch of the ditch lining the road.

"Near as a toucher," cried Clive. "Keep her up."

"Can't! The brute won't steer. She likes the ditch," came the answer.

"Then I'll stop her. Some of those wires want tightening. Then she'll steer."

But that troublesome gear lever was determined to ruin the hopes of both inventors. Perhaps it was because it had been forgotten till the very end and felt neglected. In any case, it refused to disengage, while owing to the awkward fact that the throttle and ignition levers had dropped away and gone adrift, Clive could not control his engine. It raced badly. It snorted as if it felt that it could do as it liked. It sent the swaying car hurtling along like a bullet.

"Look out!" yelled Bert. "The bally thing's pitching like a ship at sea. Stop her!"

"Can't! The brute's got the bit between her teeth badly," shrieked Clive. "I can't quite reach the throttle, and till I do she'll go plugging ahead. She runs like a demon."

"Top hole!" gurgled Hugh, whom it took a lot to frighten. "Ain't she got pace? But she'd be better if she didn't rush so much from side to side. Look out! There's a cart coming our way."

He set his teeth, endeavoured to make his figure adhere to the top of that egg box which did duty as a seat, and braced himself for the encounter. For encounter it seemed there was to be. The wondrous car which he and Clive had called into being romped towards the unsuspecting cart. It waltzed merrily from side to side of the road, seeming to take an uncanny delight in racing within hair's breadth of the ditch on either hand. It mounted the rough footpath with impunity, careless of the law and of possible policemen, its springless axles bending and bumping. It actually appeared to sight that approaching cart itself, and as if filled with fiendish delight at its unaccustomed freedom, and filled with knowledge of the helplessness of its inventors, it sped toward the vehicle, pirouetted before it, skidded badly, removing in the space of a bare five seconds one of the Rector's expensive back tyres, and then, mounting the pathway again with startling abruptness, it pitched its nose into the air, shuddered with positive glee, and having thrown its drivers into the ditch subsided into match-wood and scrap-iron. Those back wheels and their axle, borrowed for this memorable occasion, had the appearance rather of a couple of inverted umbrellas with the sticks tied together. The framework was torn asunder, and only the engine remained in recognisable condition.

As Clive and Hugh picked themselves up from the ditch and surveyed the wreck, with the driver of the cart and Bert giggling beside them, there came a horrid shout from behind them.

"Eh? What's that?" demanded the baker, for he it was who had so wonderfully escaped annihilation.

"Someone in trouble," said Bert. "Calling for help. Let's go."

"You ass!" grinned Hugh, gripping him by the sleeve. "Can't you guess? It's that Rawlings cad. We've bagged him."

"It's someone as is in trouble," exclaimed the worthy baker, not hearing the above. "Wonder if it's that Mr. Rawlings?"

"Young Rawlings?" asked Clive, with a horrible presentiment of coming trouble.

"Mr. Rawlings," came the emphatic answer. "Him who's bought the house. I seed him walking to the path through the spinney. He's been away up to Lunnon."

Clive and his fellow conspirators looked at one another painfully. Then they regarded the wreck of the motor. That was bad enough. Admission must be made to the Rector, and his axle and back wheels brought for inspection. Common honesty demanded that of them. It wouldn't be playing the game to borrow and smash and then hide their guilt in some underhand manner. And here was an addition.

"I'm a-going to see what's up," declared the baker. "You young gents had best come along too."

They couldn't very well hang back, and had perforce to visit the scene of their late labours. And there was the fat Mr. Rawlings, imprisoned in a pit which needed no adhesive clay pudding to hold him. For this London gentleman was of portly structure, and the narrow pit held him as if his fat figure had been poured into it. He could hardly shout. Even breathing was difficult, while his rage and mortification made him dangerously purple. Then, when at length the efforts of the four had released him, and he sat at the side of the pit besmirched with clay from head to foot, his rage was almost appalling.

"HIS RAGE WAS ALMOST APPALLING."

"You little hounds!" he stuttered. "You did it. Don't tell me you didn't. I know you did. I'll set the police on you. You were trespassing. This is my property. I'll send Albert down to give you a hiding, and he'll be glad to do it. I'll—I'll——" His breath was gone by now, and he sat back gasping. But his anger did not subside, and Clive's prediction of coming evil was speedily realised.

"I shall send you off to school," said his mother. "You ought to have gone long ago. I really do consider your conduct to have been disgraceful."

"A piece of unmitigated mischief, and not of a harmless character," growled the Rector, who was given to choosing long words where possible. "Unmitigated mischief, Bert and Hugh. First you have the temerity to carry out something approaching a theft, a common and nefarious business. Then you implicate a respected neighbour in a catastrophe which might have terminated in his entire and total undoing. Bert, bend over."

Dear! Dear! It was a painful and humiliating week which followed. Young Rawlings up at the house giggled secretly at his father's discomfiture. But he threatened openly when he happened to come across Clive one morning. As for the three conspirators, they were not allowed to see one another, nor to communicate.

"You'll go on Wednesday," said the Rector. "I've written about you."

That was ominous. "We'll catch it hot," said Hugh. "I don't care. I'm jolly glad to be going. A chap ought to go to a big school, not stick always at home. There'll be a workshop. That'll be ripping."

"And cricket. That's better. Wish Clive were coming to the same school. Old Tom tells me he's led a dog's life these last few days."

Clive's existence had been wretched. He was glad, delighted in fact, when the day for departure arrived, and he took his place in the train for Ranleigh.

"That cad travelling too," he said, seeing Rawlings entering a distant carriage. "Glad he's going to some other place than Ranleigh."

He saluted his mother, waved to Old Tom, and sank back on his seat as the train started. If Bert and Hugh were glad to go to a public school, so also was Clive. He had longed to see life outside the village of Potters Camp with an intense longing. And here he was on his way. What would it be like? Was there bullying? Would he have to fag? and what sort of a place was Ranleigh?

CHAPTER III

OFF TO RANLEIGH

Going to school arouses a variety of emotions. In the case of Clive they were decidedly confused and jumbled, happiness, however, at the prospect before him predominating. For residence for a high-spirited lad at home, tied to a somewhat doting mother's apron-strings, is somewhat dull, and hardly conducive to good results, while the absence of a father had not improved matters. Indeed, it may be agreed without debate that the incident of that wonderful motor-car contrived by Clive and Hugh and the ingenious trap they had set for Rawlings had not been entirely mischievous. For here was Clive about to be launched on the schoolboy world, while Hugh and Bert, having listened to a long and verbose lecture from their father, hitherto their tutor at home, had entered a train and gone off likewise.

"What'll this Ranleigh be like?" Clive asked himself again and again. From taking an interest in passing scenery, he soon began to look forward to another stop with eagerness. For at each station there were boys. Some big, some small; some jolly and whistling, others glum and thoughtful. Not that glumness was the order of the whole day. For at one station Clive observed with some amusement one youngster under the escort of a fond father and mother. The lad had much ado to keep the tears back as the train departed, while his mother wept openly into a handkerchief of diminutive proportions. Within a minute, however, there came shouts of laughter from the next carriage into which this hopeful youngster had stepped, and peering in at the next station, Clive found the lad as merry as a cricket. He was beginning to wish that he could join them.

"I say," he began, somewhat lamely, "going to Ranleigh?"

A fat youth, with a greasy, pallid face, pushed his head out of the window and surveyed Clive as if he were an inferior beetle.

"Who on earth are you?" he asked, with some acerbity. "Who invited you to speak? that's what I want to know. Jolly cheek, I call it!"

Clive was taken aback rather considerably. This was not the sort of treatment to which he was accustomed. His gorge rose at it.

"Cheek yourself! Who are you, then?"

It seemed for a moment as if the fat youth would have an apoplectic seizure. His pallid face became suffused a dull purplish red. His neck swelled in fat folds over his collar. If looks could have killed, Clive would certainly have been slain on the spot. But the engine shrieked just then, while someone within the carriage seized the tails of the fat youth, who disappeared precipitately.

"Come in, Trendall," he heard a voice shout. "One would think you were a king, never to be spoken to. But who is he? My word, I got a glimpse of his phiz, and he looked as if he'd hammer you with pleasure."

Another mile on this almost endless journey and the train again panted into a station. Clive hung out of the window, and then became aware of the fact that two individuals were approaching his carriage, while from the one next door the youthful Trendall glared at him. Rawlings was one of those approaching. He descended with majestic step from his own compartment and hailed a porter.

"Hi! Portar!" he called. "Carry these things along heear. Someone's wanted to keep ordar."

Tall for his age, decidedly podgy, and with a cast of countenance which was not too attractive, Rawlings just lacked that brisk, clean appearance belonging to young men who go to our public schools. Despite expensive and well-fitting clothes, an immaculate tie and hat, and socks of most becoming pattern, the fellow did not look a gentleman. His air was pompous. His manner of addressing the porter ludicrous. He stepped up to Clive's compartment, nodded grandly to Trendall, and pulled the door open.

"He-e-ear, portar."

The magnificent one proffered a tip without looking at it, and Clive noticed that the man took it with alacrity.

"All fer me, sir?" he grinned.

"Of course! I'm not a pauper."

Rawlings waved him away magnificently, flopped on to a seat, taking the far corner, arranged his feet on the one opposite, and then began to take close scrutiny of our friend Clive. Meanwhile, another individual had entered the compartment. He was a tall, broad-shouldered, shambling youth, of decidedly foreign appearance, with clothes which spoke of a French provincial city. He stooped a little, was slow and ungainly in his movements, while his powerful shoulders were bent forward. But the face was striking and taking.

"Pardon," he said politely, lifting his hat as he entered. "This is for Ranleigh, is it not so?"

Rawlings regarded him stonily. "The cheek!" he muttered. "Is one to answer every bally foreigner? I'm not a portar!"

He thrust his hands deep into his pockets and glared at the intruder. For the new-comer was an intruder. Rawlings had made his way to this compartment with a view to discussing certain matters with Clive, and letting that young gentleman thoroughly understand who was the master. But that last movement was his undoing for the moment. The fingers deep in one pocket struck upon certain loose cash, and withdrawing the same, Rawlings was at once stricken with a terrible discovery. He had had certain silver coins there before, and twopence in coppers. Those he had intended to present to the porter. But they were still there, while two half-crowns were missing. In fact, in his lordliness he had presented the grinning fellow with five shillings! No wonder the man smirked and touched his hat. That had pleased Rawlings at the time. Now, as the train swung out of the station, he dashed to the window.

"Hi! Hi! Portar!" he bellowed. "Hi! You come back with those half-crowns. It was a mistake."

But the whistle drowned the sound of his voice, while the porter, half hidden behind a barrow, waved a farewell to him. Rawlings threw himself back in his seat with a growl of anger.

"You're going to Ranleigh, aren't you?" he demanded fiercely of Clive.

"Yes."

"Then just you look out for squalls. What dormitory are you in?"

"Don't know," came Clive's sullen answer. This Rawlings was considerably bigger, though little older, but still Clive was not going to be bullied. "How should I?" he demanded. "What's the place like?"

"You'll find out in time. And don't you try any traps there, youngster. See?"

Rawlings was determined to let there be no misunderstanding. He stretched across the carriage and took Clive by the ear.

"None of your caddish games at Ranleigh," he said, "or you'll get something worse than this, by a long way."

Clive beat him off with a well-directed blow on the arm. In fact, with such heat and violence that Rawlings, still enraged at the loss he had so stupidly made when tipping the porter, lost his temper, and it looked as if he would at once take in hand the chastisement of the lad who was such a near neighbour. But the third individual suddenly distracted his attention. Could Rawlings really believe his eyes! This new chap, whoever he might be, a froggy probably, had asked if the train went to Ranleigh, and therefore, obviously, was bound for that destination, and must be a new boy. He was actually stretching himself out across the carriage, with one boot resting against Rawlings's immaculate trousers, while—worse than all—he had a cigarette in his mouth and was setting a match to it. It wasn't the fact of smoking that horrified Rawlings. He had broken that rule himself, and been dreadfully ill, much to his chagrin. But

Rawlings was getting up in the school. He was in the lower sixth, would probably be a prefect this term, and such an act was an outrage to his dignity.

"Well, I'm hanged!" he spluttered. "What on earth do you mean by that? Smoking! Here, stop it!"

But the one addressed merely viewed him mildly. His brows went up questioningly, while he stretched himself a little more at his ease, causing Rawlings to remove his immaculate trouser leg with swiftness.

"Do you hear?" he cried threateningly. "What's your name?"

"Richard Feofé."

"Hang the Richard! Feofé, then. Look here! Stop that smoking."

But Feofé still regarded Rawlings mildly, and taking a deep inspiration filled the carriage with smoke.

"You do not like it, then?" he asked. "Monsieur can then get into another carriage."

Rawlings went crimson with rage, and then pallid, while Clive began to enjoy the joke immensely, for long ago he had sized his near neighbour up, and knew him to be nothing more than a purse-proud bully. But for the disparity in their two weights and heights he would have long since openly defied the fellow. But it was better to see someone else do that. And here was a hulking, good-natured Frenchman doing it splendidly.

"Where do you come from? Who's your father?" demanded Rawlings roughly, as if to gain time in which to decide how to act.

Feofé was not to be hurried. He had never been to a school of any sort before, save the local one he attended in France. But he had met boys and youths in plenty. And always this quiet, shambling boy, with his broad shoulders and appearance of hidden power, had won respect without recourse to violence. He took another puff at his cigarette, a habit, by the way, rather more indulged in by boys in France, and regarded the resulting smoke with something approaching affection. His eyes twinkled. He shrugged his massive shoulders.

"Monsieur is somewhat curious," he said, using excellent English. "I am from Lyons. My father, he is a banker. My mother, ah, she is his wife, you understand. Then there is a sister. Susanne, Monsieur, younger by a year than I am. That is the sum of the family, but I will tell you all. There is a dog—yes, two—and a cat, and——"

Rawlings was purple. Beads of perspiration were breaking out on his forehead. Catching a sight of Clive's grinning face he ground his teeth with anger.

"Hang your family!" he shouted at Feofé. "Who wants to hear about Susan?"

Feofé shrugged his shoulders. "You were so very curious," he said. "But I will proceed. We live at Lyons, but sometimes we go to Paris. There I have an aunt and two uncles, Monsieur. Ah! Yes, I must tell you all. The aunt is Susanne also. A pretty name, Monsieur."

Rawlings was on the point of exploding. His dignity had long since gone to the winds. If he dared he would have seized this Feofé by the neck and shaken him. But the young fellow's broad shoulders and smiling, easy assurance warned him that that might be dangerous. But he must assert himself. He must show this Frenchman that he was a superior, and that that must be the light in which he must view him.

"Look here," he said at length, smothering his anger, "no more of your confounded cheek. Susanne's good enough for you, so just remember. You're going to Ranleigh, and it's just as well to tell you that I shall be a prefect. Know what that means?"

Even now he hoped to impress Feofé with his magnificence. But the lad merely raised his brows enquiringly, and shrugged his shoulders still lower against the upholstery of the carriage.

"A prefect. Someone in authority. Well?"

"And to be obeyed. Just chuck that smoking."

"But," began Susanne mildly—we call him Susanne at once, seeing that that name stuck to him forthwith—"but, by the way, what's your name?"

Imagine the impertinence of such a request! A new boy actually having the temerity to coolly ask the name of one who had been three years at the school. Rawlings gasped; he mopped his damp forehead.

"Rawlings," he growled.

"Then, Rawlings, you're a prefect, yes?"

"Not yet," came the somewhat confused answer. "But I shall be this term. It'd be a confounded shame if they passed me over."

"Quite so. A confounded shame. You would be a loss to the other prefects."

Susanne took another appreciative suck at the weed, while Rawlings went hot and cold. Satire went to the depths of his being. This Feofé was covering him with derision.

"Look here," he began threateningly, "it's about time you understood who you are and what I am."

"You're a prefect, yes?" answered Susanne, not the least distressed, his little eyes twinkling, "or will be, at Ranleigh. But you are not one here, in any case. Is it not so? Therefore, Rawlings, get into another carriage if you don't like smoke, and do let us be pleasant."

Never was a man more demoralised than Rawlings. He had made an entry into the carriage with the set purpose of bullying Clive, and of letting that young gentleman see who was to be the master. The commencement of the movement had cost him five precious shillings. That was sore enough. And then, naturally enough, he had addressed himself to this new boy—and had been worsted. It goaded him to madness to see Clive grinning still.

"Well done, Susanne!" called out that worthy, delighted at the turn events had taken. "Rawlings ain't a prefect yet, and in any case we're not at Ranleigh. I say, I'm a new boy too. He lives quite close to me."

He pointed a deprecating finger at Rawlings, and crossed to join Susanne. That young man welcomed him with open arms. The twinkle in his eye brightened, while he eyed Rawlings in a manner which made that individual squirm. In fact, never was the wind taken out of anyone's sails more completely. Susanne had reduced him to silence. Thenceforth Rawlings sat screwed into the corner, regarding the landscape with a face which showed the severest displeasure, while his lips muttered and twisted angrily.

"Wait till I get 'em to Ranleigh, that's all," he was promising himself. "The first thing I do is to kick this Darrell fellow. Then Feofé shall have a turn. I'll get my own back whatever happens."

Clive was no smoker. He was sensible enough to know that it would be harmful to him just as it would be to any other fellow, and for that reason refused the cigarette Susanne offered him. He wedged himself up close to his new chum, and commenced a long and intimate conversation. Meanwhile, other boys entered the train. Some in the next compartment, from which howls of laughter sounded, some in their own. Fellows nodded curtly to Rawlings. The fat Trendall came in at one station to have a chat with him, and found his chum curiously glum and silent. He couldn't understand him at all, nor fathom the movements of the two opposite. For Susanne and Clive regarded Trendall with the smallest interest. According to all the canons of school life they should have looked askance at a fellow who had been at the school a couple of years or so. In Clive's eyes Trendall should have appeared enormous. And, no doubt, had Clive been alone in this adventure, he would have been far less uppish. But Susanne was incorrigible. If he had never been to school before, he was at least not to be frightened by what was before him. To Clive, his easy, calm assurance was refreshing. To Trendall it was inexplicable. Finding conversation lagging he took himself off at the next station, his place being taken by two big fellows, who nodded cheerfully to the occupants of the compartment.

"Hullo, Rawlings!" called one, a very tall, slim young man, on whose upper lip there was a respectable growth of downy hair. "Not dead, then?"

"No," answered that individual sourly.

"New youngsters, eh?" was the second question as the tall fellow turned to Clive and Susanne.

"Yes," answered the former. Susanne took his hat off politely.

"Help!" called Harvey, for that was the name of the youth speaking, grinning at this quaint exhibition. However, he returned the compliment by lifting his own. "We don't do that sort of thing in England," he said, quite kindly. "I shouldn't if I were you. Fellows would start rotting. I say, can you play footer and cricket?" Susanne's eyes sparkled. "I like them both tremendously. But play, ah, that is another question. In England fellows get a chance. In France you may say that games are only beginning."

"Book him for a trial next scratch footer," exclaimed Harvey, addressing his comrade. "Look here, you two, I'm Harvey. This is Bagshaw, secretary of our Games Committee, and of everything else that's useful. He's head bottlewasher to every institution at the school, and don't you forget it. I say, how do you call yourselves?"

How different was his manner from that of Rawlings. Feofé gave his at once, while Clive was not backward. The latter took an instant liking for Harvey. Of course, he must be a tremendous fellow at the school, top of all probably. Or was he a master? He looked almost old enough. Besides, he had a moustache, quite a decent affair. As to Bagshaw, he was a delicate-looking fellow of eighteen, perhaps, with a kindly, wizened face. A calm, studious man. The scholar of the school, no doubt, but not a games player. Nor was Clive far out in his reckoning. For Harvey was head scholar, a man head and shoulders above his comrades. Good at work, keen on books and such things, a decided master at debate, he was still a first-rate man at games, and perhaps shone still more as a leader. His clean-cut figure was the observed of all observers in School matches. His had been the fortune to listen to howls of appreciation when he had carried off the hundred yards, the quarter mile and the long jump at the School sports, while one and all, his football team or his cricket eleven watched his every move and gesture, loyal observers of all his wishes.

As to Bagshaw, he was almost as popular. No one expected him to play games. It was well known that he had a weak heart, and with that, of course, no fellow could play. But his Ranleighan Gazette was a masterpiece. His poems were enthralling; while, strangely enough, this delicate-looking fellow, a scholar also, could hold the boys spellbound. When taking "prep." Bagshaw was not one to be trifled with. There was no nonsense about this delicate, ascetic fellow. He was cool, calm and commanding, and to those who had the sense, a real help in difficulties.

"Ranleigh. All change!"

The lamps at the station were lighted now. Clive tumbled out on to a platform seething with boys of every age. Boys laden with footballs and bags. Boys clad in warm overcoats, and others nobly discarding the same for the walk up to the school. Caps were lifted in recognition of one of the masters. Clive found himself doing likewise and wondering whether all masters were the same. For this one, a fair giant, of ample proportions, smiled down upon them all. He gripped Harvey's hand with a vigour there was no denying, while still smiling round at the company. And then in twos and threes, and here and there in forlorn ones, for your new boy is not quick to discover chums, the contingent of Ranleigh boys took the road for the school. Through a portion of the village they went, leaving the Village Jubilee Memorial behind them. Up towards the common, all railed in, where sports and cricket matches are held, up past the butcher's shop, with its slaughter-house close handy, and so onward through the tree-clad lane, past the master's entrance, giving access to the Sanatorium also, past an even more important institution, the tuck-shop to wit, and so to the gates of the school. Above, a third way down the hill, myriad lights flashed from the building. Clive forged his way up the front drive with Susanne beside him, up the steep slope to the front doors, never entered except in the case of a few, save on arriving or departing on the first or last days of the term. And so into the wide space past the chapel entrance, between Middle and Second Form rooms. And there, swept continuously by a seething mass of boys, stood a short, bald-headed master, nodding here and there, smiling all the time, evidently delighted to welcome everyone.

"Darrell!"

Clive heard his name and stopped. The lynx-eyes of the bald-headed master had espied him.

"Sir," he gulped. He felt almost frightened. There were so many boys, and there was such an uproar.

"One South, Darrell," he heard. "How are you, boy? Glad you've come. Hop up the stairs there and you'll find One South dormitory. Your name's on one of the beds. Put your bag down on it, and then go to hall. You'll get tea there. Chapel'll be in ten minutes."

How did he know that this was Darrell? Clive found himself wondering that. And what about Susanne?

"Feofé," he heard, as he ascended. And then less distinctly, "One South," with the same instructions.

"I'm glad," he thought. "Susanne'll be with me. Wonder about that howling cad Rawlings. What a downfall! He'll not meddle with Susanne whatever happens. But he'll have his pound of flesh from me if the chance comes. Wish Harvey was to be in One South also."

He clambered up the steps and turned into a dormitory but dimly illuminated. But it was big and clean and airy, and bore an appearance of comfort, some thirty beds being covered with cosy-looking red coverlets.

Clive found his bed, deposited his bag, and then enquired his way to hall. Thick slices of bread and butter—known colloquially as "toke"—appeased a ravenous appetite. He had not even time to admire the huge proportions of the Hall, the many long tables, the names of boys long since departed who had won honours at the school, and the few pictures and portraits. A clanging bell summoned him he knew not where. He found himself processing with a number of others. Through that gallery they passed, with Middle and Second Forms on either side; then sharp to the left down a paved corridor, to a wide, arched entrance. They were in the chapel. Clive passed through the handsome raised seats of the choir, down the central aisle, and drifted aimlessly to one side.

"Here," someone whispered. "One South?"

"Yes."

"Then this'll do. Squat here."

The fellow made room for him. Clive squatted and listened. The organ was filling the whole beautiful chapel with the sweetest sound. Boys had ceased entering. He raised his eyes to the entrance through which he had come, just to be seen above the choir. "Be sure your sin will find you out," he read above the doorway. The bell ceased ringing, the notes of the organ were hushed, a low "Amen" came from the vestry. And then the choir processed to their seats. Harvey was amongst them, and Trendall, his fat cheeks shaking. There was a string of masters, of all ages almost, all appearances and all sizes, looking somewhat out of their element. And last of all came the Head. Not so very tall, not big, not imposing, there was yet something about him which called for another look. But the organ was pealing again, filling this magnificent building, with its high arched roof, to the depths of every crevice.

Clive cast his eyes aloft over the screen—in itself a thing of surpassing beauty—to the curtains about the organ loft, above which showed the foreheads and eyes of two of the school. And then the notes died away in a sob, which somehow seemed to have a welcome in it. The congregation kneeled. Then the voice of the Head broke the silence with the opening of the evening service, calm and dignified and musical. His eyes wandered round the assembled boys, not curiously, not with recognition in them, but with a welcome for all.

Ah! Clive shivered just a little. Of a sudden it had come to him that he was one of them, that he was a Ranleighan, that the school honour was his honour, its prowess his, its victories his to boast of. And then the singing of the choir thrilled him as he had never been thrilled before. He felt as do those old, loyal

Ranleighans who visit their Old School after the lapse of years. The music, the lighting of the chapel, the very scent of the stone and bricks awake old memories, sweet memories and thrill them. So with Clive. He sang lustily with the rest, and then sank to his seat to listen to the lesson. There was Harvey at the lectern. Harvey the hero of the school, looking magnificent in his simple surplice. Harvey with head erect, his fair moustache curling, reading to them in a voice that showed no sign of trembling. How Clive would have shrunk from such a task! He shivered again at the thought of such a possibility.

Then came a hymn, the last prayers, and the thunder of the organ following. The choir filed away as they had come, the school remaining motionless till they heard the last "Amen" from the vestry. Then came movement. The boys were beginning to file out of the chapel and Clive prepared to follow. His eyes strayed this way and that, as he waited for his turn. All of a sudden he received something in the nature of a shock, something which set his heart thumping. For opposite him, waiting also to take their place in the procession of slippered boys, were two with familiar faces. Clive could have shouted their names. He almost did in his excitement and delight. For within a short dozen yards of him, as yet unconscious of his presence, were Hugh and Bert, his fellow conspirators, sent from their home as a direct result of that booby trap prepared for the unpopular Rawlings.

CHAPTER IV

SOME INTRODUCTIONS

"At last! Got you, you little demon! I'll teach you to laugh when a beggarly froggy gives me sauce. This'll help to make you remember manners, and is just a sample of what's to follow."

The amiable Rawlings, still smarting after his downfall in the train, had waylaid Clive Darrell. He pounced upon that youngster just as he issued from the chapel corridor, and with a heave and a jerk forced him through the narrow entrance into Middle School. A dim gas jet only served to show the immensity of the place, and its uncomfortable bareness. It was tenantless, save for the two who had now entered.

"No use your howling, my son," exclaimed the brutal Rawlings sneeringly, twisting Clive's arm till it was a wonder it did not break, and holding it so firmly behind his back that the lad could not move. "We'll commence with your lessons now, before school begins to-morrow."

He kneed the youngster unmercifully, shaking his whole body till it was a wonder his teeth were not jerked down his throat, and repeated the dose promptly. Clive shouted and kicked. His face was pale with pain, for his arm was terribly twisted. And yet he was powerless to get free. He wondered if he were going to faint. He certainly felt very giddy. Beads of perspiration were rolling down his forehead, and no doubt, in a little while, had the torture been continued, he would have actually fainted. But there came a sudden interruption. A stout, square figure lounged into the class-room, while a head appeared at the door behind. The figure belonged to Susanne.

"Pardon," he began, with that peculiar politeness for which, in the course of a few days, he became notorious, "but you are hurting Darrell."

Rawlings swung round on him, thereby nearly completing the fracturing of Clive's arm.

"You get off," he cried angrily. "You've nothing to do with this affair, and if there's any more of your sauce I'll serve you likewise. Hear that?"

Susanne seemed to be completely deaf. Not for one second did he forget his politeness. Indeed, it came to be said of Susanne, the good-natured, stolid Frenchman, that nothing ever put him out, and that even in the heat of footer he was always himself, the essence of politeness. But he could be deaf to threats.

Moreover, such a thing as temper seemed to be foreign to him. He strolled up to Rawlings, took him by the nose and pinched that organ very thoroughly—pinched it, in fact, till Rawlings holloed. He let go his hold of Clive instantly, and clung to the injured organ, while his vengeful eyes flashed over the edge of his hands at Susanne. What precisely would have happened next it is impossible to state, for there came now a second interruption. Harvey's voice was heard. He had entered the class-room and was just behind the three.

"Serve you right," he said bluntly; "and look here, Rawlings, understand this from me: while I'm Head Scholar and Captain of the School this sort of thing's got to be put a stop to. I'll have no bullying, mind that. And have the goodness to remember that Darrell's a new boy. Now, youngster, cut. It's time you were upstairs in your dormitory. Same in your case, Feofé. Rawlings, you can come along to the scholars' room. I want a chat with you."

Clive clambered briskly to One South. True, he became a little muddled between the passages and the staircases, and found himself in the wrong dormitory. But a howl from a fellow hardly as big as himself sent him running like a rabbit.

"Here! Who's this kid?" he heard, while a youth with red hair sticking up abruptly from his forehead, as if he had received a severe fright when very young and had never recovered from it, stretched out and snatched at his collar. "What dormitory?" came the curt question.

"One South."

"Then out you go. We don't have One South kids fooling about in Two South, I can tell you. Clear off!"

Clive was actually staggered by the insolent arrogance of this youngster. He bolted, whereas, with all his wits about him, it is probable that there would have been at least a wordy warfare for some few minutes. And then he dived into his own abode, and made for his own particular bed. The dormitory was almost full now. That is to say, there was a boy to every bed save one. Clive sat down on the box placed between his bed and the next, and looked curiously round. There was silence in the place. There came to his ears merely the pattering of many restless heels upon the floor, while from the other three dormitories which went to make up the four in the south of the school buildings there came not so much as a sound.

Was Rawlings in the place? Thank goodness, no! Then Harvey? Of course, he'd gone off with the bully to the scholars' room. So there was still the chance that ill luck might put Rawlings in One South. Opposite, smiling at him, was Susanne, his peace of mind apparently unruffled by the scuffle in which he had so recently taken a part. As for the rest of the thirty odd fellows, they were large and small and medium, shock-headed, sunburned after their holidays, rather clean and well groomed for schoolboys, but then they were fresh from home, and as jolly looking as one could wish for. Compulsory silence, however, muzzled them for the moment. At the call of "speak" within ten minutes such a babel of voices arose that Clive was almost deafened. Susanne grinned now and crossed to speak to him.

"I say," he began, "who's that fellow I caught twisting your arm?"

"Rawlings; he lives near us at home. He's an out-and-out bounder."

"Ah! And a bully. He'll not try again when I'm near. But when he catches you alone, then there'll be trouble. I say, er——"

"Darrell."

"Then, Darrell, pity we're not next to one another here. Wonder if it could be managed?"

The suggestion was hardly made before a hand was placed on Susanne's shoulder.

"Look here, you're a new boy, aren't you?" asked a voice. "Well, I'm Sturton, you know, prefect of One South, and chaps aren't allowed to move over and speak to one another without getting leave. Now you know, eh?"

Susanne apologised in his best manner, while Clive inspected the one who had spoken. He hadn't seen him before, for the simple reason that Sturton was one of those who ascended to the organ loft at chapel time, and was there invisible. He had come up to the dormitory after "speak," and here he was, admonishing and advising Susanne as if he were another Harvey. Clive liked Sturton at once, liked his clean-cut figure and features, his bold brown eyes, his crisp and yet friendly way of talking.

"I say, please——" he began, and then became somewhat abashed.

"Eh? Fire away! You say——"

"I was wondering, sir, if——"

"Oh, come now, none of your 'sirs.' What is it?" asked Sturton, thinking that Clive was quite a decent little fellow, an acquisition to the dormitory.

"Well—er—oh, I don't know."

Sturton laughed outright. Susanne grinned. If Clive suffered from bashfulness, at least he didn't.

"He doesn't like to say it; but we're chums—isn't that the word?" he asked. "You see, I got into the same carriage with him. There was another chap there, and he'd come to make himself disagreeable to Darrell. So I—er, chipped in, eh?"

"Got it right—chipped in's the word," admitted Sturton, looking interested, while Clive nodded vigorously.

"Chipped in, and together Darrell and I made him look foolish. Darrell's wondering whether we could have our beds close together, then I needn't bother to ask leave."

"Why, of course! Bring your bag over. Change places with one of these fellows on either side. I dare say they won't mind."

The exchange was made promptly, and Clive found himself chatting away with his new friend. He was half undressed when that fair giant whom he had first seen at the station, and then again amongst the masters processing into chapel, entered the dormitory. He went from boy to boy, shaking hands heavily but with sincerity and friendship.

"Well, Darrell," he began, accosting our young friend, and speaking in so gentle and subdued a voice that Clive wondered if he had a bad cold, or if the voice really belonged to him, "been digging any more pits of late, eh? Or making motor-cars? Tell me all about them."

There was such genuine interest in this master that Clive told the tale, till Mr. Branson—for that was this master's name—wiped tears of enjoyment from his eyes. Also the same eyes sparkled when the boy spoke of his motor-car, and forgetting all else in the depths of his interest plunged into a description of levers and gears, of throttle and ignition apparatus, of lubrication and cooling. Was Branson—Old B., as fellows spoke of him usually—was he a fellow enthusiast?

"So you like engineering things, then, Darrell?" he said in his sing-song drawl, "and digging pits too? Well, so do I. Er—that is, I like the first. You'd like to join the carpenter's shop, eh? and the smith's shop? But no motor-cars. Ranleigh can't afford to have its boys rushing about the roads. And there are the police to be considered. Well, boy, I'm your dormitory master; I hope you'll like Ranleigh."

It was Susanne's turn next. Clive watched the slouching figure of the young fellow bend politely, and marvelled as he discussed his coming with Old B. as if he were his grown-up equal. But that was the peculiarity about Susanne. Perhaps he had mixed more with men than with boys. Certainly he had an old-fashioned manner about him, while his self-assurance was far in excess of that usually displayed by one of school age. Then came the turn of other new boys, while the place of the master was taken by Sturton armed with pencil and paper, and rattling silver in his pocket. There were silver coins to be paid for the support of the football club run by One and Four South, a request to which Clive assented readily enough, though it depleted his purse sadly.

It was striking half-past nine when at length all had turned in save Sturton and Massey, the other prefect. They sat on the edge of the table occupying the centre of the dormitory, on a line with the two rows of basins running down the middle. Snuggled down on his pillow Clive watched them debating in animated manner, and rose on his elbow as a pair of heavy feet came thundering into the dormitory. A young man dressed in a blue cotton jacket hurried from jet to jet of the gas pipes, and with the help of a notched stick extinguished all but one. He was gone in a moment, his thunder resounding from the other dormitories.

"Good night, Darrell," called Susanne.

"Good night, Susanne."

Darrell dropped asleep feeling happy and entirely peaceful. He liked Ranleigh so far, liked it immensely. If there was a great drawback to the place, if Rawlings did happen to be there, and to have shown the most unfriendly intentions, at least there were good fellows enough. Bert and Hugh, for example. What luck their being at the school! And Susanne too, and Sturton, and Harvey. Yes, Harvey held pride of place. He was Captain, lord of all he surveyed, immeasurably above the head of the humble Clive Darrell.

The violent ringing of a bell awakened Clive. He started up in bed to find daylight streaming in through the high-placed dormer windows. That same youth who had operated the gas taps on the previous night was thundering through the dormitory with his hobnailed boots, swinging a bell of generous proportions. Later, Clive gathered that he was known as a "beaky." He crossed to a door at the near end of the place and tapped heavily upon it. Then he disappeared as if in a perpetual hurry, and the ringing of the bell resounded from the other dormitories. Clive hopped out of bed, thereby arousing the inmate of the next bed. That young gentleman raised a very sleepy face from his pillow, hit rather snappishly at the hand which Clive had laid on his bed thereby to steady himself, and dropped back on his pillow.

"Hang you, waking me!" he grumbled, his eyes half shut, as if, too, there had been no such thing as a bellman. "It's always the same with new kids. Get funked when they hear a bell. Want to hop up at once. Here, you Darrell, call me when it's twenty past the hour. I give myself ten minutes the first morning, afterwards just five. Any decent fellow can wash and dress in that time."

Clive followed Sturton and a few of the others out of the dormitory, slippers on his feet and a towel about his waist.

"Swim, eh?" asked Sturton, giving him an encouraging nod.

"Rather!"

"You're the sort of chap we want then. Hullo! Masters still fugging. None of those old games, Masters," sang out Sturton, whose manner of addressing the one in question showed that he meant to be head of his dormitory whatever happened. "Here, out you come! Fugging may be allowed at home, but at Ranleigh, never!"

The unfortunate individual who lay next to Clive, and who had declared his intention of sparing a bare ten minutes on this, the first morning, for the purpose of ablution and dressing, was dragged out of bed without ceremony.

"Hop into your shoes and no skulking," said Sturton, standing over him. "I've had enough of your slackness, Masters. Every chap over twelve in this dormitory goes down for a dip every morning. The kids can, too, if they like. Same with those in Four South. I tell you One and Four are going to come out cock dormitory in footer this term if I can manage it."

Grumbling was of no use. Indeed, Masters showed no great inclination that way. Clive found him, after a while, when they had become more intimate, a merry, contented fellow, but dreadfully lazy.

"A regular slacker," Sturton declared on more than one occasion. "There's a cart-load of sisters at his home, and they molly-coddle the fellow. If he imagines an ache or a pain, even in his toe, he lies abed in the morning and is fed by one of the many sisters. But there's no bringing chaps up here on the spoon. No hand-rearing at Ranleigh if I know it. When a chap's ill, he can go to the sick-room. That's right enough. Or to the 'sanny' if he's really bad. Otherwise he's got to be fit—fit as a fiddle, Darrell."

Sturton was nothing if not open and straight-forward. Clive found in him something strangely akin to Harvey, the idol of the lower school, the man admired and envied by all the seniors. For Sturton was fresh and breezy in his ways. He addressed the juniors, not as if they were so many nuisances, or as individuals vastly beneath his notice—a manner much resorted to by Rawlings and the fat-faced Trendall—but as equals, cheerily; but always in a way that showed that he expected instant obedience.

His motto was perfection. He set an example of the strenuous life, and allowed no shirking where games were concerned. Nor was he backward where work came into account. His figure, dressed in an overcoat over his pyjamas, often with a towel about his curly head, was familiar to all in the dormitory who happened to open their sleepy eyes in the early morning. For Sturton was "swatting." He had some examination in view, and since the rules of Ranleigh forbade the burning of the candle at both ends, and indeed compelled the shutting down of all lights by ten o'clock at night, Sturton perforce had to burn the candle at one end only, and that the daylight one. Five o'clock found him poring over his books at the dormitory table.

And now he was ready to lead his juniors for the morning plunge. His conquering eyes viewed every bed in the place. Peremptorily he called to certain fellows. And then the procession set out for the bath, not sedately following Sturton, but in a rushing crowd, which went like an avalanche down the stairs, out of the wide passage between Middle and Second Schools, and then into the corridor about the quad. Clive peeped through the open windows, innocent of glass till the coming of December, when the school carpenter would put the frames into position. He saw a wide quad, smoothly asphalted, and rising by steps on the north side to a central doorway. Those open windows ran round it on three sides, and doubtless there were corridors within them. But he had little time for observation, for as part of that scampering throng he went pell-mell down the corridor, swung sharply to the left, and then along the east side of the quad. Up a short flight of steps, worn into deep hollows by the shoe-leather of many a Ranleighan, to the right abruptly, and so down a whitewashed passage with an abrupt turn at the far end, and then through a doorway into the dressing-room of the bath. A stretch of water lay between concreted walls.

"Cold as ice," shivered Masters, still begrudging the comfort of his bed. "Sturton's a demon for hardening fellows. All the same, a fellow feels frightfully fit when he's had a dip in the early morning. But a bed pulls; I could always do two hours longer any morning."

What fellow in his schooldays couldn't? A cosy bed pulls very hard on a cold, dark morning; but, with a peremptory Sturton about, there was no shirking. One and Four South boys mingled with others from West, a single, large dormitory, with those from North and East, and splashed into the bath. Sturton had his own ideas as to how the plunge should be taken.

"Can't stand a chap who walks in," he said. "Might just as well have three inches of water in a tub in one's room. A fellow ought to dive, and he can go in off the board if he wishes. For me, there's no place like the shallow end. You've got to be canny when you dive, for there's not three feet of water, and if you scrape the bottom, why, concrete on a naked chest acts like a rough file on soft wood. It draws blood every time. So you've got to remember that. Now, young Darrell, show Susanne the way. Follow me to the deep end. The first plunge'll freeze you to the marrow. The swim down will warm your blood. You'll come out again with your skin on fire, feeling as fresh as a daisy."

Off he went, cutting the water obliquely. Indeed, the dive was bound to be almost a flat one. Sturton did not appear again till he rose at the far end of the bath. Down he sank again, pushed off from the far wall under water and came up under Clive's nose, to that young gentleman's wonder and admiration. Then Clive attempted the same thing, flopped badly, stinging his hide severely. The ice-cold water sent a chill to his very marrow as he entered it. And then, as Sturton had said, his blood seemed to boil up as he took a first stroke. He was in a beautiful heat when at length he returned to the shallow end and clambered out to watch Susanne. That young man—known already to his dormitory by the name Clive had given him—looked somewhat doubtfully at the bath.

"Swim?" asked Sturton, who had not yet got his measure, and who with insular pride and prejudice was apt to look down upon a foreigner. "Eh?"

"Yes, but——"

"What? Funk the dive?"

"Yes," admitted Susanne frankly. "But I'll do it if it kills me."

He went souse into the water, sending a huge wave before him, and rising a moment later to rub his knees and elbows.

"Come to ground?" asked Sturton sympathetically. "Well, you won't to-morrow. Nothing like having one jar to teach you to be careful. Off you go. We'll all of us have to be nippy."

Clive had never before had much need to practise haste, for at home breakfast had not been an early function, while the school he attended was within easy distance. But at Ranleigh he soon learned what it was to be something of a speed merchant where dressing was concerned. He could scrub his skin dry after his morning bath in a mere jiffy. The rush back to One South dried all the parts he had missed in his hurry. To dive into his clothing was a process facilitated by many an artful dodge. Masters, in fact, was a promising instructor.

"Stick your things overnight so as you can hop into 'em all together," he advised. "Vest and shirt always as one, mind you, and tie still on the collar. Of course, any juggins knows the dodge of getting into pants and socks at one operation, while if you don't bother to undo your shoes, you can push your feet into 'em in a jiffy. Five minutes is my time for washing and dressing."

"Was," corrected Sturton, who happened to overhear this edifying conversation. "Was, Masters. I've been doubtful about the efficacy of the washing part. Chaps in One South have got to be known as fresh-water fellows, and a piece out of your short allowance won't help us. Besides, you're over twelve. Don't you let me catch you missing your dip in the morning."

Once dressed on that first morning Clive drifted down the stairs to Middle School. There was no particular reason why he should go there. But numbers of the school were entering the narrow doors, and he followed. Bert was just within, looking thinner than ever, his eyes still more dreamy. And Hugh was beside him, vivacious and very wide awake.

"I say, how ripping!" he exclaimed. "But wouldn't the Governor be riled if he knew what had happened? It was the last thing he wanted to do to send us to the same school. What about that beast Rawlings? Thought I saw him in chapel last evening."

"Impossible! The lordly Rawlings go to Ranleigh!" exclaimed Bert. "Nothing less than Eton'd suit him."

"All the same, he's here. I travelled a part of the way down with him," said Clive. "I say, I'll tell you all about him later. He's a beast, and no mistake. But I want to get hold of that fellow. Hi, Susanne," he called.

The Frenchman shambled awkwardly towards them. His provincial clothes were in marked contrast to those of the other fellows. Not that that fact seemed to distress him. Susanne cared not a rap for popular opinion. Half-way towards Clive a big fellow jostled against him while deep in conversation with another, and jarred by the contact turned angrily upon him. It was Rawlings, with the oily, fat Trendall beside him. At once the bully's face reddened. He looked threateningly at Susanne, while the Frenchman regarded him with something approaching amusement.

"Pardon," he began, for he deemed himself the cause of the collision.

"Hang your pardon! Look here, you Frenchman, there's just one thing you've got to understand. I'm a prefect, and——"

"You're a new kid," chimed in Trendall, looking distinctly unamiable. In fact, this greasy, fat fellow had thrown in his lot with Rawlings since the previous evening. There had always been some sort of attraction between them. But Rawlings was to be a prefect. To the self-seeking Trendall that was sufficient, a friendship with him promised many advantages, and here was an opportunity to cement that friendship.

"Precisely," said Rawlings, "and the sooner you get to know it the better. You'll do well to sheer clear of this Darrell."

There was surprise in his eyes as he saw Bert and Hugh. A sneer gathered on his face, and then a scowl of anger. For Hugh grinned a grin of recognition. He remembered the pit, and the manner in which it had captured the wrong individual.

"You're here too; then you'll catch it," growled Rawlings, moving on with Trendall.

"Pleasant," smiled Hugh, when he had gone.

"A gentleman, eh?" asked Susanne, with a lift of his dark eyebrows. "But——"

"My friends, Bert and Hugh Seymour," introduced Clive. "That Rawlings is an out-and-outer. With Trendall as his toady, and perhaps another crony, they can make life unbearable here for us. That is, for Bert and Hugh and I."

"And Susanne," said that worthy, smiling. "Remember that I have been dragged into this matter."

"Tell you," cried Bert suddenly, "we'll send the beast an ultimatum. Tell him we'll hammer him if he interferes with one or any of us."

That scheme had to be put aside for the moment, for there came a clamour at the door. There arose a shout of "*Cave!* Old B.," and an instant later that fair giant entered the form room, obviously having easily overheard the warning. Boys ranged themselves up into line, and there began Call Over, Clive's and other new boys' names being tacked on at the end.

"'Sum, 'sum, 'sum," the answers sounded, and then were punctuated by the ringing of the chapel bell. The door, shut a few moments before on those who were late, was swung open, and they processed to the chapel. After that there was breakfast in the Hall, and, later, form work began with a vengeance, Clive being placed in the Lower Third, while Bert attained to the Upper; Hugh ascended only as high as Upper Middle, while, to the surprise of all, Susanne romped into the Upper Fourth. It followed, therefore, that some time elapsed before the little quartette met again. But when they did, Clive drew up a letter, which, having received the signatures of all concerned, was duly posted to "Albert Rawlings, Ranleigh, Local."

"This is to inform you," it ran, "that we, the undersigned, have decided to lick you every time you touch one of our band. We refrain from giving you our private and confidential opinion of you. As gentlemen, we feel that we have no right unduly to hurt your feelings. And also, this opinion of ours must be very well known to you. Just sheer off and leave us alone is the sincere advice of

Clive Darrell,

Bert Seymour,

Hugh Seymour,

Richard Feofé (Susanne)."

CHAPTER V

AN ULTIMATUM

"What'll you do?" asked Trendall, breathing heavily as he leaned over Rawlings' shoulder in Lower Sixth Form room and perused the ultimatum which Clive and his chums had sent. "Lick 'em all straight off, eh? But, of course, you'd have to catch 'em singly. That Feofé cad is as strong as a horse, and though he can't fight as an Englishman can, he'd kick like a horse."

It seemed likely enough that the lordly Rawlings had considered that side of the question, or perhaps was even then considering it. For he turned a furrowed brow to his comrade.

"I'm going to lie low," he said. "One thing's certain, the first chance I get I turn the Darrells away from our place. Of course, you know, Trendall, that we own the whole show that Darrell's father had. He made a mess of things, and my father came in and bought. That's why he hates me so much. As to this letter, pooh! I'll get even with 'em all before I've done. Feofé doesn't frighten me, not a bit."

Certainly not. Yet Susanne had pulled the great Rawlings' nose, and that brilliant and magnificent bully had not retaliated. But he would, some day, when the moment was propitious. For the time being he left the little quartette alone, and Clive and his fellows were therefore at liberty to forget the feud; which they did promptly. In the meanwhile, Ranleigh had many things of interest to show them.

"Look here, Darrell kid," observed Masters one day, presuming on his two months' seniority of Clive, and on the fact that he had been two terms at the school, "I don't mind taking you along to show you the sights. Been to the tuck?"

"What's that? Oh, tuck-shop, I suppose?"

"Of course, booby! You don't suppose it's a sort of place where they do the washing! Well, suppose we go there and introduce you? Eh?"

Clive agreed readily enough. He was beginning to find that life at Ranleigh opened up a wider prospect for him. At home he and Hugh and Bert had been the best of chums, and no one had been admitted into their close friendship. But here the matter was different, and better. For the difference in forms separated the chums often enough. True, Bert and Hugh were in the same class-room as

Clive, for it accommodated the two Middle and the two Third Forms. But at Ranleigh every hour saw a change in the class-rooms occupied by the various forms. Sometimes Clive was in Middle class-room, a little later he'd be in the Lower Fifth, and yet again in the "Stinks" room, a department that began soon to fascinate him, and which proved to be the one particular attraction to Susanne.

Circumstances, therefore, separated the chums often enough, for Bert and Hugh were in Four South Dormitory. Not that that prevented communication when in their respective dormitories, for the inventive Clive soon had a species of life-line manufactured, and this, when Sturton's attention was occupied elsewhere, could be tossed over the partition right on to Hugh's bed. Notes could thus be dragged backwards and forwards, and continuous communication kept up.

"But it can be improved, of course," said Clive, to which Hugh readily assented. "We'll make a telephone, nail the wires up the walls of the partition so that no one can see 'em, and then we can talk just as much as we want."

It never occurred to either of them that they might get all their chattering over in the daytime. But that is just the little point which people sometimes fail to comprehend. It was the novelty of clandestine conversation which attracted, and set these two inventors to work to construct a telephone from plans and descriptions given in a book they had managed to borrow.

In One South itself, Clive had Susanne always beside him, and very soon a firm friendship grew up between them. While on his other side lay Masters, the slug, as Sturton called him, a decent fellow, nevertheless, and now anxious to act as guide and faithful friend to our hero.

They passed along those endless corridors to the back doors, through which law compels the boys to emerge, and sauntered down between the Fives Courts. On the left lay the Gym, where Hugh had already been practising. Then beside the Tennis Courts, and away across the field which fronts the school. And who could wish for a better place? What father or mother or fond uncle or guardian could hope to find a healthier, better spot than Ranleigh? The world has heard of the school. It has made its mark in many a walk of life, so that there is no great need to describe it minutely or to mention its precise position. Suffice to say that it is situated in Surrey, that it projects three parts of the way up a sloping hill, which is bathed by the sun on every side. There is not a musty spot about it, not a corner nor a crevice in which injurious germs may hide. See it, then, a red-brick pile, clad with creeper, with its clock tower and its chimneys and pinnacles. Cast your eyes upon the surrounding country, and admit, as admit you must, that never was there a more ideal position. For the village is a mile away. The school stands beautifully isolated. Fresh breezes sweep direct from pine tree and heather across its roofs and into its windows. Add to these charms playing fields which vie with those of schools of greater antiquity, and you have a description of Ranleigh.

But we are forced to admit that Clive gave not a thought to it. He scudded across the field with Masters, dashed through the front gates and away down the road till they came to the tuck. It is a fascinating little shop, and here again we must admit that its contents appealed more strongly to Clive than did the surroundings.

"Never been in before, eh?" asked Masters slyly, well knowing the fact that Clive had not.

"Never; wish I had. Rippin', ain't it?"

"Not half bad," admitted Masters casually. "A chap can stuff himself full here for next to nothing. By the way——"

"Eh?" asked Clive, who was regarding a pile of apple tarts with close attention. "How much, please?" he asked the attendant.

"A penny each, sir."

"Cheap!" murmured Clive. "Oh, what where you saying, Masters?"

He was carefully inspecting the contents of his purse by then, and not looking particularly at Masters. It was not precisely what that young gentleman wanted. He coughed loudly. "Oh, never mind," he said lamely. "I—I didn't say anything."

It was such an obvious fib that Clive stared at him.

"Oh, did I?" then remarked Masters. "Oh, yes, I remember. But it doesn't matter."

He thrust his hands into his pockets, turned to the door, and beckoned to Clive. "Come on," he said, somewhat sadly. "Let's clear. I'll take you in some other time."

That was just the very thing that Clive could not agree to. He had been thick-headed before. But now he was beginning to grasp the situation. It was awfully nice of Masters, too, he thought, though, to be sure, he didn't see the smile on the face of the attendant.

"What's up?" he demanded. "You're never going to leave the tuck without eating something?"

"Must," came the answer.

"Why?"

"Oh, never mind." Masters shrugged his shoulders, and went from the cottage, Clive following. "Fact is," he admitted, once they were outside, "I've forgotten to bring money with me. It's a beastly nuisance."

"But it don't matter," cried Clive. "I'll lend you some."

"And then, of course," Masters hurriedly interjected, "it's a sort of custom here, you know, for new kids to—oh, never mind, let's clear."

"To what?" demanded Clive, beginning to fathom the mystery.

"Well, if you must know, it's a sort of custom at Ranleigh for new kids to stand treat the first time they enter the tuck. But it don't matter, as I said. Let's clear. I never borrow money."

The generous-minded Clive could see only one way out of the difficulty. Indeed, he was eager to show his hospitality. And so five minutes later found the two youngsters securely seated in the little room beyond the tuck, their feet over a gas fire, their teeth busily engaged with apple tarts, while steaming cups of cocoa stood beside them. By then, Masters' modesty had entirely departed. It had been a wrench, of course, to allow a new kid to treat him! But in for a penny in for a pound wasn't a bad motto.

"Tried those big chaps?" he asked, pointing to a box of squares of chocolate. "Ripping! They're only a penny, and there's different colours all the way through. Tony—met Tony yet? He's a fellow with red hair in Two South— well, Tony swears that there's regular pictures worked up in those squares, and that if you bite carefully you can see 'em. I don't believe it myself, but it's a joke trying."

Clive did know Tony. He was the red-headed fellow who had shouted at him and been so very pugnacious on the first night of the term when Clive had entered the wrong dormitory. As to the squares, well, it would be rather a joke to test this theory of Tony's.

"We'll test 'em, then," he said. "How many, eh?"

"Well, of course," said Masters guardedly, "a fellow could do it with one, I suppose. But he'd have to be clever. Two'd give a chap a better chance, while— —"

"Sixpenn'o'th of those square things, please," demanded Clive, who was warming to Masters, and who happened to have received a useful present from a distant uncle that very morning. "You try first, Masters."

"And those brandy balls are just the things for prep.," remarked Masters, some little time later, as if it were an afterthought and he had not meant Clive to hear. "They're hot with peppermint, and you can smell 'em all over the class-room. It makes the chaps look round and long for some themselves, while the prefect who's in charge of the room gets raging. Come on, Darrell."

It was perhaps a fortunate thing that Clive's stock of sixpennies was becoming small, or he would have listened further to the blandishments of the crafty Masters. As it was, he purchased a liberal quantity of brandy balls, divided them with his friend, and then went off to other fields.

"Sundy tuck's there," Masters informed him as they skirted the common, where cricket matches are played. "Of course, the Head knows that there is one, and would give his ears to catch chaps there. My word, they would get a licking! But he can't succeed, and for a very good reason. You see, a chap can slip in without being seen, and if the Head or any other inquisitive master happens to come along and suspect, why, you can bolt from the back door, up the garden and over the wall at the end. I've done it. So have other chaps."

Before three weeks of his first term had passed Clive had a nodding acquaintance with all the surroundings of the school, and with most of the fellows. Moreover, he had witnessed the first great footer match of the season, and his youthful chest had swelled with pride because of the prowess of Harvey and other men. In fact, he was slowly and steadily imbibing that spirit of *esprit de corps* which helps a school along. He was beginning to understand that self-effacement is a good thing at times, and that the good of the school as a whole is what should be considered. Else, why did Harvey work so hard to train the team while still doing his best in school time? Why also did Sturton work so loyally to support him, and still rise at cock-crow every morning so as to prepare his own tasks?

But early frosts somewhat upset the plans of the Captain, and saw letters innumerable despatched to some three hundred homes, demanding that skates should be sent immediately.

"Another day's frost and we'll be able to go anywhere. They say the canal's good," said Hugh, who had been making diligent enquiries. "But my mark is the lake at Ditton."

"Private, isn't it?" asked Masters, who had joined the little band of friends, and who, in fact, was often with them.

"Yes. But what's it matter? The Delarths are away from home. They'd never want to keep good ice all to themselves. We'll take french leave."

"Or write and ask. Why not?" ventured Bert mildly.

"Why not?" repeated Susanne, with sparkling eyes. "It will make the fun better. Besides, it is rude, is it not, to trespass on private property?"

They scoffed at him promptly, and the very mention of rudeness put aside the intention to write.

"It'll be part of the lark to go without being invited," said Hugh. "I know the place already, for I've been skirmishing round to discover likely spots for nesting. In the spring I'll be there. And if this frost continues, I mean to try what it's like on the ice. So there, Susanne."

Two days later, after an intervening thaw of some five hours' duration, whereat the hopes and the faces of every member of the school, save the Captain and the footer team, fell dismally, the ice was reported to be bearing on neighbouring ponds, and particularly on that one down by the common in front of the butcher's shop. It had frozen very hard overnight, and the ground was as hard as a stone. After dinner, therefore, Bert and Hugh and Clive set out, Susanne being in their company also, with Masters following behind as soon as he could get away, an "impot" of some length having detained him. Indeed, the self-same Masters had made a valiant attempt to complete the task during dinner-hour in Hall. A pen of Clive's own invention had been brought into request. Thereon were fixed no fewer than three nibs, all of which would write at the same moment.

"You see, it's not one of those clumsy things one's heard of," said the lordly inventor when he produced this wonderful time-saving implement. "Anyone can tie three nibs on to one holder and try to write with 'em all. But the blots he makes, my word! One nib rests nicely, but has too much ink. A second is too short to reach the paper, while the third sticks the point through and tears a hole. This pen gets over all three difficulties. So long as you dip her carefully, she'll write, for all the nibs are carried on spring holders. It's a champion. I'm going to bring out a self-filling six-line automatic writer before I've ended. I'll sell 'em by the ton to chaps at school."

No doubt he might if he were fortunate, and if all "impots" were of the same character as that given to Masters. That worthy having incurred the displeasure of his form master had been very politely and in dulcet tones requested to deliver five hundred repetitions of the following statement. "There's a time and a place for everything."

"And all because he scented peppermint," declared Masters hotly, when he reported the matter to his cronies. "That chap Canning's a bounder. He's always finding fault somewhere."

"But," ventured Bert cynically, "perhaps he doesn't like peppermint."

"Doesn't like peppermint! Rot!" cried Masters. "Who doesn't?"

"Well, you do," grinned Susanne.

"And so does any decent fellow. But that's where it is. Canning isn't a decent fellow. He's always grousing. Masters, you're talking. Masters, you don't answer. Masters, you're a fool. Masters——"

"You're a glutton," grinned Hugh, enjoying the indignation of that individual, and receiving a buffet for his pains. "Well, he cobbed you sucking brandy balls, given you by Clive."

"And told me that they were beastly, that I was making a beast of myself to suck 'em in class time, and that there was a time and a place for everything. Then gave me an impot."

"Which has to be done."

"That's it, and there's skating this afternoon. I'm going."

It followed that Clive's inventive genius was called in to help, and that day at dinner, Masters, having gobbled up his meal, spent the rest of his time crouching over a book resting on his knee, on which was stretched the paper on which he was operating. And all would have been well, for he was making amazing progress with that patent pen, but for the fact that a sudden and unforeseen difficulty had arisen. The penny bottle of ink he had requisitioned had the most idiotically narrow neck.

"Asses!" he growled, showing the difficulty to Clive, who sat next him. "What makes 'em turn out bottles like that? How's a chap to get to work?"

Clive had many brilliant ideas constantly occurring to him.

"Shove it into a spoon," he urged. "A tablespoon. Empty the bottle in, and then you can dip easy. It'll prevent you dipping too deep. Get on with it."

Masters realised the brilliance of the suggestion, and at once put it into practice. He took the biggest spoon to be had, buttressed it around with bread-crumbs, and then emptied his ink from the bottle. That was famous.

"One gets along like a house on fire," he told Clive triumphantly. "And the writing's ripping. Old Canning'll remark on it. George! Darrell, you might sell him one of your pens. Look! There's fifty of the beastly lines written. Here we go again. 'There's a time and a place for everything.' So there is, my boy. Hall's the place for writing rotten impots, specially when there's skating."

Hall, no doubt, was an excellent place. But accidents will happen, and here with the most surprising result. For Masters, after much diligence, had actually managed to complete three hundred lines when his sleeve got anchored in the handle of the spoon filled with ink. It jerked over, and in one brief instant the writer of the "impot" had the contents of the spoon in his lap, while some of the inky mess flowed over the table, making an excellent black map on the cloth.

"What a mess!" he groaned, when he had vainly mopped at his trousers with his handkerchief. "I'm sopping wet, and as black as a hat. And look at that beastly tablecloth. Here, Darrell, suggest something."

The best that Clive could do was to propose a covering of bread-crumbs and salt, with which the huge stain was promptly covered. But all to no purpose. The eagle eye of the Captain of the School going the round of the tables in Hall after "knock up," when there was compulsory silence, discovered the map which Masters had painted so unwittingly.

"Whose is that?" he demanded.

"Masters'."

"Ah! Writing at table. An hour's drill to-morrow, Masters. And that mess'll cost half a crown. Perhaps more. Why, your seat is smothered also. You're wet to the skin. Report to the matron afterwards, and get a change. I'll talk to you this evening."

There was Masters in trouble with a vengeance. His "impot" had to be commenced again, for ink had flown liberally over it. His trousers were ruined, and doubtless his under garments. There was half a crown at least to pay, and a visit to Harvey into the bargain.

"When there'll be a whacking," grinned Bert, always the cynic. "That'll be merely as a precaution. He'll lay it on hot so as to warm you and drive off the chill you'll be sure to have contracted."

Masters was not in sufficiently good frame of mind to trust himself to answer. But skate he meant to. So at the moment when Clive and his friends left the building, he was seeking new raiment in his dormitory, having already obtained fresh underclothing from the matron. Then, by dint of running, he caught up the little band who were bent on trespass, just before they reached the ring fence that surrounded the property of the Delarths.

"Just look round and make sure there's no one about," cautioned Clive, glancing over his shoulder. "Now, Hugh, you've been here before. You lead the way."

"Then over the fence. Into that copse at once, and then bang straight ahead. The only fellows we have to look out for are the keepers. Of course, they'll hate our going through their covers. But then, something's got to give way when there's skating. Over we go. Last man take a look round when he's joined us."

It took them perhaps half an hour to creep through the wood into which Hugh led them. Sometimes they imagined they heard voices, and when that was the case they cast themselves flat on the frozen ground and listened with bated breath. But there was nothing else to alarm them, and pushing on they arrived at length—after much exertion, for the cover was thick and brambles had a peculiar fascination for their persons—at the edge of the lake on which they proposed to skate.

"Well, I'm jiggered!" declared Hugh, his face flushing, his steaming breath a cloud all round him. "There's someone on the place already."

"Someone? A dozen people," Bert corrected him.

"And—I wouldn't like to swear to it, but I do believe that that's old Canning," said Masters, glowering on an individual who suddenly came into view from the misty distance and swept across the smooth sheet of ice towards them. "Just like him to set a fellow an impot so as to prevent his skating, and then, when that chap had taken no end of pains to get finished and——"

"Including half drowning himself with ink," grinned Bert, as a gentle reminder.

"And getting a half-crown fine marked up against him," laughed Clive, giggling at his friend's misadventure.

"And," proceeded Masters severely, ignoring the interruption, "and was working like a nigger, it's just like this cad Canning to turn up at the very spot and spoil fun entirely."

That was where the sight of this master affected the whole party. His imposition was merely a matter between himself and Masters. Of course, they were all awfully sorry for Masters, though his getting soaked with ink was a jolly old joke, whatever he thought of it—but Canning was a cad, all the same.

"What's he want to come along here trespassing on our property?" demanded Hugh hotly.

"But—it isn't ours, is it?" asked Bert dryly, whereat Susanne threatened him with violence.

"Of course it's not," the slouching Frenchman answered. "Not actually, you know. But we thought of the place first. We've the most right to it. What's Canning want hanging round the ice we've selected?"

"Cheek! Beastly impudence!" declared Clive grandly, while Masters still glowered on the unconscious master. For it was Mr. Canning without a doubt, a kill-joy on this occasion. For, having gained the lake after such great trouble, Clive and his friends dared not venture upon the ice they coveted.

"There's that cad Rawlings," suddenly whispered Bert, for Mr. Canning was close to them, and had sat down to smoke a cigarette.

"And the greasy Trendall. He's always sure to be somewhere within distance," growled Masters.

"And if that isn't Harvey, with Sturton near him, I'm not worth listening to," observed Clive, as if he were speaking of a certainty. "Yes, there's Harvey, hand in hand with Miss Withers."

"But—I don't understand," said Bert, smiling grimly when some few minutes had passed. "There are hundreds of our fellows. They're arriving every minute. Surely——"

Slowly it began to dawn upon the little band that perhaps all their secrecy and all their effort had been wasted.

"Supposing leave was given for the school to skate here," suggested Hugh, aghast at the thought.

"There's Smith Primus. Let's ask him," cried Clive, catching sight of a fellow of his acquaintance.

"But there's Canning still there," said Masters, with something approaching a groan. "Supposing leave's been given for the school to skate here——"

"And supposing—which seems a moral certainty—that we've made out-and-out fools of ourselves," interjected Bert satirically.

"Oh, shut up, do!" growled Masters, while Hugh caught his brother by the collar. "Supposing that's the case——"

"What?" demanded the incorrigible Bert. "That we've made asses of ourselves? That's dead certain."

Masters looked as if he would gladly slay him. But he was determined to continue. Moments were flying as they discussed matters, and if they were to skate at all they must clear up this mystery.

"Supposing that's so. Well, in any case, these woods are out of bounds and we're trespassing. Unless we can slip out on to the ice without that cad Canning seeing us, why——"

"Skating's out of the question," groaned Clive. "Look here, you fellows. I'll slip on my skates, wait for Canning to turn his head, and then go swinging past him. If I signal you on, you'll know skating's allowed, and can slip on to the ice one by one as I've done. Eh?"

They agreed to the proposition. Clive, moreover, was successful, and in a little while was diligently waving them on. And then his chums followed, all contriving to escape the eye of the smoking Canning, except Masters.

"Oh, Masters, that you?" he demanded, swinging his head as that young hopeful happened to emerge from the wood and approach the ice. "Been trespassing, eh? Been into the wood?"

There could be no denial. Masters could merely glance at Mr. Canning as if he wished the most dreadful thing to happen to him.

"Yes, sir," he said curtly.

"Then you've forgotten our little conversation, and the lines you've no doubt waiting at the school to give to me. Let me see. Yes. 'There's a time and a place for everything.' Those were the words. Well, they're true of this occasion. This isn't the time for trespassing when Mr. Delarth has so kindly given the school permission to skate on his lake. He particularly wished that there should be no disturbance of the covers. Masters, you must have sadly forgotten the lesson I attempted to teach you. Let me have those words written an additional five hundred times by to-morrow afternoon."

"There's a beast!" said the unfortunate delinquent, when he rejoined his friends. "I'd fifty times rather be sent to the Head with a note and take a whacking. This impot business is breaking my spirit."

But you wouldn't have thought so had you seen him ten minutes later. He was hurtling over the surface of the lake at lightning speed, with a string of boys on either side of him. It was an hour later when there came a shout from a far corner. Clive, dashing in that direction, saw that the white surface of the ice was broken and flooded. There were dark heads floating above the water. One was that of a girl. Susanne's face was amongst them. Trendall's, too, fat and oily.

"Help!" shouted Clive, and at once set about a rescue.

CHAPTER VI

CLIVE AND HIS FRIENDS TRIUMPHANT

That shout for help brought a scurrying crowd swooping over the frozen surface of the lake toward the spot where the ice had broken. It was taken up by more than a hundred. Small boys—kids, as Masters scoffingly designated them—gave voice to the call in high-pitched falsettos. Those of the senior school gave ear to the calls, and bore down upon the spot in silence. Canning—Masters' *bête noire*—threw away his cigarette and scuttled over the ice at a rate which was marvellous. But Clive was there first, and we speak the truth when we say that he was flabbergasted. Talk about a fellow being trained to be ready to meet any emergency! Clive was out of the running. He hadn't an idea. For at least twenty seconds he stared at Susanne's face, peeping out of the water, as if the sight robbed him of reason. And then his inventive brain set to work.

"Hold on to the edge of the ice," he bellowed. "There's a ladder back over there. We'll send for it. Look out, I'm coming."

Susanne nodded cheerfully. He had his arm round the waist of the lady who had been immersed, and grinned at Clive.

"Hurry up, then," he bellowed. "Don't mind myself, you know, but there's the lady."

What was Trendall doing? Clive saw him grip in frenzied fashion at the ice and slip off. He made another effort, and then stretched his arms over his head. Was he sinking? wondered Clive.

"Look out," he yelled, slipping to his knees and crawling toward the dark and jagged-edged hole. "Look out for Trendall."

Susanne cast his eye over his shoulder, hitched the elbow about the lady on the edge of the ice and gripped Trendall. He pushed him against the edge of the ice, and then finding his own grip slipping, he let go his hold.

"Hold tight there," he shouted.

"Hold to the ice," bellowed Clive, sliding nearer and now flat on his face. "Hold to the ice, Trendall. Get away from Susanne."

But Trendall was not only exhausted; he was in a panic. Slipping from the ice again, he touched Susanne's shoulder, and then gripped it. Out shot the other hand and fastened about him. The three—Trendall, Susanne, and the lady—bobbed down beneath the water.

"Let go! Let go, Trendall, you idiot!" shouted Clive, and then glanced over his shoulder. There was a ring of fellows round the gap in the ice, kept at a respectful distance by two of the prefects. Behind them again were some dozen of the seniors scudding away for the ladder for which Clive now shouted. Harvey was coming in Clive's wake, very cautiously, but not for fear of his own safety, while Rawlings stood irresolute, and when he saw that he was attracting attention, slunk to the rear of the gathering.

"Go quietly there, Darrell," Harvey called. "The ice is awfully rotten and will let you in if you're rash. I'll be as near as possible, and as soon as the ladder comes I'll push it right out to you. Ah! That chap Trendall will drown the lot of them. Leave go there, Trendall!" he shouted peremptorily.

But the fat and greasy senior who had toadied to Rawlings, and who had taken his part against Bert and Hugh and Clive, may be said at the moment to have been completely out of his element. Such a catastrophe as this was just the thing to test a fellow's courage, and Trendall did not shine at all. Susanne, on the contrary, might, but for the awkward turn events had now taken, have been merely enjoying a bath. But matters were too desperate for enjoyment. Trendall had firm hold of him, and though Susanne made a valiant effort, the hulking senior was dragging him down and the lady also. It was then that Clive acted. The crowd gathered behind first held their breath and then cheered him. In his enthusiasm Masters dashed forward, and throwing himself on his face wriggled towards him; while Hugh skated over the ice reckless of the consequences, till a stern command from Mr. Canning caused both to halt. For Clive had plunged forward.

"Look out, Susanne!" he called. "I'm coming in to help. You hand the lady over to me and then tackle Trendall. The fellow's gone stark, staring mad."

"LOOK OUT, SUSANNE! I'M COMING IN TO HELP"

Wriggling his way rapidly forward he was near the broken edge within a few seconds, when, as was to be expected, the ice broke with a soft, grating sound, letting him into the freezing water. And it was high time that someone came to Susanne's help, for that young fellow had more to fight against than he had strength for. He struck savagely at Trendall, but without result. He was dragged under by the combined weight of the lady and the lout who had now seized him. Clive even noticed that his face had gone a purply red colour, while when he came to the surface Susanne gasped for breath frantically, showing how immersion was telling upon him.

"Hand over the lady. Beat that cad off," bellowed Clive, striking out for the trio. "Now Susanne, hand over."

Fellows would have laughed at Clive at any other time, for it was ludicrous to see one of his small stature grasping the waist of a lady decidedly bigger than he. But the event was too serious. Also there was so much movement. For there were others bent on rescue. Harvey was there, and with one glance over his shoulder, and a caution to the prefects to keep the crowd back, he floundered across the ice and broke his way into the dark fluid in which the four were now floating.

"Push that ladder out quick," he shouted, as he sank into the water. "Send young Seymour and Masters forward. They can both swim and are light weights. Ah! Sturton, get together one or two of the senior fellows, and if things get worse come in in a body."

Then he left the edge of the ice and struck out. As for Sturton, if Harvey had not already gone to the rescue, he would have done so most certainly. But as we have said before, he could be counted on always to back up his senior loyally. He swung round on the crowd of boys instantly.

"Newman, you'll do," he said, beckoning a stoutly built fellow to him. "Collins Primus too. There's Jimmy Pritchard. Coming, eh?"

"Rather. Ready for anything," was the quick answer as the young men selected skated forward.

"Then Gaspard also. He's a swimmer, and you, Rawlings."

All came to the front. All? No. Rawlings seemed to be deaf. Sturton had recognised him standing at the back of the crowd, and at the summons Rawlings had sidled away. In the distance, coming towards him at a fast pace, he espied a group of fellows bearing the ladder for which Clive had shouted. In a second he seized upon the opportunity and turned away. But Sturton knew his man, and summoned him again in a voice there was no denying.

"Rawlings," he called. "I shouted for you. You're either deaf and did not hear, or—coming?"

There was no way out of it. The lordly youth who had made matters so disagreeable both at home and at the school for Clive and his friends turned with as good a grace as he could summon, and pushed his way through the crowd.

"Did you call?" he asked lamely.

"Did he call?" echoed one of the prefects satirically, a chum of Sturton's, one, too, who had taken Rawlings' measure long ago. "Every man in the school heard your name."

"But you," interjected Barrold, a puny Sixth Form fellow, who made up for lack of inches by inordinate go and good spirits.

"Perhaps he didn't though," broke in Bagshaw, the scribe of Ranleigh, the scholar who was most often to be seen arm in arm with Harvey. Everyone knew that Bagshaw was the prince of good fellows, always anxious to save a row. They knew, too, that footer and cricket and swimming were forbidden to him. And yet Bagshaw pushed himself forward.

"Here, Sturton," he said brusquely, "let me come. I'm always put in the background. Rawlings is a strong chap and can help to manage the ladder."

And thus the incident was passed over. In the heat and excitement of the moment, too, there was every opportunity for fellows to forget it. Few, indeed, had overheard the satirical words uttered by Barrold and the other prefect. Still fewer had noticed the flush which came to Rawlings' face to hide the pallor with which it had been covered a moment before. And none were witness of the mutterings he gave vent to as he turned to meet the bearers of the ladder. But Sturton knew, the delicate Bagshaw also, that Rawlings had funked. Hugh Seymour learned of it, too, on the morrow.

Meanwhile, all eyes were fixed on the figures struggling in the water. Clive had relieved Susanne of his burden, and clung with his free hand to the ice. As to the jovial Susanne, things were going hard with him. Had he been called upon some three minutes earlier to free himself of the fellow clinging like a limpet to him, he would doubtless have succeeded, though not with ease, for the arms and grip of a drowning man are not quickly to be thrown off. But the young chap had been pulled beneath the surface of the water so often that he was already exhausted. Trendall still clung firmly to him. Even Clive could make no impression on those clawing hands, though he made an attempt to do so, hooking his elbow on the ice as Susanne had done. He was feeling desperate indeed, in his helplessness; for Susanne was more often under the water than above it.

"Supposing he gets under the ice! That chap's drowning him. Hi! Help!" he bellowed.

And then Harvey came into view. The Captain of the School cleft the ice debris and the water with lusty strokes, and was soon close to Susanne. He tugged, too, at those encircling arms, but they defied him. Then, while the crowd watching held their breath, he lifted one arm, doubled his fist, and brought it crash down on the head of Trendall. And that had the desired effect. The grip slackened. The two drowning lads separated. A second or so later there was a loud splash near at hand, and Sturton plunged into the icy water.

"Saw you'd more than you could manage, old chap," he said curtly to Harvey. "So came along to help. You fix that chap Trendall. I'll manage Feofé. Well done, Darrell! One South's looking up, eh? How's the lady?"

"Insensible, I think. She's very heavy. But I can manage. Ah! I'm awfully glad you've got him."

Sturton had gripped Susanne by then, and now had his head clear of the water. The big head of the Frenchman, with its dripping, tousled mat of hair, lay on his shoulder. The face was deadly pale, as pale as that of the lady he had been supporting, as white and blanched as that even of Rawlings as he heard Sturton's summons. His eyes were tightly closed. The cheeks seemed to have fallen in. A frightful feeling of despair assailed Clive Darrell. At that instant he seemed to be able for the first time to measure his friendship for Susanne.

"Hooray for Ranleigh! Hold on to them, you chaps! Well done, Darrell! Three cheers for Harvey and Sturton!"

The crowd went frantic and delirious with delight at the dash and success of their comrades. Now that Harvey and Sturton had gone to help, not one but deemed the rescue certain, if not quite complete. The boys yelled themselves hoarse. Some danced on their skates with excitement. Mr. Canning alone seemed to retain his self-possession. Dodging from side to side all this while, anxiously watching what was passing, he had long ago slipped off coat and waistcoat. Perhaps he was fifty years of age. At any rate, his hair was white at the temples, and from the point of view of the fellows at Ranleigh that stamped him as an old man. But he was active enough, though not so much so as Harvey. Still, he was ready himself to plunge to the rescue should more help be needed, and for the moment he kept the boys back, and kept his head, which was, after all, a more important undertaking.

"Ah! There's the ladder," he exclaimed in tones of relief, as Rawlings and a number of others appeared. "Hand it to me. That's right, slide it flat over the surface. Now, keep that crowd well back. Well done, young Seymour! Hullo, that you, Masters?"

This latter individual gave his form master a curt nod. There was no rudeness meant. Only Masters was intensely excited, intensely eager to see his chum Clive in safety. He answered Mr. Canning just as he would have answered any other fellow at the moment.

"Gently does it. I'm too big a weight to go too far forward. Seymour, you're light enough. If the ice gives and lets you in I'll come after you. Now, on we go. As quick as we can."

Hugh made up his mind how to act in a moment. He stepped on to the rungs of the ladder, lay flat down on it as if it were a sledge, and then called back to Masters and to Mr. Canning.

"Push her along," he said, unwinding the long scarf he had wrapped round his neck. "The ice is cracking a little, but I think it'll bear. Farther. A little farther."

Thrusting the ladder before them, the two behind soon had the satisfaction of seeing Hugh within reach almost of Clive. Then there was an ominous cracking. The surface of the ice sank beneath Hugh and was swamped with water. A moment or two later it gave way, letting him into the lake. Then a coil of rope swished across Masters' shoulder, tossed by a keeper who had suddenly come upon the scene.

"Shunt the ladder round to the far side, sir," he called. "There's a spring over here, and that makes the ice rotten. Shunt it round, then tie the rope and go ahead. You'll have to be quick. Them chaps is more'n half frozen."

Clive felt numbed through already. He could see Harvey's lips shivering, and his teeth chattering. Sturton, too, looked blue, while Hugh, who had swum over to join him, looked pinched and desperately cold. Anxiously they watched as Masters tied the rope to the end of the ladder, and then with Mr. Canning's help changed its position. Once more it was thrust forward, this time with Masters flat upon the narrow end.

"Heave!" shouted the keeper. Masters took the coil and sent it twirling over the group in the water. Harvey caught it.

"Here," he gasped, nodding to Clive. "Take it. Seymour'll help you with the lady."

They made a turn round her waist, and then as Masters drew upon the rope they pushed and helped the body of the unconscious lady on to the ice. A terrific cheer greeted this successful operation. Masters drew the lady toward him, swiftly threw off the rope and tossed it back to his comrades, and then backed with his burden.

"Well done! Well done, indeed!" cried Mr. Canning. "Here, Bagshaw and some of you others, carry her away to safety. Ah, they're sending Feofé next."

The ungainly form of the gallant Susanne was slowly hoisted on to the ice and dragged towards the crowd. Bert was the first to make his way to the front to receive him, and once with Bagshaw's help having carried him to the rear of the crowd, he set about reviving him in a manner quite scientific. He rolled and squeezed Susanne till one might have accused him of positive roughness. He worked till his breath came in gasps, and until another of the fellows came in to assist him.

Meanwhile, there remained in the water Trendall and four others, and soon enough the former was sent to safety.

"Now," said Harvey, when the rope came swishing over them again, "Darrell." But Clive showed no keenness.

"Quick!" commanded Harvey. "Off you go."

"Please," began Clive, for to argue with the great Harvey seemed a sacrilege— "please, Harvey——"

"Eh? What on earth's the matter with the kid?" demanded that latter. "Look here, we're all of us jolly well frozen. I am, at any rate. Ranleigh don't want to have to record a death on this occasion. So out you go."

But again Clive objected. "Oh, I say, Harvey, please——" he began. "I—you know——"

Harvey scowled. The pleasant-faced captain of the school actually scowled. Had he been on terra firma and this Darrell dared to disobey his glance even, Harvey would have booted him.

"Yes, I'd boot the little beggar," he said angrily, for he was still fearful of what might happen. But Sturton knew his man to a T. He leaned over, all dripping as he was, and whispered to Harvey.

"Leave the kid," he said. "He was first here, and he makes it a sort of point of honour. Leave the kid, Harvey."

Thereat the Captain grunted. He looked closely at Clive, and then motioned to Sturton.

"You go, then," he said. "But you'll explain. It's the place of the captain of anything, whether ship or school, to go last out of danger. But, dash it, this kid's worth making an exception for. Heave up, Sturton. I'm keen to get out of this water."

And that was how it happened that Clive left the hole in the ice last. The cheers which greeted the coming of each one of them were thunderous. They even brought a chilly blush to Clive's cheeks. But he was given very little time in which to listen.

"Get off back to the school," commanded Sturton. "Here, you Hugh Seymour and Darrell, cut quick. Report to the matron when you're back. Run all the way. I'll boot you if you don't. Do you hear? Skip, then."

"And ask Mrs. Tyndal to have hot bottles and blankets ready," shouted Mr. Canning, who was bustling from Feofé to Trendall, and back to the still unconscious lady. "We'll get some sort of conveyance and send them up. Now, you boys, strip off your skates and help to carry our patients."

Thanks to the fact that the Headmaster of Ranleigh was an enlightened individual and believed in teaching his scholars other things than merely Greek,

Latin, and Mathematics, there were numbers of the fellows who, like Bert, had more than a smattering of the art of First-Aid. Still, the surface of a frozen lake is not the best of places on which to revive semi-drowned individuals. And then, unconsciousness in all three cases was due perhaps in great degree to cold and exposure. There were not wanting willing hands to carry Susanne, the lady, and Trendall to the big house adjacent to the lake, where hot baths administered by the housekeeper and her attendants soon helped matters wonderfully. But it was late in the evening before Mr. Canning set out with two blanketed figures. By then Clive and Hugh had put in an appearance, glowing from head to foot after their sharp run up to the school. Sturton and Harvey were not long in following, and by tea time a hot bath had made the glow about their bodies permanent. They descended to the Hall in a body, the school being already assembled, and we record only the truth when we say that their appearance was the signal for an outburst of enthusiasm entirely unprecedented. Never before had Ranleigh been so stirred. Never before had there been an event quite so exciting. Ranleigh was known far and wide for the strength of its lungs, for the liberality and genuineness of its applause. But now the school went mad. Defying fines, boys stood on the tables and cheered as Clive and Hugh and Sturton and Harvey went to their places. The fellows cheered themselves hoarse, and called for speeches. Then the sudden appearance of the Headmaster put a damper for the moment on their enthusiasm.

Let us more fully describe the one who held in his hands the administration of Ranleigh. Not tall, as we have said already, not perhaps very striking in appearance, Dr. Layman yet attracted and held the interest and sympathy of any body of people he cared to address. Clean-shaven, save for a pair of whiskers, grey-headed, he presented a face which was the essence of kindness. A pair of twinkling eyes were wont to look down upon the school, whether from his seat in Chapel, or from the dais in Hall. Austere some would have called him, those who looked but once at his face. A jolly, rollicking fellow the boys knew him to be, save when there was occasion for severity. And now he stood of a sudden before them. Did he notice those who, contrary to all regulations, contrary, indeed, to all precedent, had mounted the tables in their enthusiasm? If he did, he showed no sign of having done so, while they slunk back to a more decorous position.

"Boys," he began, shutting his eyes as was his wont when addressing an audience, "boys of Ranleigh, to-day I am a proud man."

They made the old Hall ring with their cheers and shouts. Evans Tertius even, the smallest of all there, raised a shrill voice to swell the cheering of his comrades. And then silence fell again, a silence that was trying.

"Boys of Ranleigh, I feel that I have reason to be proud of this school to-day. For some of your comrades have behaved with heroism, while all have shown coolness in time of danger. I need mention no names. Those who have done best of all are well known to you. I congratulate them, and I congratulate the school on having them amongst us. That is all. Trendall and Feofé and the lady are now recovered, I am glad to say. Boys, there will be no preparation this evening."

Yes, Ranleigh cheered again. The boys shouted themselves hoarse, even when the Doctor had left them. And then, Nature asserting herself, they sat down to discuss the meal, for appetites were keen after the skating. We can believe, too, that the affair was discussed threadbare before evening was ended, while glances turned frequently towards Clive and the others. Some, too, were turned in Rawlings' direction.

"The fellow funked," said Barford deliberately.

"No," corrected Bagshaw politely. "Look here, Barford, don't say that. I'm not too fond of Rawlings, I own. But if the school got to think a thing like that he'd never have another decent minute. Let him have the benefit of the doubt. The thing'll be a lesson to him."

As for Masters, delighted with the ending of such an adventure, and forgetful for the moment of his ill luck when at dinner, he sat down after tea with that wonderful pen of Clive's invention and began upon the task which Mr. Canning had set him.

"Beastly cad," he told himself, but with far less bitterness than on that same afternoon. "But he bucked up awfully well to-day. You could see he was ready to go in and help the others. All the same, what's he want to give me such an impot for? Beast, I call him."

"Oh, hullo," called a voice at the doorway. "That you, Masters?"

The owner of the name admitted the fact with reddened face. "Yes, sir," he said lamely.

"Writing?"

"Yes, sir."

"Home?"

"No, sir."

"Or doing impots?"

Mr. Canning grinned. It was like the cad, thought Masters for a moment. Then, catching something out of the usual in the master's smile, he permitted himself to smile back in return.

"Impots, sir," he said.

"Ah! There's a time and a place for everything, eh, Masters?"

What could the young fellow do but grin? Mr. Canning looked absolutely genial. Now that Masters came to look at him more closely and less severely he was bound to admit that he wasn't a bad sort of fellow.

"Though beastly fond of giving impots," he thought.

"Doing it now, sir," he said.

"But there's no prep.," suggested Mr. Canning.

"Impots aren't prep., sir," came the answer.

"No, but there's a time and a place for everything, and to-night's the time for enjoyment. Leave that impot, boy. I'll take it as presented."

He was gone in a moment, leaving Masters with a very red face indeed. "Well, I'm jiggered!" that young hopeful exclaimed, when at length he had recovered his balance. "I say, Seymour, Canning isn't a bad sort, is he? Did rather well to-day, eh? Not half a bad fellow. Think I shall patronise him in the future."

The climax of all came when they were ranged in order for Chapel. The great Harvey, smiling and serene as ever, passed down the lines of boys, and happened to hit on Masters.

"Hullo," he called. "I say, Masters, thanks."

The words almost caused another paroxysm of cheering. Masters went the colour of a beetroot.

"And, by the way," added Harvey, "about that ink stain. Expect it was an accident. I'll see the right people. Half a crown's too big a fine. Supposing we forget it?"

CHAPTER VII

PLANS FOR AN OUTING

Round about the "tortoise" stove in the workshop at Ranleigh the tongues of certain of the boys wagged with a vigour there was no denying and no checking. Susanne held the post of honour, seated on an up-turned box in front of the stove, his feet on the high, bent-iron fender which kept the hot cinders from coming into contact with the piles of shavings littering the floor. Clive lolled back, his shoulders against the corner of the nearest bench, while Masters occupied a place on the same form.

"My! They don't smell half good," reflected Hugh, sniffing with decided appreciation at the roasting apples placed on top of the stove. "There's apples and apples."

"And orchards and orchards," chipped in Masters.

"And some of them are easier to get at than others, eh?" smiled Bert, prodding a baking potato with the broken prongs of an old fork. "There never was a place such as this is for a wet day. Of course, when one's a senior it's easy enough to bag one of the Fives Courts and have a game. But not being a senior, of course——"

"You have to descend to the workshop," laughed Susanne. "It's good enough for me, anyway. I suppose if we all did as you'd have us, you'd be at Fives, Hugh in the Gym, and Clive hammering iron in the forge. As to Masters——"

"Ah!" grinned that unabashed youth, "I know what you're going to say. Of course, I'd be sweating at impots for that cad Canning. Now, would you believe it? after letting me off the one about a time and a place, the very day after he set me another. That's Canning all over."

There was a grimace as he ended. Masters had found Mr. Canning a strange mixture indeed, for whereas he had experienced his benevolence on the night after the rescue of those who had been plunged into the water, the master had been down upon him like a ton of bricks on the following day.

"Masters, you're not attending. What was the passage we were then construing?"

Masters made a wild shot, one which went very wide of the mark too.

"And that's what we were doing, then?" asked Mr. Canning sweetly.

"Yes, sir—at least, that's the best I can remember."

"Indeed. Your memory is very defective. We were not even dealing with the page in which that passage occurs. As I said, you were not attending, and as you have thereby lost the benefit of the excellent rendering given us by Martin Secundus, you had better write me out page 46, both in Latin and English."

"The beast!" Masters had muttered. "Always down on me! Wish I'd never come to Ranleigh. Talk about freedom and fair treatment! A fellow's down-trodden at this place. That Canning's a tyrant."

But he was whistling within a few minutes, at the end of the lesson, and would have forgotten the "impot" but for a reminder addressed by one of his fellows. That sent him post-haste to discover Martin Secundus.

"What did you want to give that Canning a rendering for?" he demanded roughly, for Martin was of the small order. "See what you've let me in for, too! I've got to write out page 46 in Latin and English."

"Sorry, but your own fault," was the retort, small comfort for Masters.

"Oh, my own fault, eh? Look here, Martin, you've landed me into this impot and will have to help."

"Have?" smiled the other. "I like that!"

"Like it or not, you'll help," came the answer. "Or——"

"Or what?" demanded Martin, not in the least put out. He wasn't afraid of Masters, not in the least, for they had had many a scuffle. He rather liked the fellow, as a matter of fact. But "have"—that was a large order.

"Or——" began the desperate Masters, and then relapsed into a smile. "Oh, look here, Martin, you can do these things standing on your head. I hate Latin. It gives me a headache. Come along to my tuck-box. I had a hamper arrive last week, and we can talk about the impot while we're feeding."

Wise Masters! More than one at Ranleigh had found their way to his notice, if not to his friendship, by offering food. And here he was using the same method of persuasion. However, the "old firm," as Clive, Bert and Hugh, Masters and Susanne had designated themselves, were engaged in discussion round the workshop stove, and we must not forget them.

"As to Masters," declared Susanne, having been interrupted by that young fellow, "as to our friend Masters, he'd probably be found asleep, or at the tuck, or washing himself in ink."

The sally brought a howl from the others. Masters was not likely soon to be allowed to forget that incident. The mere mention of it roused him to a fury. He shot up as if he had been kicked and leaned across to strike at Susanne. But Clive cocked a leg on to the top of the stove and thereby intercepted him.

"Look here," he began, "do let's talk sense."

"Then you shut up altogether. That's the only way to make it possible," retorted the angered Masters, sitting down with a bang.

"And decide what we're going to do and how it's to be done," went on Clive, without notice of the interruption.

"We've decided to go, then?" demanded Bert.

"Rather!" cried Hugh.

"I wouldn't miss the show for worlds," declared Clive.

"There'll be heaps of Frenchmen there," suggested Susanne, with a cool shake of his head. "I'm nearly sure to know some of them. That'd mean a feed, eh?"

The idea was wonderfully attractive. "Of course," suggested Masters, with furrowed brow, "if you didn't know any of them it wouldn't make any great difference. They'd be awfully glad to see you, and——"

"Me, yes," agreed Susanne. "But my friends—well, that's a tall order."

There were signs of dissension at once. "But you'd never be such a sneak as to accept a feed and leave us in the lurch," blurted out Hugh. "If we go, we all go together. If there's a feed——"

"We all feed together," grinned Masters.

"But we aren't there yet," Clive reminded them. "Now, do let's get to business. There's to be a meeting of aeroplanists at Guildford. That's settled."

They all nodded their agreement. Hugh interrupted further conversation for the moment to lift the frizzling apples from the stove and hand one to each of the gathering. "Can't talk without eating," he said. "Now let's get on with it. There's an aeroplane meeting."

"The old firm's going, lock, stock and barrel," interjected Masters, with decision.

"If it can be arranged."

"It can," Clive corrected Bert. "What's to prevent us?"

"The Head! Guildford's out of bounds, in any case. There'd be ructions if a Ranleigh boy were found there."

"But one won't, that's just it," asserted Clive. What "it" was exactly he failed to explain. However, he soon cleared up the resulting mystery.

"Who's going to be such an ass as to go in a school cap?" he asked haughtily. "We'll sneak our bowlers out of store and no one'll be the wiser."

"But how are we to get there?" asked Bert. "That's the question we started with. Everyone knows there's to be such a show. Guildford's a long step away, and the train's out of the question."

"Ah, but you've forgotten Higgins. There's Higgins," Clive reminded them.

Yes, there was Higgins, one of those artful, ingratiating scoundrels ever the dread of a Headmaster, ever the attraction of fellows at school. For this man in question, like many another at other schools than Ranleigh, stocked articles contraband at the school but much sought after by boys. The master of a sweet-stuff shop, wherein was combined a tobacconist business, he could be visited by those who had obtained a pass to the village. Stores of cigarettes were obtained from him. Susanne, whose bad habits had commenced with a somewhat liberal or free education in France prior to coming to England, had no difficulty in purchasing there what smokes he required; while one boy of Clive's acquaintance had even bought a revolver, though for what purpose even he could not say.

"There's Higgins, yes," reflected Clive.

"Who's all serene. He's offered to take us in a brake he can hire. We can join him up at the back of the school and none be the wiser. Call the trip ten miles there, and the same back. Well, we're on the spot in a little more than an hour."

Masters turned a glowing countenance to his friends. But Clive showed disapproval.

"An hour or more. What's the use of wasting all that time on the road? Let's do the thing in style or not at all. Let's go by motor. Higgins can manage that just as easily."

"At a price! He don't forget to open his mouth too."

"Well, what price?"

Clive dragged out all his available coins and counted them carefully.

"Three bob a head by trap. Five, if there's a motor," said Masters. "I talked it over with him. Not a bad chap, Higgins. He knows how to keep his mouth shut too, which is something."

The discussion waned for a while, for each one of the group was busy with his finances. Then all eyes went to Susanne. He was the Crœsus of the party. Never a day but he had money in abundance, the reason being perhaps that his father was a banker.

"Wish mine were," Masters had groaned on more than one occasion. "Then I'd have a few coppers to spend now and again, instead of a beggarly allowance. My Governor seems to think that a chap hasn't need of cash. He rams thrift and economy down my throat till I'm almost afraid to buy even a biscuit."

"Five bob a head," said Bert reflectively. "Is it worth it?"

"Is it worth it?" they shouted derisively at him.

"Ever seen an aeroplane?" asked Clive hotly. "Think of being able to say we'd watched fellows flying. Besides, we might get up in one ourselves. I mean to try."

"And there's the feed," Hugh reminded them.

"Feed? What feed?" demanded Masters eagerly. "Higgins don't include it in his price. I tried to make him. Where's the feed?"

"Susanne's, duffer!"

"Mine?" asked the astounded Frenchman. "It's the first I've heard of it."

"There's a oner. Never heard of it, when only a minute ago he was telling us of his friends and how they'd ask us to lunch with 'em," shouted Masters. "Don't tell us you've forgotten, Susanne."

"Ask *me* to lunch. I never said a word about you fellows. It was you who suggested the thing. Oh, yes, I dare say there'll be a blow-out for *me*," said Susanne complacently. "But for you, doubtful. You fellows had better sneak some bread and cheese at supper the night before and carry a store with you."

He grinned provocatively at them, and then calmly tackled a roasted apple. "Yes," he reflected, "I've no doubt I shall meet one friend at least. There's Levallois, a flyer. My word, he can fly! He comes from Lyons, and'll be awfully glad to see me."

"Us," suggested Masters desperately.

"Me. What's he want to know you for? I shall go off to lunch with him as a matter of course. It'll be sickening to leave you fellows, naturally, and no one'll be more sorry than I, er—er—or you—but then, there it is."

So saying he buried his teeth in the apple, taking not the smallest notice of the glaring eyes of his comrades.

"Of all the selfish beggars!" began Masters, whose energy was always pronounced when there was a question of food. "Susanne don't deserve to come with us. It's sickening to hear him jaw about a feed all for himself, and to listen to him advising us to take chunks of bread as hard as bricks, and cheese that's only fit for use as cart grease. It's simply sickening."

His disgust was great—so great, in fact, that he might have pressed the question still further, thereby bringing about a termination of the hitherto comparatively pleasant nature of the meeting. But the practical Bert intervened.

"What's the use of grousing," he asked, "and gassing about a feed that's never been offered? Why, Susanne's friend mayn't be there. He may find no one to invite him."

"I shall. Certain," declared that individual, grinning. "If there's one Frenchman there, he is my countryman. He pays toll. That's quite regular. He'll be awfully glad to meet me."

"Oh, well, then you get an invite. What's it matter? Bread's good enough for me so long as I see the fun. Let's settle the matter. Five bob's a heap. That Higgins is a Shylock. He'll take every cent from me."

"Same here," asserted Hugh, pulling a face. "I shall be short for the rest of the term."

Susanne produced a sovereign. "How much for the lot?" he asked.

"Twenty shillings, and five extra for you," cried Masters.

"Then take it as settled. I'll write home to the people and tell 'em I've had heavy calls. A motor's a call, isn't it?" he asked naïvely, seeing his friends smile. "I pay the motor. If there isn't a feed, then we've something left to buy grub with. How's that? Pass another apple, Clive. You hang over them as if the store belonged to you."

It got dusk before they had finished talking. The far ends of the workshop were hidden in gloom before they rose from their places about the stove. And then there came the sound of a scraping match. A flare lit the gloom in the distance. A tall figure stretched upward to a swinging lamp and lit the wick. It was Hole, the school's carpentry instructor, unchanged after years of service, with an eagle eye for old faces and a keen recollection of incidents gone and forgotten by the majority. If only every school existing had such a workshop, and made attendance there almost compulsory, instead of an extra to be paid for by parents! For there, in the workshop provided by Ranleigh, boys learned a thousand and one things. Handiness came quickly to them, and better than all, perhaps, here was at hand a means to fill many an hour which might otherwise have been idle.

Benches down the centre bore a host of tools, while the special property of individuals was housed in lockers near the entrance. The stove was placed half-way along the shop, and beyond, one entered a second shop provided with turning lathes. See Clive there, with the faithful and interested Hugh in attendance, both lads working the foot pedal with might and main, while dust and shavings whirled about them. Or follow them to the blacksmith's shop, an adjacent institution. There, dressed in leather aprons, with sleeves tucked to the shoulder, they might be seen many and many a time beating out some piece of spluttering metal on the anvil. Or the metal-turning lathe held their attention, and they slowly and laboriously pounded at the pedal while the hardened tool took off shavings at a pace which was slow to the point of exasperation.

But there were days also in this shop when flames and sparks flew up the chimney wildly, when either Hugh or Clive, or even Susanne on occasion, turned the handle of the mechanical blower. Coke heaped high on the hearth glowed redly, while the heat within the shop was stifling. Perhaps these conditions existed for an hour; perhaps for longer, Clive or the shop instructor ever and again lifting the lid of a crucible buried in the glowing coke. And then, with a joyful shout, it was announced that the brass was molten. Think, then, of the joy these young mechanics experienced. The boxes placed so carefully over in the corner had cost them many an hour's labour. Packed with sand, and divided at the commencement, the two halves of the moulds fashioned from their own patterns were now assembled, and the moment had arrived to pour the molten brass into the narrow openings left for that purpose. And imagine the impatience of these model-makers awaiting the setting of their castings.

Those were the days which Clive enjoyed most. It was after a bout of casting that his lessons were worse prepared than on other occasions, while drills and "impots" showered upon him.

"Darrell, inattentive again," Old B. would exclaim sadly, as if the matter were a personal grief to him. "Half an hour's drill to-morrow."

Or Harvey, the great Harvey, would rouse his curly, shapely head from his desk in the middle of prep., strange sounds having disturbed him.

"If that isn't young Darrell again," he'd exclaim testily. "Come here, Darrell."

Fearful of the consequences, but unlikely to be robbed of his love of mechanics by any amount of punishment, Clive would leave his seat and come to the front.

"Well?"

"I—er——"

"What's it this time?"

"Only a wheel. I was just filing it so as to be ready for after school."

The culprit would hand forth a file of gigantic size, and a casting of his own making. Prep., Clive had found, was an excellent time for the doing of such little jobs. But there was the difficulty of drowning noise. Harvey had been annoyed on more than one occasion.

"Oh, only a wheel! Let's see, what was it last time?"

"Another wheel. You see, there are two, and——"

"There generally are two. Look here, Darrell, I'm sick of this nonsense. You not only shirk your own work, and get into trouble with your form master, but you disturb the other fellows and keep them from work. Come along to the Scholars' room after supper. I shall give you a whacking."

And, as a matter of course, Masters would be grinning delightedly as Clive went back to his seat, while Hugh or Bert or Susanne would pass short notes of compassion to him. Sometimes they were shot over the heads of the others in the form of darts, duly labelled with the name of Darrell. Or they were passed from hand to hand, or better still, the wily Susanne's invention, they were rolled into the shape of a fine pencil, inserted in a pea-shooter, and sent hurtling at the head of the one for whom the correspondence was intended. Let us record, too, that Susanne became an expert with this instrument. Such was his dexterity, and such his strength of lung, that with the aid of wet blotting-paper rolled into balls, and essentially of red colour, he could actually eject them at the high ceilings of the form rooms, where the moist condition of the shot caused it to adhere, and—so good was the aim after long practice—that with patience and a sufficiency of these moist pellets Susanne could write his name on the ceiling. That term many a form room ceiling bore in thin lines of red dots the letters Feofé, with "Susanne" close alongside in brackets.

But there was the question of the aeroplane meeting to be settled.

"Masters will see Higgins and fix it," Clive explained to Hugh in a hoarse whisper, when they were seated at prep. that evening. "It's lucky that to-morrow's a saint's day. That'll give us heaps of time, for the meeting don't begin till after midday."

Numerous were the notes which passed between Clive and Masters and Hugh during that hour and a half's prep. The many items to be settled caused the exchange of missives even when they had reached their dormitories, and that fascinating, home-made telephone being as yet incomplete, and, in fact, stubbornly refusing to work in spite of the scientific aid and knowledge of Susanne, they had recourse yet again to the weird series of wheels and strings passing over the partition. And, of course, as fate would have it on this the most important of occasions, Sturton discovered what was happening.

"What the dickens——" he suddenly demanded, swinging round in the chair in which he was seated at the dormitory table. "Here, Darrell, up to something more? I told you last week I wouldn't have any further chucking of notes over the partition. Suppose it's to young Seymour again? Bring that note here."

It was a desperate moment. Clive clambered out of bed and stepped across to the prefect, the note in his hand.

"Here it is," he said grudgingly, eyeing Sturton askance, for that note contained a résumé of the details of their escapade of the morrow. Dished up in finished style, as it were, were full particulars of their intended movements. Anyone glancing through the scrawly and badly spelled lines could not fail but discover the depths of the conspiracy.

"Higgins is a brick," the words went. "Masters saw him to-night after prep and just before chapel and Higgins said he was reddy and didn't want twenty five bob but twenty and that's awfully decent of him and the car's going to be wating over by the windmil at twelve. Won't it be ripping, eh. There's heaps of room for the lot of us and Higgins'll have smokes. Susanne says they're nesessary to him and'll make him look like a blud, and Higgins knows a shop where we can get a blow out for next to nothing. There a bob each to pay to go into the plais where the aroplaynes fly, but Higgins can manage to pass us in free as his frend's the gatekeeper. So all's serene and to-morrow'll be ripping.

74

"The Firm."

That was the communication. Sturton handled it and turned it over curiously. As a matter of fact, he was rather amused at these notes so constantly passing. It not being so very long since he himself was a youngster, he had a friendly recollection of his own eccentricities.

"What's this?" he asked sternly, causing the pyjamaed Clive to quake. "One would think you young donkeys hadn't a chance for gassing during the daytime. As it is, I know this sort of thing goes on the whole of prep. time. Look here, Darrell, an hour's drill to-morrow."

An hour's drill. Why, that meant that Clive, with a number of other forlorn individuals subjected to the same punishment for their various crimes, would have to assemble in the quad after dinner, and there be marched to and fro and round and round by a prefect as weary of the task as they were. At least, that was the general rule. Sometimes the commander of this squad was a martinet. Sometimes the master for the week wreaked his vengeance on boys in general and these unhappy wights in particular by taking the quad himself, or standing at the entrance to the quad, his mere presence stimulating the prefect till the boys undergoing punishment groaned at the numerous orders to "right wheel," "left wheel," "form line," "form fours." Form every sort of formation that the drill-book allows for or the fertile mind of an ingenious prefect can devise. And Canning was the master for the week, and Rawlings the brute of a prefect who would be on duty on the morrow.

Clive groaned and shivered.

"But to-morrow's a saint's day, Sturton," he ventured in tones of protest.

"All the better. You'll want something to do. Time hangs heavy with you youngsters on saints' days. A drill'll keep you out of mischief."

"But——"

"What's in this precious note?" asked Sturton, holding it up to the gaslight. "Secrets? Let's see 'em."

He handed the note to Clive and invited him to open the folded paper. That young fellow went a sickly yellow colour. The drill could be got over, he reflected. He could miss it. He'd have to do it every day after, that was certain, and Sturton might invite Harvey to give him a slogging. But the cause was worth this sacrifice. But to open the note and show Sturton the contents meant wrecking the whole affair.

"It's private," he managed to say at length.

"Oh, private, and awfully important. Let's see."

In one second Sturton fell in Clive's eyes from the giddy pinnacle on which he had been placed. "Never thought he could be such a cad. Opening fellows' letters. Beastly dodge!" thought Clive, glowering on him.

"Here, open it and read," said Sturton severely.

"It's private."

"Can't help that. Read it."

"It's private, I tell you."

Clive was distinctly angry and stubborn.

"Oh!" Sturton looked him up and down, his brow furrowed. He had not the smallest intention of opening the note himself, nor even of listening to its contents. He was merely gauging Clive's character. "Then you won't?" he asked coolly.

"No, I won't."

"You know what to expect, eh?"

"Yes. I don't care."

"Look here, Darrell, don't be a donkey. Fellows don't look at other chaps' notes, or listen to secrets. You're right not to split. Get back to bed. Promise not to send any more and I'll let you off the drill."

"Not after this one," said Clive. "It's important."

Sturton grinned. He could thoroughly sympathise, and he rather liked Clive for his show of obstinacy.

"Pitch it over then," he said, "and let it be the last. I'll whack you if you break your promise."

"But a chap can telephone, and we'll have to work like niggers to get that thing going," said Clive, when he had whispered to Susanne.

"That won't be sending notes. I wouldn't break a promise to anyone, least of all to Sturton. He's a decent fellow."

The morrow found the Old Firm jubilant and expectant. They slipped off after Chapel, raced down to the common and espied a panting car over by the windmill. All together they changed their school caps for bowlers and donned their overcoats. Susanne and Masters, who always did these things in superior style, had donned the tallest of tall collars, while the former had blossomed forth with an eyeglass. And we are bound to confess that Susanne thus decked out made quite a handsome and impressive foreigner. Masters had the appearance of a third-rate actor, for, as we have said, his collar was of the highest, while his fancy waistcoat would have roused the envy of a Cockney. Patent leather boots, spats, and a cane of huge proportions completed a turn-out which was distinctly startling. However, who thought of that, for were they not off on an expedition which promised huge excitement?

"I mean to get a lift in one of the machines," said Clive deliberately.

"While Susanne ain't forgot his promise," interjected Masters.

"Promise!" exclaimed the gallant Frenchman.

"A blow-out," Masters reminded him.

"For me—yes. Rather!" came the tantalising answer.

"All aboard!" cried the rascal who was to drive them. "Ready? Then off we go!"

The engine roared. The clutch went in with a jerk. The car bounded off for Guildford and the long-anticipated flying meeting which the Old Firm had determined to patronise.

CHAPTER VIII

BREAKING BOUNDS

Never before did a distinguished party of strangers come to the ancient town of Guildford more jubilant. Heads were craned over the side of the car which the ruffian Higgins had provided, staring eyes looked in all directions, but mainly skyward.

"Perhaps we'll see 'em flying," suggested Clive breathlessly, for his mechanical mind was stirred to the highest pitch by the thought of seeing men launched into the air.

"Hold hard!" shouted Masters, whose quick eye had lighted on something decidedly alluring, and who was ever alert to make the very utmost of the smallest opportunity. "Hold hard!" he almost shouted as the car crawled jerkily along the high street and past a pastry-cook's window, in which were displayed a tempting mass of tarts and cakes. It was like this greedy fellow. When food was about, when it happened to be anywhere within sight or scent, he had not a soul above eating. What mattered it if there were an aeroplane meeting? What did he care if men were to fly? Food was food, and Masters had always a healthy hunger.

"You chaps," he began, "here's our chance. If we miss it, ten to one we'll be hanging about without so much as a crumb, and I'm jolly empty."

"But—but, Susanne's friend is going to stand a feed," Hugh reminded them. "Don't forget that."

Masters pooh-poohed the suggestion, though on the previous day he had waxed indignant at the thought that such a treat could not be in store. He had called Susanne a sneak. Now, with those alluring cakes within his ken, he chose to forget what had happened. Also there was such a thing as remembering the saying, "A bird in the hand is worth two in the bush." Masters had coins in his pocket, thanks again to Susanne, and, as we have said, he had a perennial appetite.

"Blow Susanne's feed!" he declared. "If it comes off, all the better. I for one'll be ready. But I'm famishing now. So stop her."

The band descended straightway, and without much need for further persuasion. When they mounted the car again sundry well-filled bags accompanied them. Then on to the field. Crowds were making their way thither on foot, others in motors and traps. Outside the gates there was a seething mass of people, through whom Higgins drove the car at reckless speed. And then the gates opened. They were passed in after a nod and a few words between Higgins and the gatekeeper.

"Look out! Duck!" whispered Bert, suddenly, in hoarse tones of alarm. "Bothered if that isn't Old B. Duck, I tell you."

With one accord the car load bent their heads till it appeared as if one and all were engaged with their boot laces. Clive glanced askance into the crowd, and there beheld the tall, bulky form of Mr. Branson, his dormitory master. The sight of that tall, genial giant set him quaking. Not that Mr. Branson was at all of the fierce order. Rather, he was an easy-going fellow, who had as perfect an understanding of boys as ever master had. But he could be roused to anger— anger which as a rule resulted in the bestowal of a cuff, for Mr. Branson took the law into his own hands as a rule, and did not favour sending boys to the Headmaster with one of those short, explanatory notes which resulted in a caning. No, Old B. was a good, slow, well-meaning giant whom all adored, and none more so than Clive. But he feared him also.

"Old B.," he murmured. "Old B. right enough, and looking this way."

"Seen us?" asked Bert desperately.

"Never!" declared Masters. "He's too sleepy for that."

"Then he's spotted the car," suggested Susanne. "He'd know it, as he and others of the masters use it at times. What's he doing?"

"Gone off into the crowd. Looked awfully hard at this car," said Clive, suppressing a shiver. "Smiled, that tired sort of smile of his, and then cut off in the opposite direction."

The statement brought all heads to their normal elevation again, while questioning glances were cast first at the crowd, now left behind, and then at one another.

"What did Old B. mean by that, then?" asked Bert, after a painful pause. "Stared awfully hard, and then sloped off."

"As if to avoid us. As if he guessed there were Ranleigh boys in the car and didn't want to spot 'em," suggested Clive.

"Good Old B.! Just like him," cried Masters, regaining his composure, for the sudden information that Mr. Branson was in the neighbourhood and eyeing them had thrown him into a flutter.

"More impots," he had groaned inwardly. "More drills, and a whacking as a matter of course. Ranleigh's an awful place for a fellow to be sent to. Tyrants, the whole lot of 'em!"

"In any case, he's here, and means to watch the flying. A beastly nuisance," reflected Susanne. "Of course, we shall have to keep our eyes open. But I know a dodge to beat him. I'll look out for Levallois, and if he's here, why, he'll invite us to his hangar. Old B.'ll never dare to enter."

Thus relieved for the time being of their fears the party tumbled out of the car, and having agreed with Higgins to meet him precisely two and a half hours later, struck across the huge field in which the meeting was taking place toward the half-dozen hangars in which the flying machines were housed.

"That's Levallois'," said Susanne, pointing to one over which the flag of France flew. "I'll cross direct."

"But—but you can't," Bert told him, for Bert was one of those youths who somewhat lack assurance. He had a huge respect for authority and order. He often envied Masters his cheek, and Clive and Hugh the dash and persistence which carried them through difficulties. "You can't, Susanne. The place is roped off, and there are scores of police."

"Can't! You wait," laughed the Frenchman. "See that bobby. Looks a good chap, eh? See me get round him."

They allowed the voluble Frenchman to go ahead of them a few paces, as if he were not attached to the party, and watched with breathless interest as he nonchalantly ducked under the ropes which kept the crowd back. Susanne, his monocle in position, strolled away across the enclosure.

"Hi! You stand back there!" came the summons from the nearest constable. "Get out of the enclosure, please."

Susanne might have been deaf. It was not until the officer of the law actually had his hand upon his shoulder that the young fellow showed the smallest attention to his order. And then, in the inimitable style of Feofé, a style somewhat spoiled by the jeers and laughter of his schoolfellows, but nevertheless a style which was part and parcel of the young fellow, Susanne raised his hat and swept it from his head. In wonder and amazement his comrades heard him addressing the constable in French, speaking volubly, waving his arms, pointing to the hangars opposite. And then he dived into a waistcoat pocket and produced a card.

"What's this?" demanded the constable, a young man, evidently puzzled. "Can't read it. You're French, eh?"

Susanne nodded energetically. He beckoned to Masters, and at the signal that young fellow dived beneath the rope and ran to join him. At once Susanne fired off a string of words, totally unintelligible to the constable, and mostly so to Masters, who was no great French scholar. But he knew what Susanne wanted, and knew also what he and his friends required. Also Masters was just the youth to carry a matter like this through in splendid style. He had cheek enough for a dozen.

"It's like this, don't you see, constable," he said, smiling sweetly at the officer. "Monsieur Feofé—that's French, you know—Monsieur Feofé comes from France, where all the flying's done, and Monsieur Levallois's one of the flyers. That's his shed over there, with the French flag over it. Well, of course, Monsieur Levallois expects Monsieur Feofé and his friends. We've come here to see him. He wants us over at his place, you see. I'm sorry you can't understand Monsieur Feofé. But that's the worst of these fellows who can't speak English."

An older constable might even have been taken in, though to be sure he might have noticed the half-suppressed grins on the faces of the party of young fellows stationed by the ropes. Also he would certainly have been surprised at the youth of these visitors. But he was a young man, on duty almost for the first time, and somewhat confused.

"I've got my orders, strict," he began.

"Of course, of course!" interjected Masters hurriedly. "Of course, constable, orders to keep the crowd back. Quite right for you to obey 'em. But we're not the crowd. You see, Monsieur Feofé's a swell sort of fellow. It'd be rude to refuse to pass him and his friends through. He wouldn't understand it. Monsieur Levallois would be furious, and I dare say the inspector in charge of the police'd get a wiggin'. So it'll be all right, see?"

That young constable wasn't by any means too sure. But Susanne's apparent ignorance of English, his obvious impatience at this delay, his embarrassing politeness, for he continued to sweep his hat from his head on occasion, while firing off a long string of unintelligible words at Masters, all had their effect. The man wavered.

"My orders is to pass no one——" he began again.

"Come on, you chaps," sang out Masters, whose cheek was tremendous. "The constable understands. We'd best hurry, for Monsieur Levallois is waiting. Thanks, constable. If there's any trouble refer the inspector to me. Sorry to have bothered you."

The arm of the law passed them through, reluctantly and doubtfully. It was as much as Hugh and Clive could do to suppress their mirth till out of hearing of the policeman, and Susanne's behaviour made the task even more difficult. For that young fellow heartily enjoyed every item in this manœuvre. He bowed low to the constable, covering that unhappy and uncomfortable young fellow with blushes. He swept his hat from his head for perhaps the twentieth time, and rattled off his thanks in French. And then, following sedately across the field,

81

he looked about him with inimitable coolness, and turned to survey the gathering crowds through his monocle, which was still screwed into his eye.

"Of all the cheek!" gasped Bert, to whom such an adventure was a revelation. "Come on, Susanne. Old B.'ll spot you the instant his eyes fall on you. Do stop fooling and come along!"

"Grand!" declared Clive, thoroughly enjoying the entertainment. "That bobby was finely flustered. But, I say, supposing Levallois won't have anything to say to us. I've heard that lots of these flying fellows get pestered with people in their hangars and throw them all out. Supposing Levallois don't want us."

"Supposing he ain't there," grinned Hugh, bringing up another difficulty.

The suggestions caused the little band to close in as if for mutual protection.

"Well?" asked Bert desperately. "Supposing Levallois isn't over there, or don't want us?"

Susanne's serenity was undisturbed.

"There's some sort of a Frenchman, anyway," he observed. "He'll be glad to see me in any case. Of course, if he don't want you fellows, it'll be awkward—for you."

He grinned openly at them till Masters could have struck him. It was perhaps just as well that a stop was put to the argument at that moment by the wheeling out of an aeroplane from one of the hangars. That set the party hurrying till they arrived at the line of sheds. Here there was much movement. Officials came and went, more than one eyeing the boys with evident suspicion. An important-looking inspector of police was posted adjacent to the very hangar over which the French flag flew, and promptly pounced upon them.

"What's this?" he asked severely. "No one but gentlemen flying, their mechanics and managers are allowed here. What fool's broken orders by passing you in?"

But again Susanne and Masters saved the situation, the one by his embarrassing politeness and his volubility, the other by his specious explanation.

"Oh, Levallois, that's the French gentleman's name, is it?" asked the inspector, mollified, but not entirely convinced. "Well, if he says that he's asked you here, suppose you must stay. But none of the other flying gents are having friends, least of all youngsters. Still, we don't want to be rough on a foreigner. He might not understand. Here, sir," he called, putting his head into the hangar over which the French flag flew, "here's a parcel of young gents come to see you; and some of them's out for a lark, I'll bet."

A smile stole across his face. Masters' get-up was perfectly ludicrous. As to his fellows, not one but wore his obvious youth in awkward manner, save and excepting Susanne. The composure of that young fellow was wonderful. He stepped into the hangar, leaving his comrades outside to listen in trepidation to his conversation with its invisible owner. It was with a sigh of relief that they saw him appear at the door and beckon.

"It isn't Levallois, after all," he grinned, "but Dubonnet. But it's all right and square, Monsieur Dubonnet's a sportsman. Come into the place and feed. He's going to have a meal now, for the wind's too high as yet for flying."

Masters' eyes were wide open with amazement. Bert could hardly believe his ears. As for Hugh and Clive they were bubbling over with excitement. Nor were they intensely astonished. The latter, at any rate, had seen so much of Susanne as to convince him that what that young fellow took in hand he accomplished. For Feofé had that happy knack of winning friendship, a knack which it behoves all to acquire. Also he was far more at his ease with his elders than any of the others. It seemed almost natural, therefore, to Clive that he should have brought about this introduction. Clive bobbed to the young fellow whom Susanne presented, and then, forgetting all else, stepped up to the aeroplane and began with Hugh's help a close and critical examination. Then a call from the smiling owner sent the two of them to the far corner where a board table was erected, with a ham and a joint of beef upon it, together with other items.

"Help yourselves, gentlemen," said Monsieur Dubonnet. "Accident has given me friends to-day, and I needed them. Now, let's get the meal started and then tell me how you managed this business. I suppose you're from Ranleigh?"

"Yes," admitted Masters, his mouth already half filled with ham, his eyes protruding at the directness of the question.

"Know it?" asked Clive.

"Rather! There myself, you see. Breaking bounds, eh? Well, I don't blame you. But, by the way, I'm expecting one of the masters. My old dormitory master, you know—Old B. Know him? Of course you do."

The bombshell produced an impressive and painful silence. Masters looked desperately across at the door. Even Susanne reddened, and then Monsieur Dubonnet relieved the tension by laughing uproariously.

"Had you all badly," he grinned. "All the same, Old B.'ll be paying me a visit. But we'll make that right. There's a place screened off at the back of the hangar and you can get cover there. I'll post one of you fellows to watch at the door."

And so for the following hour they took it in turn to watch. The meal finished, Clive and Hugh plied Monsieur Dubonnet with questions—questions, too, of such an intelligent nature that they aroused his interest. Indeed, the enthusiasm of these young fellows gained for them an invitation to try a flight.

"You'll like it awfully," declared Monsieur Dubonnet. "Of course, one feels scared at first, but that's natural. Accidents do happen at times, I know, but I don't think you need be fearful."

It was with beating hearts that our two young friends, half an hour later, smuggled themselves into the cab mounted on the machine. Two mechanics appeared and wheeled it from the shed, while Susanne and the others kept carefully in the background.

"See you later," sang out Bert.

"Alive or dead," grinned Masters, who was envying Hugh and Clive greatly. "Think of me, Darrell, when you're falling."

But no amount of chaff had any effect on our two amateur flyers. The starting of the engine brought the red to their cheeks. The rush of air over their heads sent their pulses dancing. The roar of the exhaust passed almost unnoticed as the machine started forward. And then up they went, swooping over the heads of the people gathered to watch the flying. We need not record here their impressions. Suffice it to say that a very proud and gratified couple at length descended from the machine and joined their comrades.

"Time to be off," Masters reminded them. "Higgins'll be wondering what's happened. And besides, if we don't move soon we shall be late for call-over."

Taking care to view their surroundings before issuing from the hangar, and having volubly thanked the great Dubonnet for his kindness, the little party made their way across the enclosure, under the ropes, and so to the spot where the car was to await them. There was no Higgins there on their arrival, but a search discovered him in an adjacent booth where refreshments were provided.

"Looks as if he'd had his full share too," Hugh whispered to Clive. "Suppose he can drive?"

"Hope so," was the laconic answer, though there was doubt in the tones. For Higgins had been refreshing himself with a vengeance. He was none too steady as he issued from the booth and leered at his passengers. However, there was no doing anything in the matter.

"The beast!" growled Bert in tones of disgust. "I've always disliked Higgins, and I hate him now. If it hadn't been for the fact that he could get the use of the car and so make it possible for us to come to this meeting, I'd never have consented. The brute's drunk."

"No, not quite," corrected Susanne. "But the drive home'll be exciting."

It proved to be filled to repletion with excitement, for Higgins scooped through the town of Guildford as if police did not exist and pedestrians had no right to the pavements. His course was followed by howls of rage from passers-by, to all of which he paid no notice. He sent the car whizzing out into the country, and dashed along the high-road at giddy speed, while Clive and his fellows clung to their seats as best they could.

"Settling down nicely to it," reflected Susanne, after a while, for it took a great deal to shake the coolness of the French youth. Indeed, he seemed rather to have enjoyed the recklessness of the driver. "He don't steer into the footpath quite so often, and he isn't going so fast. In another twenty minutes we ought to be back near the common."

"And mighty glad I'll be too," admitted Bert. "Of all the brutes, this Higgins is the biggest. But he does seem to be settling down. No, he doesn't. He's putting on the pace again."

"Racing," ejaculated Masters, as if the admission pained him. "Look, there's a car ahead and Higgins means to pass it."

Perhaps a quarter of a mile ahead they could see the back of another car, one, too, with which the boys of Ranleigh were familiar. For they knew it to be one of the three which plied for hire in the neighbourhood.

"Slow as a beetle. We'll beat 'em easy," declared Hugh, stimulated by the thought of a race.

"Walk past it if Higgins can manage to steer decently," agreed Clive.

"Shove her ahead," cried Susanne, springing to his feet and leaning over the driver. "Keep her straight, Higgins. Now, let her go. We'll beat those other fellows into a cocked hat. Hullo, they're looking back."

There were two passengers in the vehicle in front, and at this moment they looked behind them, and then turned to urge their own driver to greater speed.

"Whew! Did you recognise 'em?" asked Hugh, staring after the other car.

"Who?" demanded Clive.

"Those fellows?"

"No. Why?"

"Ranleighans," said Hugh with conviction. "Spotted them at once."

"Rawlings and Trendall," declared Susanne. "I knew that it was they all along. Just fancy catching a prefect breaking bounds! Saw 'em at the flying meeting. They were in that booth with Higgins, and slipped out when I went in to fetch him. Anyway, they can't give us away. We're all in the same boat this time, though if it had been different, and Rawlings could have caught us out, there'd have been trouble. We've got him nicely this time."

If it were in fact the two mentioned in the car ahead, then Clive and his friends need have no fear of the consequences of recognition. For what a prefect can do, that also can smaller fry. Also, if Rawlings had broken bounds with Trendall, then his lips were sealed.

"Hooray! He's bound to hold his tongue," cried Masters; "and if he tries it on with any of us after this, why, we've only to rake this matter up. Now let's whop his car, and pass 'em. Go ahead, Higgins."

Higgins needed no encouragement, and to speak the truth the cold air seemed to have steadied him. There were now few of those frightful swervings to which he had treated his passengers earlier on. He kept the centre of the road, and accelerated his engine till the car dithered and vibrated from end to end. As to the driver of the car ahead, he jerked at sundry levers, opened his throttle and tried to make the best of what was a hopeless case. Gradually he was being overhauled. He cast a glance desperately over his shoulder and again jerked at his levers. But all to no purpose. Higgins' car drew abreast, then level, in which position the two cars thundered along for a while, the two sets of passengers glaring at one another.

"Hooray! We win!" shouted Masters, half standing and grimacing at Trendall.

"Pass them! Pass them!" bellowed Susanne, waving his arms in truly French style. And then he must needs lift his hat. The action set Rawlings scowling. He was angry enough already at the thought that he, a prefect, had been discovered in the act of breaking bounds, discovered too by a group of boys who held him as an enemy. And now to be passed by them in a race was more than he could put up with.

"Stop that racing!" he shouted. "There'll be an accident. Order your fellow to slack down and let us go ahead."

"Order your own," responded Masters, careless of the consequences. "We've as much right to go fast as you have. Fall behind. You're the slower car."

Rawlings shook a big fist at them. Susanne acknowledged the threat by once more ironically lifting his hat. Masters grimaced at his seniors. And Higgins stirred his car to even greater efforts. They shot ahead, leaving the occupants of the rival car fuming with rage. All heads were turned to watch them. Faces were reddened with excitement, and eyes shone at the thought of such a brilliant victory. A hoarse cheer was even uttered by Clive and his friends, a reckless cheer, just to let Rawlings know what they thought of him and how little they feared. And then all gave vent to a howl of dismay. For, of a sudden, something went wrong with the following car. It swerved to one side, recovered a straight line, and then turned into the pathway. A moment later the rear end had risen into the air, and as Clive and the others watched, first Rawlings, then Trendall were tossed out into a dense mass of bushes lining the path. The driver followed them, smashing his way through the glass wind screen. They heard his body thud to the ground, while the up-turned car fell on him. Their shouts and shrieks caused Higgins to cram his brakes on and bring their own vehicle to a standstill. A minute later they were gathered about the up-turned car.

"FIRST RAWLINGS THEN TRENDALL WERE TOSSED OUT INTO A DENSE MASS OF BUSHES."

"Quick! Pull it off him," commanded Susanne, seemingly as cool as a cucumber. "Now, all together. Ah! He's killed."

"Killed?" It was Rawlings who asked the question, his lips bloodless, his knees almost knocking. "Killed? Then—then what happens? Do we have to appear?"

It was like him to think first of himself, and not of the unfortunate man. But the question he had asked was one which was bound to be asked. It was one which intimately concerned one and all of the boys of Ranleigh who had broken bounds. They turned from the body of the man to one another.

"I'm awfully sorry for that poor chap," said Susanne at last. "As for us, we're in for it, eh?"

"Absolutely," agreed Masters. "Right in the soup."

"Unless——" began Rawlings.

"Unless what?" asked Clive curtly.

"Unless we can get out of the mess by——"

"Telling lies?" asked Hugh, backing Clive up swiftly.

Rawlings nodded ever so little.

"Thanks, Rawlings," said Susanne coldly. "You and Trendall do as you like. We'll be getting onward."

CHAPTER IX

HONESTY'S THE BEST POLICY

The short run from the spot where the poor fellow driving the rival car in which Rawlings and Trendall had been passengers had met with his death was anything but a pleasant experience for Clive and his comrades. In the first place, Higgins, hitherto reckless as to his driving, now went at a snail's pace, as if he were in a funeral procession. And then there were two additional passengers in the car. The boys eyed one another in silence. Susanne, as if to break the spell, and careless now, as ever, of the lost authority of Rawlings, fixed his monocle upon that worthy reflectively.

"Best 'op as soon as we gets to the common," suddenly cried Higgins over his shoulder. They heard the brake grind. The car came to a standstill. Then the rascally driver turned upon them, thrust his cap to the back of his head and invited all to listen.

"See 'ere, young gents," he began. "Just at this point you gets off and 'ops it up to the school."

"Yes." Susanne answered him in a mono-syllable, though his brows were furrowed and his eyes scowling. Rawlings slid from the car, and Trendall likewise. Then the others followed, till they were gathered around the bonnet.

"Well?" demanded Susanne curtly.

"And jest at this 'ere point I goes right off to the village. See?"

"No," declared Susanne and Clive together, obstinately determined to give the fellow no encouragement, for they guessed at what was coming.

"There isn't anything to see," said Bert coldly. "The thing's plain. You're here at this spot. We divide. You go off to the village and there give information to the police."

"That's just where you're off it," cried Higgins at once, savagely, "and don't you get a layin' down the law to me, Mr. Seymour. I 'ops it to the village, and I says nothing. I leaves it to the police to find out what's happened. I didn't cause that accident. It was the steering gear that broke and upset the car. So it's no fault of mine. You ain't fools, you young gents?"

"No," declared Rawlings eagerly, for he was listening.

"Certainly not," ventured Trendall.

"Depends," said Susanne. "Go on."

"And no one knows as Mister Rawlings and Mr. Trendall were on that car. Yer see, it's only them as you've got to think of. It ain't known as they was there. My car don't come into the question. So I says, just 'ere we 'ops it and says nothing."

"Quite so. Hear, hear!" cried Rawlings, plucking up a vestige of courage.

"And supposing we're asked," demanded Masters, looking Rawlings coolly up and down till that immaculate young fellow felt intensely uncomfortable. "Eh?"

"We know nothing," said Rawlings and Higgins together.

"Nothing whatever," declared the latter with emphasis. "Not a word. We wasn't out on the car. We wasn't at the meeting. We don't know nuffin' about the death of that poor cove."

"And why should we?" chimed in Trendall. "We're not responsible. It isn't as if he had been murdered. The car overturned, and Rawlings and I were jolly lucky. The police won't need any explanation. There! That satisfies you, eh?"

Clive Darrell went a dull red as he listened to this conversation. He had forgotten for the moment the fact that Old B. had seen the car at the meeting, and that he alone could put the police on the right track if information were needed. To Clive it did not seem that there was any other action than a straight one. For supposing some other driver of a motor-car were accused of having caused this fatal accident? It was quite possible. Then the position would be dreadful. And in any case, though he was ready for a lark at any time, and would doubtless break bounds on many another occasion, still he wasn't going to lie to save his own skin or that of Higgins, Trendall, or Rawlings.

"Come on, Susanne," he said coldly, tucking his arm within his friend's.

"Good day, Higgins."

"Good day," repeated Masters, linking his arm in Clive's.

"Er, good evening," cried Bert and Hugh together.

"'Ere! Stop!" shouted Higgins, his face aflame with passion.

"Well?" asked Susanne placidly; for he had the most even of tempers.

"Do I understand as you four's a goin' ter give us three way?" demanded the ruffianly Higgins, squaring up to them in threatening manner, while the Old Firm stood arm in arm watching him closely. "Eh?"

"You have managed to gather something of our meaning, at any rate," replied Susanne, without raising his voice in the slightest.

"Then you're going to give information yourselves?" asked Rawlings, two spots of red colour in his otherwise pallid cheeks, his eyes blazing.

"In other words, you're going to act like a parcel of fools and sneaks," shouted Trendall, his temper aroused like that of Higgins'.

"One moment?" asked Susanne coolly. "You really take the words out of my mouth. Our action will be decided after discussion. If the police want information, as seems certain, we shall volunteer it. I am not quite sure that we shall not at once report the circumstances. In any case, we do not intend to lie. As for you, Rawlings and Trendall—you must do as you like. Your movements and your actions have no interest for me and these other fellows."

"You mean, then, that if you're asked who were in that other car you won't say?" demanded Rawlings eagerly, breathlessly in fact.

"Certainly, that is, if the request comes from the school authorities. If from the police it is a different matter. Now you know. Lie as much as you care to yourself. This firm don't go in for dirty behaviour of that sort."

The great and placid Susanne carefully focussed his monocle upon the figure of the prefect, regarded him, from the sole of his dusty boots to the crown of his somewhat damaged bowler, with something akin to scorn, and then set out for the school with his comrades. They left the trio behind them in earnest conversation, a conversation which, before it was ended, became somewhat heated. Nor did it bode much good to Clive and his comrades. It may be said, indeed, that all Rawlings' vindictiveness was centred upon the young fellow who lived so close to him at home. But in the case of Trendall we are bound to confess that the condition of his mind was essentially wavering. To commence with, at heart he was a better and a more generous-minded fellow than Rawlings. And then, try as he might, he could not forget his indebtedness to Susanne. Rawlings had chided him for it. He had argued against that feeling as unnatural.

"Feel as if you ought to be grateful!" he had scoffed now on many an occasion, for he was ever fearful of losing the alliance. Rawlings had, indeed, felt the coldness of his fellows for many a day after that episode on the ice. Fellows who had been quite content to know him before, to be even jovial with him, though never actually friendly, were now always busy when he happened to accost them, and hurried off. Or they turned cold looks upon him, which sent him off with his tail between his legs and his lips muttering. Trendall might do the same. Susanne and his friends had helped to save his life. Trendall had even thanked them, though lamely it must be admitted.

"Call that saving your life! Rot!" Rawlings had told him. "What followed? For a week and more the chaps were never tired of hooting you. They told you that you had acted like a muff. That you had nearly drowned the whole party. And now you speak of gratitude, and to fellows such as they are."

It was always the memory of the uncomfortable and indisputable fact that Ranleighans had jeered at him that turned all Trendall's better intentions and feelings to gall and wormwood. Hyper-sensitive where his own dignity was concerned, and having for a long while had perforce to put up with a great deal of chaff, he had found, up to that affair of the ice, that friendship with Rawlings improved his position. There are snobs in every school, we suppose. Rawlings was decidedly one. Trendall was, perhaps, another. In any case, alliance with Rawlings had brought him comfort and affluence, for his friend was blessed with even more money than was the case with Susanne. And chaff had ceased, for Rawlings was free with his hands and feet. But that ice episode had set fellows jeering. Trendall forgot a natural gratitude to Susanne and his friends in the bitterness of the ridicule poured on him, and this, fanned by Rawlings, made him almost as great an enemy as was that immaculate but detestable young fellow.

"So we sticks together, eh?" asked Higgins, as the trio were about to separate. "If them young sneaks says as you was in that car, I says you wasn't. If I'm axed who was there, why, I don't know."

A ponderous wink and an ugly leer accompanied this statement.

"But I knows who was along with me, oh, yes, I knows all about that. I was going to Guildford shopping, yes, and these here youngsters sees me and asks for a ride. I gives it to 'em. Yes. That's right. And their names is Feofé, Masters, Darrell and two Seymours. You're clear, Mr. Rawlings. Thank ye, sir. Sovereigns is useful every time. You say as there'll be another by the end of the week?"

"When my allowance comes; but on conditions."

"In course. Conditions that I gives them young sneaks away and knows nothing about you."

The conspiracy thus hatched boded ill for Clive and his fellows, for when one began to analyse the circumstances of the case, it would be their word against that of Higgins. Whereas he stated that they had hailed him on the road, their statement would be that he had taken them by arrangement. If they said in addition that Rawlings and Trendall were in the second car, Higgins would strenuously deny the statement, and there again there would be conflict of testimony, which would be useless to convict either of the two. Gold had, in fact, won over the rascally Higgins, just as it may win over any similar scoundrel. Rawlings felt that his money had been well expended, and he followed Clive and his friends to the school in a distinctly calmer frame of mind. The trouble which had been staring him in the face was gone. He was chuckling at the fix into which Susanne and his band would certainly tumble.

"We've just to sit tight and keep our mouths shut, Trendall," he said. "Of course, we shall have to appear indignant at the charge, and—ah, that's lucky, we shall want an alibi."

"Eh? How much? What's an alibi?"

"Duffer! Someone to prove that we were elsewhere."

"Higgins then."

"Idiot!" Rawlings rounded on him angrily. "How can he prove that when he was off at the flying meeting? What about Tunstall?"

Tunstall was another of the same kidney as Higgins. Ranleigh was, in fact, at this period, somewhat unlucky in this particular, for Tunstall was one of those oily wretches ever on the look out for favours from anyone. In a smaller way than Higgins he had more than once procured contraband articles for Ranleighans, and was ready at any time to do a service. Better, too, for Rawlings' purpose, he occupied a shop somewhat isolated and away from the village. A prefect had the right to go there. Doubtless the fact of his taking a friend would be overlooked.

"He's the very man," agreed Trendall. "But—look here, Rawlings, I don't like all this business. Supposing it were found out?"

He never thought of the dishonesty of it all. Like his friend, he feared only the consequences of discovery.

"Rot! Of course the thing'll pass. Don't be an ass," growled Rawlings. "Let's sprint off at once. We've time to see him now and still be in for call-over."

Everything seemed to be working in their favour, for the wily Tunstall was at home, and tumbled to their meaning instantly. He was a shock-headed, unkempt individual, with a crooked back and a chin which seemed to have settled down on his chest from infancy. A straggling beard depended from the same chin, while long, untidy eyebrows overshadowed a pair of cunning orbs.

"Say as you was here the whole afternoon, a drinkin' corfee and sich like; of course, Mr. Rawlings," he leered, "but—well, yer see, bein' only a poor man, with this here shop to depend on, I can't afford to give nuffin away, don't yer see, nuffin, not even a promise."

"But we'll make that all right," came the instant and eager response. "Look here, Tunstall, what's it worth?"

The wily one screwed his eyes up till his long brows mingled almost with his unkempt beard. "What's it worth? Well, see here, supposin' I don't stick to the tale. Supposin'——But you ain't yet told me why you've axed for this here alibi. Is it a robbery?"

"A robbery!" shouted Trendall angrily, his fat cheeks wabbling and flushing red. "What do you take us for?"

Tunstall might easily have replied that he took them for what they showed themselves to be. But he had his own terms to make, and caution was necessary.

"No offence, gents," he said silkily. "No offence, I'm sure. I wasn't thinkin' that, of course. But what's the reason for wantin' this here alibi? You've got into some sort o' mess, I suppose. What mess, then? I has to ask, 'cos I has to protect myself, and besides, though I may only keep a small shop, I've got me own feelin's, and me own pride."

The task was not so easy a one as Rawlings imagined. Or, to be precise, that young gentleman was not half as clever as he thought himself. Had he been so he would have seen through the artifices of this rascal at once, and would not have shown concern at his lack of keenness to undertake the work asked of him.

"I'll—I'll make it worth your while, Tunstall," he said desperately. "As to the cause, why, we've been to Guildford. There was an accident on the way back. The steering gear of the car went wrong and we were turned over. That man Ranger, who was driving, was killed. Now, the police will find him and the car on the road. It's plain he was killed by accident, and there's not the smallest need for our names to appear. All we could do would be to corroborate the story of the accident. But we don't want to do that, for we'd been breaking bounds. Now, a sovereign if you help us."

Tunstall held out a grimy palm.

"Put it there, sir," he leered. "I'll swear as you was here all day a drinkin' corfee and——"

"Not all day," Trendall corrected him. "We came just before twelve and left at three. That makes it impossible for us to have been at Guildford."

"Then you come here at twelve and left at three. You was drinkin' corfee and jawin' and what not. Put it there, Mr. Rawlings."

"I can't now, but at the end of the week," came the lame answer. "I've given my last sovereign to-day. But I'll easily get more, and——"

"Oh, ho!" cried Tunstall, looking cunningly at them. "You ain't got the stuff on you, but you've got promises. Well, any man is rich with them. Gold's gold, Mr. Rawlings, and without it a man can't speak, nor take risks, which is a deal more, I can tell ye."

"But—what do you mean?" asked Rawlings desperately, afraid to lose his temper and abuse the man. "My word is good enough, surely? If I say I will pay you a pound, that money is as good as paid."

"In course. In course, sir. But gold's gold, as I've said. Promises ain't worth half, or even that. I could ha' done this here job for twenty shillings, but for a promise of twenty, no. It ain't possible."

"Then how much?" asked Trendall, his fat cheeks shaking with apprehension, for he could now see the importance of possessing an alibi. "How much for the job?"

"Five quid. Not a penny less," came the leering rejoinder.

The mention of such a sum caused the two Ranleighans to stare hard at one another. Rawlings' brow was deeply furrowed, his eyes had a far-away look. Trendall watched him anxiously. For his part five pounds was out of the question. Masters could have raised such a sum almost as easily, and that was saying a lot, for Masters was for ever grumbling at the smallness of his allowance, and the meanness of his people. But Rawlings had a wealthy father, one, too, who boasted of the expense caused by an expensive son. He liked to feel that his offspring was cutting a dash, and for that purpose gave him ample funds. Still, even he might kick if too great a demand were made.

"Got it!" cried Rawlings, snapping his fingers with delight. "Five pounds, you said, Tunstall?"

"That's the figure. It couldn't be done at a halfpenny less."

"There's that parting present we're giving to Tarton, the 'Stinks' master," suggested Rawlings. "They're asking for subscriptions to the fund, and——"

"You could get it for that, eh?" demanded Trendall eagerly.

"Easily. Tell the Governor I want to do the thing well. He'll never be any the wiser, and'll never ask questions. Very well, Tunstall, it's a big price, but I'll pay it. Five pounds for the job, half as soon as my next allowance arrives, the rest before the term's ended."

The wretch looked at him artfully, his eyes screwed up to narrow slits again.

"You promise?"

"Certainly."

"On yer—on yer honour?"

"What next! Of course!" growled Trendall. "As if we were likely to break our word."

"I dunno. I dunno," muttered Tunstall, but so that they could hear. "Honour's a great word with you gents, and me and the likes of me don't understand it. But I should ha' thought that young chaps as wanted a job o' this sort done hadn't— well, five pound then, half within a week, the rest as you say."

A flash of indignant anger in Rawlings' eye, and a sudden heightening of Trendall's colour, had warned him to refrain from further speaking. He nodded to them both and showed them out obsequiously. As for the two who were to pay him for this job, they slunk away from the shop as if they were afraid of their own shadows. That last unmeant thrust on the part of Tunstall had gone home with a vengeance.

"The cheek of the brute," growled Rawlings. "What'd he mean about honour? What business is it of his, anyway? Eh?"

But in their heart of hearts they knew that the thrust was deserved. What honour could they have, indeed, when they were parties to such double dealing? However, a sharp run up to the school made them forget the incident. They were in good time for call-over, and went in to tea as if nothing unusual had happened. By the following morning they had persuaded themselves that their fears had been needlessly aroused, and that their precautions were unnecessary.

"Wish I hadn't been quite so free with that fellow Higgins," Rawlings whispered to Trendall as they went into Chapel. "The chances are the police have found the car and the man, and have decided that it was an easily explained accident. There was the broken steering gear to tell them its cause, and nothing to show that there was another car there or anyone else in the wrecked car, for that matter. I'm sorry about that sov. As to Tunstall, of course, if he don't have to swear an alibi, why, he won't get his money."

But breakfast brought a decided change to the situation. The meal was ended, "knock up" had sounded, this latter being a sharp rap given on the table occupied by the masters up on the dais. It called for silence, while Harvey made the round of the hall, inspecting table linen. Then followed grace as a rule, and immediately after the boys filed out of the Hall in regular order. Now, of a sudden, a familiar figure bounced on to the dais. It was the Headmaster. Dead silence followed, silence in which Rawlings could hear his heart thumping. It palpitated a moment later when the Head began to speak. He stood in the middle of the dais, his head thrown back, his eyes apparently closed, a smile on his face which might have deceived the unwary. But Ranleighans knew that something unpleasant was coming. The acidity of his tones even more than the words told them of his great displeasure.

"There was an accident on the road from Guildford yesterday," he said. "A man was killed. Certain Ranleigh boys were there. They will step forward."

Clive felt as if his legs would not support him. It was all very well to have formed resolutions, but acting up to them was an altogether different matter. He quaked. The severe tones of the Head, his austere manner, his obvious displeasure alarmed him. Clive hesitated. He looked across at Susanne, and saw that young fellow actually grinning. And then he took heart. He clambered over the long form between which and the table he was standing, and marched toward the dais. Susanne was already in motion. Masters followed close behind him, wearing a woebegone expression, while Bert and Hugh brought up the rear, their faces flushed with excitement.

"Ah! Five of you. You were present at this accident?"

"Yes, sir," came from Susanne, a wonderful ally on such a stern occasion.

"Yes, sir," repeated the others.

"And you declare that the cause of this man's death was due purely to accident?"

"Certainly," from Susanne.

"Decidedly," from Masters.

"Yes, sir," from Clive and the others.

"There were others present in the car in which you were riding? Darrell, answer the question."

"The driver only, sir," Clive managed to blurt out.

"Ah! His name, Feofé?"

"Higgins, sir."

"But that is not the name of the man who was killed. Explain!" demanded the Head severely, opening his eyes to thrust a glance at the culprits.

"No, sir. We were in another car. The accident occurred after we had passed," Bert took upon himself to explain.

"Ah! That is clear enough. There were two cars. You boys had broken bounds and had been to the meeting at Guildford on the one driven by Higgins. What boys were in the other?"

No answer. Susanne was gazing over the head of the chief of Ranleigh at the glazed windows beyond. Clive looked decidedly frightened. Masters appeared not to have heard the question. For Bert and Hugh, their faces were impassive.

"I will put the question differently. There were Ranleigh boys in the other car, were there not?" demanded the Head curtly. "Masters, answer."

"Yes, sir."

Down in the body of the hall Rawlings and Trendall began to tremble. The critical moment was arriving. They must stand to their guns, and when those sneaks on the dais had mentioned their names, they must declare their innocence. It would be perfectly all right. They had that alibi. Higgins would also declare in their favour.

"And you recognised them? Feofé, answer."

"Yes, sir."

"Then their names, if you please. Seymour Primus, you will give them."

A stony silence followed. You could have heard a pin dropping. Boys in the body of the Hall hardly dared to breathe, while Rawlings and his crony found the strain almost intolerable.

"Then, Feofé? Those names."

Silence once more. Not a syllable from the Frenchman.

"Then, Darrell? Seymour Secundus?"

The Head swung round and beckoned to someone outside the door through which he had entered, one admitting directly on to the dais. There was a trying interval during which not a foot was stirred. Never had Ranleigh school remained assembled in such a deathly silence. Even Old B., standing so close to the Head, seemed to feel it. His face was flushed a dull red. His eyes were blinking. The fair giant looked decidedly uncomfortable. And then the tension was relieved. Carfort, the school butler, appeared with a cane of vast proportions beneath his arm, and handed it to the Head.

"Now we will proceed," said that worthy, regarding the culprits and the whole school icily. "You boys know what to expect if you refuse to answer. I ask you once again for the names of the two Ranleigh boys who were in that other car. They should have come forward at the first. They have failed to do so. Give me their names."

Silence. Nothing but stony silence. Susanne looked as if he were whistling. Clive's head was held high and haughtily. Masters wore the sort of look he usually had when receiving another dose of "impots." And then the school was electrified by another demand.

"Rawlings and Trendall, stand forward," cried the Head. "You others go to your places. Dismiss the school, please, Mr. Perkins. Rawlings and Trendall, who were in that other car, who witnessed the accident I have referred to, and who disgracefully failed to come forward, those two will go at once to my room. There they will be dealt with."

The school gasped. Clive felt as if a ton weight had of a sudden been shifted from his shoulders. He watched the forlorn figures of Rawlings and Trendall shambling after the Headmaster.

CHAPTER X

THE RUINED TOWER

Even the longest of terms comes at length to an end; and finally that eventful first term which Clive and his friends had spent at Ranleigh drew to a close. The last days were carefully and jubilantly marked off by every junior boy on a calendar of his own making. Boxes were packed, good-byes said, and the school divided for the holidays.

"Shall try to get over to see you chaps in the hols.," declared Masters, on the eve of departure. "Much depends, though, on the Governor. Can't do railway journeys on my allowance. Sickening, isn't it?"

"Rotten," Clive consoled him. "But it's only twenty miles, eh?"

"Barely. Perhaps a bit more. Nothing on a motor," agreed Masters, recollecting their trip to Guildford. "And you've a car, haven't you?"

Bert grinned at that, a satirical grin which made Clive boil with anger. Hugh got very red. He looked closely at Masters to see if he were poking fun at him.

"Not going to have a chap like you pulling our leg, you know," he said haughtily and somewhat threateningly. "What do you mean by a car?"

"Why, a car, of course. What else?" grinned Bert provocatively.

"Quite so," admitted Masters, a little puzzled. He had understood, in fact, from Clive's glowing description of the home-made vehicle of which that hopeful and Hugh were joint inventors and proprietors that it was something really very fine. He never imagined, indeed, and had never been given data on which to imagine, that the said car consisted of odds and ends, that the workshop engine was the propelling force, that the steering gear was of the crudest, that bicycle wheels did service in front, while the rector's tricycle had supplied that all-important part, the back axle. Clive in his descriptions of mechanical matters appertaining to himself was wont to wax very enthusiastic. He clothed his inventions in a covering of gloss, which, to the uneducated eyes of Masters, was quite opaque. That car, then, to this same Masters, had always been imagined as a car, not a collection of odd bits.

"Oh!" exclaimed Hugh at length, seeing that no attempt was being made to make fun of the invention. "Well, Clive, a bit more than twenty miles, eh? How'd she do it?"

"On her head. Easy. But we mightn't be able to get away. Train's easier for Masters. Let his Governor stump up. He ought to. What's a Governor for?"

That was just the very point of view from which Masters beheld his paternal relative. He went off in the train promising to see what persuasion would do. And then Susanne waved an adieu to his friends.

"Au revoir!" he sang out, his head projecting from the carriage window. "Wish you chaps a jolly time. Rawlings won't be interfering with you."

And that, indeed, was the thought of Clive and Bert and Hugh. To be quite truthful, the trio hardly now gave the immaculate Rawlings a thought. For the downfall of that young gentleman had been very sudden and very evident. He was no longer a prefect. His haughty, airy ways were gone. He was a changed individual. As for Trendall, the fat fellow's fat cheeks had seemed less fat of late. He had taken the lesson he had received very much to heart, and as if he realised his former shortcomings, had actually drifted away from Rawlings. They were no longer seen together. Their familiar figures, arm in arm, were no longer observed on the playing fields. Instead, Trendall had moped for a while, and then had begun to draw other friends about him. Instead of a sulky nod, he now even deigned to smile at Susanne and the others, and on this, the very last day of the term, he had made a confession.

"Look here, you chaps," he said, somewhat lamely perhaps, for it wanted no little courage to tackle the matter, "I'm afraid I've been rather a pig."

"Eh? Er—oh—don't mention it," was Masters' instant rejoinder, somewhat characteristic of that young gentleman.

"Shut up!" growled Susanne promptly. "Well, Trendall?" he said encouragingly. "We don't think it."

"Then I do. I've acted like a pig and a bounder, and I'm sorry. I've been an ungrateful brute all along and want to apologise. It's late in the day, of course, but then, there it is, I'm sorry."

He held out a hand, lamely again, as if fearful that it would pass unnoticed. But Susanne seized it instantly. It was like Susanne, the warm-hearted Frenchman.

"Good! Very good!" he said. "We're to be friends from now, eh? I'm glad."

"So am I; it's no use being enemies," declared Bert, taking the proffered hand too.

"Rotten!" reflected Clive. "It'll be something nice to look forward to after the hols."

"Ripping!" cried Masters warmly.

And thus was the quarrel made up, much to the relief of all, and particularly of Trendall. As for the guilt of the latter, together with Rawlings, it had leaked out soon after their denouncement before the assembled school that Old B. had seen both cars at the flying meeting, and hearing of the accident had at once given information.

Home at last! The escapade which had sent Clive and his friends to Ranleigh seemed to have been forgotten. The Rector beamed on his boys.

"Wouldn't have sent you at all if I'd known that young Darrell was going to Ranleigh also," he laughed. "Of course, it meant more mischief. That young Darrell's a terrible fellow. Well, here you are, back again. Let's hope you'll have a fine holiday."

"Vote we go prospecting," said Hugh, two days later, when all were settled down. "There's that place we've gassed about so often."

"Place? Lots of places everywhere, and we do nothing but gas," grumbled Bert. "Which particular place?"

"Merton Tower, of course, booby!" cried Clive. "You knew all along."

"Well, there's a place called Merton Tower. What next?"

"There's an ass known as Bert Seymour," declared his brother in disgust. "As if you weren't there when we were talking."

"Oh, I'm there nearly always," came the rejoinder, for the two brothers often sparred. "But you do the talking, you and Clive. I have to listen. It's no wonder if I forget things. Let's get along. There's a tower, a place, and I'm supposed to know that a place is this Merton Tower."

If looks could have brought punishment, Bert would have been a sad individual. He grinned at the threatening glances of his friends.

"Well?" he demanded again, impatiently.

"We're going to explore it," said Clive, forgetting his anger at the prospect before him. "It's said to be haunted."

Hugh went a trifle pale. Ghost stories and tales of haunted houses always had that effect on him.

"Haunted?" he repeated in awed tones.

"Rot!" reflected Bert rudely. "Stuff and nonsense!"

"There's a mystery about the place," Clive proceeded, ignoring the last remarks. "No one dares to enter. We tried once, Hugh and I."

"And funked, eh? Saw the ghost and bolted."

Bert chuckled loudly. It was true of him that he was as a rule a listener in the councils of these three. Often enough his dreamy eyes told that his thoughts were far away, probably on the cricket field, while the chatter of his friends passed unnoticed. But he had a habit of suddenly giving his attention, of picking out scraps which came to his ears and of ridiculing them. That was the time when Clive and Hugh ground their teeth, flashed indignant glances at him, and even threatened violence. Not that Bert minded. He often chuckled the louder.

"We tried once, Hugh and I," repeated Clive with an effort. It was hard to keep one's temper with such a chap as Bert.

"And bolted, probably at your own shadows," laughed his tormentor.

"And were met by a rough fellow a hundred yards or so outside the tower."

"Yes," agreed Hugh quickly. "He threatened to——"

"Whop you, eh?" teased Bert.

"To kill us if we didn't sling our hooks. That's why we bolted. He'd a knife," said Clive. "This time we go armed. Then, if it comes to a question of knives, why, we're ready."

"Yes," Hugh backed him up. "Ready for anything."

"And we're going to-day."

"Now," said Hugh.

"And expect me to risk it," laughed Bert. "Well, let's go. I'll back there'll be no man to greet us. A few jackdaws perhaps, an odd crow too. But a man with a knife, never!"

The conversation having come to an end amicably, Clive dived in at the back door of his mother's establishment, where with wonderful persuasive powers, often practised it must be confessed, he managed to induce the cook to supply three bundles of provisions.

"It'll save coming back for lunch, you chaps," he told them on his reappearance. "We shall have lots of time to explore. Supposing we found something."

"Buried gold and jewels," cried Hugh, his eyes bulging.

"Might happen," admitted the practical Bert. "There are lots of tales of hidden wealth, and some of it gets discovered. There's a yarn about this very tower."

"Gospel?" asked Clive with a jerk.

"True as possible. Place attacked some time in the old days. Rich old bounder in charge. Saw he hadn't a chance, and so dug a hole somewhere and buried his valuables. Supposing we came upon the spot. They say in the village that attempts have been made. Once a bangle was discovered. Then one of the searchers fell into a well and that put an end to the business. It was supposed to be haunted then, and the tale still holds. Lights have even been seen flitting about during the night."

"And there's a tale of buried treasure?" asked Hugh eagerly.

"Ask anyone in the village."

"What'd we do if we found it?" gasped Clive. "I know—buy a real car."

"Rather!" echoed Hugh.

To which the careful Bert made the rejoinder: "Don't count your chickens before they're hatched. Still, if the tale's true, and I believe it, why shouldn't we find the stuff? Clive'd buy back the place and kick the Rawlings out. That'd be good, better than a car by a long way."

By this time the trio were on the road astride their bicycles, and since the ruined tower for which they aimed was barely six miles distant, it took them but a little while to approach it. Then a halt was called.

"Better feed now and so have less to carry," suggested Hugh. "We'll be all the fitter for searching. By the way, supposing the door's shut. There was a door, wasn't there, Clive?"

"That chap rushed out of one, anyway," came the answer. "Vote we go cautiously. Last time we went to the place across the fields and were seen at once. Supposing we try through the copse at the back. That'll give us cover right up to the doorway."

The suggestion was voted to be a good one, as also that of Hugh. The three hopped off their machines, and selecting a sheltered spot by the highway, sat on a gate and opened their parcels of provisions. The meal ended, they mounted again and rode a mile farther, till they had passed the tower on their right and were a little behind it. Then they dismounted, passed through a gap in a hedge, and plunged into the thick cover afforded by a copse which extended to the tower.

"Safe to leave the bikes here," whispered Bert, who once he was embarked on an adventure put his heart into it. "Let's make for that tree over there. It's the nearest to the gap through which we entered, and also the tallest. Then we shall find them again easily."

"Supposing someone else does?" asked Clive doubtfully.

"And clears off? Mine belongs to the Governor," said Hugh, with recollections of what had happened on a former occasion when he had borrowed the Rector's belongings.

"Not worth talking about," declared Bert emphatically. "No one saw us enter the copse. We made sure of that. Then who's to find the bikes? If it weren't for the tree here we ourselves would have a job when it comes to returning. Here we are; prop 'em against the trunk. Now for the tower."

They thrust their way in Indian file through the copse, treading softly. Not that anyone was likely to overhear them. But then there might be someone, as on that former occasion, and as all there were burning to inspect the place and enter the tower they determined to take all precautions. There is this to be added also. Like many other people burning with enthusiasm, Clive and his friends had an inward consciousness that where others had failed they would succeed in finding the wealth said to have been buried.

Ten minutes later found them at the edge of the wood, within twenty yards of the tower. Brambles and scattered bunches of growth extended right up to the moss-clad walls. As for the tower itself, it was a tall, somewhat dilapidated affair, but better preserved in one quarter, where its battlements thrust upward toward the sky. Directly beneath them was a wide archway, overhung by a gallery far up, through apertures in which warriors of old were wont to drop masses of stone upon the heads of unwanted callers. Bert pointed them out to his comrades.

"Splendid dodge!" he said. "Rather a shock for the fellows down below. Bet they bolted."

"Those who could. A few hundredweights of stone fall with a bang," Clive reminded him. "Not much moving afterwards."

"And look at the narrow slits behind which the chaps with the arrows stood," whispered Hugh, pointing to narrow apertures flanking the door, and appearing at various heights till the battlements were reached. "Wonder what it feels like to have an arrow in you?"

Bert shuddered. "Ugh!" he reflected. "Let's get on. How are we to enter?"

The puzzle was not an easy one to solve, for when they had left their cover and reached the door, the latter was found to be a massive affair and in splendid order. There was a postern in it, firmly padlocked, however. Not even the most agile could have clambered up, and had they been able there was no entry at the top of the door.

"Done," groaned Hugh.

"Let's see," whispered Clive. "Let's creep on round the foot of the tower and see what we come to."

Brambles and ferns obstructed their path. A crumbling wall of stone crossed it, and halting for a moment they saw that it turned abruptly to the right some fifty yards away, and then again came towards the building.

"A courtyard or the garden in the old days," said Bert. "Wonder if that's where that old beggar hid the treasure?"

"Ah!" It was a very shrewd suggestion. Clive stared about him with added interest. "Hardly likely," he ventured after a while. "The old chap was cooped up, isn't that the story?"

"Yes; and hadn't a chance. Knew every farthing would be taken from him."

"And so buried it."

"Don't blame him either," declared Hugh. "But where would a fellow be most likely to bury gold under the circumstances? Not in the garden."

"Why not?" asked Bert curtly.

"Because the enemy were round there without a doubt. Probably sat behind the garden walls comfortably taking pot shots at the defenders. Look there, there's a hole in the tower right opposite. Bet you the cannon smashed the stones in. That old cove couldn't have got to the garden."

This seemed probable enough, and therefore the movement forward was proceeded with. They skirted the moss-covered foot of the tower for some fifty paces, and though all observed that the battlements above them had been much broken, and had disappeared altogether in parts, yet the height of the walls was still so great that climbing was out of the question.

"A flying machine'd be the thing," said Clive. "Looks as if we'd be beaten."

"And have to go back. Don't like that," reflected Bert.

"Only we'd get there in time for lunch," Hugh reminded them. "That's one consolation."

A complete circuit of the tower at length convinced them that entrance was more difficult than they had anticipated, if not utterly impossible. Clive inspected the padlock on the postern and declared it to be unpickable. Hugh gazed aloft as if he expected to discover a dangling ladder waiting conveniently for them. Then Bert made a movement.

"I'm going to get into that tower whatever happens," he said obstinately. "Even if it takes me a week I'm going to get inside."

They would have cheered him if there had not been need for silence. As it was, Clive slapped him approvingly on the back and then asked an all-important question.

"How's it to be done? Creep in through one of those slits for firing arrows?" he asked in bantering tones. "Or dig a way under the wall? That sounds the most likely."

"I'm going to climb by that ivy," was the steady answer. "You chaps can hang about down below to pick up the pieces. There's a window fifty feet up, just beneath the battlements, and the ivy goes right up over the top, and's as thick as my leg. I'm going to chance its bearing."

When his friends came to inspect the place they were bound to admit that the idea was practicable. At the same time it was risky, particularly for Bert. One would have thought that Hugh would have made the attempt with greater chance of success, seeing that he was a gymnast. But Bert was an obstinate fellow. He seldom shone in adventures entered upon by the Old Firm. His comrades had come to look upon him as an excellent follower, an untiring though sometimes absent-minded listener, and as a youth with caustic and satirical wit, who at times roused them to the height of anger. To hear him now obstinately declare his intention of undertaking this difficult and dangerous task was rather staggering.

"Think you'll do it?" asked Clive doubtfully. "Awfully steep, eh?"

"Walls usually are steep," came the grim rejoinder.

"Ivy might be rotten. You ain't much good at climbing," ventured Hugh.

"Because I'm never the one to show off," said Bert quickly. "I'm not much good. That I'll admit. At the same time I'm going up to that window, or be smashed to a jelly down here. Naturally, as I dislike the thought of being smashed into a jelly, I shall hang on for all I'm worth, so, after all, the matter resolves itself into a question of the strength of the ivy. I'm going."

They watched the obstinate and foolhardy fellow commence his attempt, and more than once shivered as he appeared to be falling. Presently he had reached a point high overhead and was still mounting. Indeed, in less than three minutes he had actually gained the window for which he was making and was seen to be entering.

"What one chap does, another can," said Clive. "I'm going to follow."

"And I'll be after you in a winking. There's Bert waving to us. Up you go. Who'd have thought the thing could be so easy?"

But when he came himself to make the attempt Hugh found it none too light a task. True, there were plenty of ivy stems to grip at, and an abundance of niches into which to thrust the feet. But the mass of leaves clinging to their stems thrust one away from the wall. Sometimes, too, one of the stems proved elusive, and broke away from its fellows. But Clive at length reached the safety of the window, and Hugh after him.

"Done it!" ejaculated Bert enthusiastically. "Now for a look round."

"And the treasure," Hugh reminded him. "Those chaps who searched before may not have been able to get into the place. The doors were locked, perhaps."

"I say," interrupted Clive, "wonder where that well is?"

That set them thinking deeply. They stood at the edge of the window looking into the dark interior of the tower, wondering which way to turn, and where they would find security.

"Beastly to fall into a well," reflected Bert. "Jolly dark in here, I think. Wish we'd brought candles."

"Come on," said Hugh. "What's the good of funking? We're here, inside the tower, and may as well make the most of our opportunities."

Very gingerly indeed did they set about the exploration of the interior. Common sense told them that care would be needed. For the results of damp and decay and neglect were everywhere apparent. There were even bushes growing on the stone floor upon which they now stood. A tree of quite respectable proportions had taken root on the roof overhead, and its boughs dangled toward the window by which they had entered.

Beyond, at the far side of the chamber to which their climb had brought them, there was a doorway, of stone like the rest of the building, though one of the blocks which went to make the roof of the arch had tumbled from its position and lay broken in pieces on the floor. Hugh led the way towards it, peered through, only to find that he was looking into another room of vast proportions. Then he made for a narrow opening in the wall to his right, and began at once to ascend the steps constructed, as one could see, in the interior of the wall itself.

"Leads to the roof," he whispered over his shoulder. "Let's have a look round first."

Perhaps they stayed ten minutes on the giddy perch to which their climb took them. They gazed over the broken battlements. They peered down through those apertures through which the defenders had been wont to drop uncomfortable masses of rock on their attackers. They even clambered to the summit of a tiny tower set up in one corner where, without doubt, the sentry in bygone days had taken up his station. It commanded a grand view of the surrounding country, and from it Clive was able to look down upon the domain which his father had owned, and which should have been his one day but for the coming of those strangers. Then they turned from the roof, descended the steep flight of steps built in the wall, and searched for an outlet to other parts of the building. Clive was the first to find it. Led by him the party descended to the next floor, only to discover that here time and decay had done its work more thoroughly. The floor was almost gone. One had to cross to a doorway opposite by walking on the top of the wall which had once supported the edge of the floor. He gained the doorway, devoid of door like all the rest in this building, peered through it into a place which common sense told him must have been the upper part of a chapel, though the roof was gone in one part. And then, of a sudden, he lifted a finger to his lips.

"Voices," he whispered incredulously. "I can hear men talking."

"Certain! Sure!" agreed Bert. "Three different people, I think."

"Down below too," chimed in Hugh, having joined them. "What's it mean?"

After waiting there for perhaps five minutes, the three gently stole across the floor of what had probably been a gallery. Peering cautiously over the broken balustrade of this they looked below them. Then they withdrew their heads suddenly. For four men were seated below about a fire which blazed brightly in the ancient hearth of the old dwelling. Who they were or what they were none could guess; but this was certain: they were disreputable-looking, and one had a face which was familiar, while in the case of a second his head and shoulders were hidden by a portion of the masonry.

"The fellow who chased us away once before," whispered Clive.

"I'm certain," agreed Hugh, jerking his head decisively.

"And—and, do you know, you fellows," said Bert, with great deliberation, "do you know that there have been a series of robberies round these parts lately?" Hugh shook his head. Clive looked the question he wished to ask.

"Well, there have been," added Bert, "and I wouldn't wonder if those are the beggars."

"Burglars?"

"Yes," Bert answered curtly to Clive's question.

"Then—er don't you think——?" began Hugh. "Don't you think it'd be wise for us to——?"

"I don't," Bert responded abruptly. "I've got in here after a bit of a climb. I'll see this thing to a finish. If they're burglars, all the better. Let's get back to the balustrade and listen."

CHAPTER XI

BERT MAKES A DISCOVERY

There had been burglaries in the neighbourhood. Bert was quite correct when he asserted the fact emphatically.

"Lots of 'em, too," he repeated in a hoarse whisper, drawing Clive and Hugh after him across the rafters, which in days gone by had supported the floor of the chamber leading to the gallery of the chapel within the deserted tower. "Just listen to this," he went on, in more natural tones, when he had conducted them back to the window by which they had gained an entrance. "There was a burglary at the Evansons', eh?"

"Big one," agreed Clive. "They're five miles away from this."

"And a heap of stuff was taken. That's three months ago."

"More—four months," asserted Hugh, thrusting his hands deep in his pockets and shrinking his neck into his collar. Hugh, in fact, wore a most severe and thoughtful expression. Then he seemed to have thought of something important. His hands shot from his pockets suddenly. He searched the belt beneath his coat, secured round his middle. "Might want 'em, eh?" he asked, fingering the dagger with which he had so thoughtfully provided himself. Clive, too, copied the movement.

"Rot!" observed Bert very curtly. "As if we could venture to fight those beggars down there. Besides, it isn't proved that they are burglars. They may be merely tramps."

"Aren't tramps burglars, then?" asked Clive hotly.

"Of course!" from Hugh.

"Rot again!" said Bert. "Tramps may be pilferers. They're not burglars—at least, not as a general rule. Burglars nowadays dress more or less like gentlemen, live in fine houses or hotels, and employ all the latest scientific appliances."

"Such as X-rays, and that sort," reflected Clive.

"And diamond drills, and dynamite, and gloved hands, and—and the rest of 'em," added Hugh.

"Right—tramps can't afford those things. They may pilfer; they don't set out to become downright burglars. Now, those beggars below aren't all the same."

"One of 'em's the blackguard who threatened Clive and me some while ago," Hugh reminded him. "An out-and-out ruffian he looks too. More of the tramp style, I should call him. So there goes bang your idea that these chaps are burglars."

"In fact, it's a mare's nest," grinned Clive. "These fellows are just tramps or out-of-works, or something of the sort. Homeless fellows, who find that the old tower gives cheap and splendid lodgings. Think of it—nothing to pay for house-rent, no rates and no taxes, no neighbours, either, no annoyance from noisy dogs, or from cocks and hens, no children playing pranks, and——"

"Dry up, do!" said Bert fiercely. "Just shows that you two chaps go about the world with your eyes half closed. That's the worst of being amateur mechanics. Everything that isn't something to do with an engine, a motor, or—or a what-not, isn't worth taking notice of."

"Here!" began Hugh indignantly, for breezes frequently arose between the two brothers. Hugh was not the lad to be down-trodden. Indeed, as a matter of actual fact, it was he who oftenmost triumphed. The easy-going, dreaming Bert usually collapsed early in such arguments and agreed to whatever was passing.

"Shut up!" he retorted curtly enough on this occasion, and to the astonishment of Clive, and, be it added, to Hugh's own astonishment also, for that young gentleman bit the words he was about to utter off short at the very tip of his tongue.

"Well?" he asked lamely.

"Who said that that blackguard didn't look like a tramp? He does—any ass can see that—but the others don't. They're better dressed—roughly, I'll admit, but better. But they're disguised. Whoever saw chaps of their supposed position—labourers you'd call 'em—smoking cigarettes out of gold-mounted holders?"

"Oh! Eh?" ejaculated Hugh, his breath rather taken away.

"You didn't notice, then?"

"Er—no."

"Nor you, Clive?"

"No. But I saw it, if you can see the difference in what seems rather a contradictory statement. What'd Old B. call that if he were taking us in classics?"

"Hang old B.!" declared Bert irreverently.

It made the others flush to hear him speak in such fashion. Bert say such a thing of Old B., one of his particular favourites! Clive and Hugh looked askance at the comrade they knew as a rule as a smooth-spoken, wool-gathering fellow. Here he was decidedly emphatic—brusque, to say the least of it, in fact quite rude, and hurling names about in a manner which might be that of Masters', but was certainly not that customary to Bert Seymour. Hugh wondered what next was coming. Clive grinned sheepishly, and then suddenly straightened his features. Half an hour before he wouldn't have minded Bert's seeing that grin of derision. Now he was positively afraid.

"Er—oh—er, yes," he said lamely.

"Eh?" asked Bert sharply.

"Oh, nothing."

"Then don't gas. Look here. What I've said is true enough. Hugh didn't see what I've mentioned. Well," said Bert, with cold scorn, "no one expects anything better from Hugh."

"I say! Look here!"

"But Clive saw it, for a wonder," the elder of the lads went on without faltering. "So it's true enough. Three of those chaps are impostors. The fourth keeps house down here for 'em, and lets 'em know how things are going."

"What things?" asked Hugh sulkily.

"What things! Why, who's away from home, or going away shortly. Who's a big swell, with lots of cash and lots of jewels. What the police are doing. Whether they suspect anyone in particular. What clue they have to the perpetrators——"

"How much?" asked Clive.

"Perpetrators. Fellows who did the job," said Bert, with cold scorn again. In fact, his tones were icy. He might have been speaking to little children. "What clue they have to the perpetrators of the burglaries, and what chance there is of cracking other cribs."

His grip of the situation was really amazing. Clive remembered all of a sudden that Bert had already made quite a name for himself in the school Debating Society. It was strange, he had often thought, that a fellow usually so retiring and so dreamy should be ready to get on to his feet and speak before an audience. He himself would have shivered in his shoes if called upon to debate. Yet Bert turned not so much as a hair.

"Ready to get on to his hind legs and gas at any moment and on any subject," Hugh had once observed. "Glad he keeps his gas for the Debating Society and don't let it off on us. Bert's a wonder."

He was a distinct surprise on this occasion—at any rate, what might with justice be described as a dark horse. For here was Bert gripping the intricacies of the situation as if he'd been thinking them out for hours. And what was more to the point, though usually content to take third place, as we have explained, he had of a sudden crumpled up all but the feeblest attempts to contradict him, had hurled scorn at his friends, and was now virtually in command of the party. He was a wonder indeed! At last he was being taken seriously.

"So we take it as agreed that these beggars are burglars," he said. "The next question is, how are we going to act?"

"The police. Send for 'em," suggested Clive.

"Yes, we will, in time, as soon as we've proved to our own satisfaction that the thing we've discovered is no mare's nest. Hugh, how long would it take you to nip down by the ivy?"

"To the ground?"

"Of course. Where else, donkey?"

"Two minutes," answered that young fellow when he had squinted from the window.

"Then you stay here and wait for a signal. I hope not to have to send it. But if I do, hop."

"Eh?"

"Clear off. Get home to father and then to the police."

"Yes. But you?"

"Clive and I will remain. I've discovered already that the stairs which once led to the first floor have fallen down. The floor's a very high one, and unless there is some easier way up elsewhere, where we haven't yet explored, those fellows wouldn't be able to get at us. That leaves us safe. While they're trying to get us down, you'll be off. See?"

"And you'll keep them trying till I can get the police. I've got it. Hooray!"

"Shut up!" commanded Bert.

Hugh showed wonderful obedience. He even looked admiringly at his brother, and that was very unusual with him. In fact, Hugh's conceit was large up to this moment. He was more than apt to lay down the law, especially where Bert was concerned. And now he had met his master. Where strength of character—real strength—was required, Bert had as if by magic suddenly become leader of the trio.

"Stay there and wait. Keep your eye open," he said. "Come on, Clive."

They went off across the old room, through the archway, and so to that other chamber across the floor beams of which lay the road to the gallery over the tumble-down chapel. What memories, what imaginations that old place brought up too! Clive recollected the tales he had so often read of times gone by when people lived in similar places, in fortified towers and castles. When strife between adjacent barons was frequent, almost incessant, when sudden raids were made, and when the surrounding people, the serfs and tillers of the soil, all who owed allegiance to one of the mighty barons, hastened, at the blowing of a horn, to the castle, driving maybe their cattle before them, and accompanied by their wives and children. He could see them here, massed in a huge square open place in the heart of the tower. He pictured himself as one of them—the sentry, in fact—perched on that high smaller tower on the roof to which they had ascended, peering out over the country and watching the blazing of the homesteads and the approach of the attackers. He closed his eyes, this imaginative Clive, and saw the galleries and roof and windows peopled by men-at-arms in leathern jerkins, armed with bows and arrows, or with clumsy arquebuses. Many, too, with huge halberds. There were others up on the roof, poising masses of rock on their shoulders, ready to hurl them down upon the enemy approaching the door. There too, amongst them, was the noble baron himself, with his spouse, while between them stood a trumpeter. He could see the envoy of the enemy approach on his horse, a white flag attached to his lance, could hear the flare of his trumpet summons, and his demand that the tower should be surrendered. And then, still with soaring imagination, he grew enthusiastic as he conjured up the haughty refusal of the baron, the first blows struck, the noise and shouts of the contestants.

"S—s—she! Go quietly. You'll let 'em hear us." Bert brought him suddenly to his senses, and perhaps it was as well that he did so, for at the moment Clive was balancing himself in the centre of one of the floor beams, wabbling somewhat giddily, and looking as if he might fall on to the massed-up debris down below, all that remained now of the massive floor on which the ancient occupants of this room had trodden. Yes, it was a place to conjure up all sorts of strange ideas. One could picture the huge oak table in the centre of this room, the rush mats on the floor, the forms and rough chairs round the huge, open fireplace. But Clive had dreamed long enough. It was strange indeed to hear of his dreaming. That was the sort of thing one expected of Bert. And here he was perfectly wideawake, the reverse of dreaming, as practical and unromantic as could well be imagined.

"S—s—she!" he whispered. "I heard 'em moving. Stop a bit. They may be listening."

No. The drone of voices came to their ears. Sometimes it appeared as if all four men must be talking at one and the same time. Then there were but two or one. Later, there was loud, raucous laughter. Then a man coughed and choked, and once more there was loud laughter, louder this time, for three joined in it.

"Just the moment to move forward," whispered Bert. "Come on."

He gained the gallery, and Clive soon afterwards. Then they crept to the ruined balustrade and peeped over. Yes, there were the four men, and now that Clive's interest and powers of observation had been stimulated he remarked at once that whereas the three men, strangers to him, were clad in rough clothing, as if they were labourers, two were certainly smoking cigarettes from gold-tipped holders. At least, it looked as if the bands surrounding the holders were gold.

"Might be simply cheap gilt," he told himself. "All the same, it's fishy to see 'em smoking cigarettes from holders. That's the sort of thing Susanne'd do. He don't think anything of a fellow who don't use one, and says that cigarettes aren't worth smoking otherwise. Wonder when I'll be able to smoke and enjoy it?"

It was one of Clive's ambitions, one destined, it seemed, to be long deferred. For we must be perfectly candid on this subject. Clive, like a huge number of other young fellows who attempt to smoke, in their heart of hearts abhor the thing. Only the fancied grandness of the practice lets them repeat it. Perhaps, also, it is because smoking is so strictly forbidden, and is such a severely punished offence because of its decidedly harmful effects, that boys dare attempt it. In any case, speaking of Clive, we have to faithfully record the fact that a cigarette went far to make him feel positively sick, and being a sensible fellow he had decided against the practice. Even Susanne had lost his keenness, while Hugh and Bert had never once shown an inclination in that direction. Indeed, to do the "Old Firm" but simple justice, they were models where smoking was concerned.

Down below, in the body of the ruined chapel, beneath an expanse of roof still supported on some half-dozen pillars, and situated so close to the edge that the two above could easily perceive them, were the four men whose voices they had heard, the head and shoulders of one of them, however, being still invisible. They sat for the most part on masses of stone which had once been portions of pillars. But one occupied a chair, while now that he had more time for observation, Bert saw that, far in the background, and only partly visible, was an iron bedstead, on which lay a bundle of blankets. A wood fire blazed in the centre of the circle formed by the men, and propped on iron legs above it was an iron pot. Near by, also, were glasses and a bottle.

"A chap could easily get across over there, and lie down immediately over their heads," whispered Bert, of a sudden, when they had been looking downward for some few minutes, vainly trying to overhear what was passing between the men. "I suppose it's all right trying to overhear, eh? Don't like sneaks of that sort as a rule. But here, eh?"

His eyebrows went up questioningly. Clive jerked his head.

"All's fair," he answered. "If they're burglars, why it's——"

"Playing the game?"

"Exactly."

"Then you think we could get over there? I'll try, at any rate. You stay and watch. If I succeed, you follow."

Bert went off at once along the gallery, creeping close beside the wall, for the balustrade had in parts disappeared entirely. Nor was it such an easy task to reach the spot he had pointed out, for once more it was necessary to cross a part where the roof of the chapel had disappeared as completely as had the balustrade. There was, in fact, simply a stone archway left, across which he must walk to gain the position he sought. And it must be remembered that that archway was not by any means low. The pillars supporting it towered upward a considerable height, so that looking down made one giddy. A few hours before, Bert would have hesitated. The masterful Hugh also, fully conscious of his prowess in the gymnasium, would in all probability have elected to leave the task unaccomplished. But Bert was transformed. He swept difficulties aside as if they did not exist. Measuring the height of the archway, and its breadth, he stepped on to it, held his arms widely outstretched, and commenced the passage, while Clive looked on, his heart in his mouth.

"He'll fall," he thought. "Just fancy Bert's venturing. George! He's across, and now he's beckoning. I've got to chance it too."

He felt dismayed. Where there was a difficult tree to be climbed when he and Hugh were bird's-nesting, Clive made light of the business. He scoffed at heights, at weakened and rotten branches, and laughed at the very idea that he should fall. But walking the tight-rope was an altogether different class of undertaking, and what was this feat but tight-rope walking?

"Jolly well like it," he thought. "Of course, the arch is steady. But it's awfully narrow, and it's such a height. If one tripped, one would be over. That'd kill a fellow."

He crept along the gallery, stole softly to the arch, and then looked over. It made him feel quite queer when he peered down into the ruined chapel. Clive felt like funking. He was on the point of shaking his head in Bert's direction. And then he changed his mind. What Bert could do, he would.

"As if I'd let him beat me!" he thought. "He'd call me a funk. He's been slinging names around freely since this began. Like his cheek! Just fancy Bert slinging names at a fellow!"

A hot flush rose to his cheeks at the thought. If he had hesitated to make this attempt to cross a moment earlier, he was now eager to set out.

"Just fancy being licked by Bert. Not me! Rather get smashed into mincemeat down below than have him jeering."

And off he went across the narrow archway, with Bert watching him anxiously, as if doubtful of his capacity to cross. If Clive could have read his friend's thoughts he would have flushed even redder than he had done a little while before, for conditions were reversed with a vengeance. It was always a matter of doubt with Clive and Hugh, and with the somewhat bumptious Masters, to tell the tale fully, whether Bert, when accompanying the Old Firm on some of its more reckless expeditions, would ruin its success by his natural timidity. And here he was ready to call Clive a funk if need be, and anxiously wondering whether he were capable of doing what he, Bert, had done!

"Ah! Glad you managed it. Thought you might get giddy and fall," he whispered. "Now lie down and don't kick up a beastly row. I want to listen."

There was sudden movement down below. One of the four under observation—and now that Clive and Bert had changed their point of vantage, invisible to them, for they were almost directly beneath—rose from the stone seat he had been occupying, kicked the logs on the fire till they sent a stream of sparks upward, and then sauntered out into that part of the chapel exposed to the sky. Where a roof should have been, there was now nothing but the broken ends of what had, doubtless, once been finely carved stone arches. They poked their shattered tips from the farther wall like so many fingers, and attracted the attention of the fellow below. Seeing him suddenly appear, Clive lay even flatter, and he, too, took stock of those remains of broken arches. And then, straightway, he pictured the chapel as it had been, with its carved and ornamental roof, its beautiful stone pillars, its aisles, its pews. And in amongst the latter those people of a bygone day. Men in armour, ladies in the fashion of the time, retainers stationed everywhere. He even fancied he heard the low-voiced music of the organ, the chanting of the choir, the deep bass notes of the priest in attendance. And then he was startled into the reality of things as they were. For the man below was speaking. Despite his clothes, one would have sworn that he had some pretensions to being a gentleman. He was still smoking a cigarette, and now knocked the end against one of the pillars of the chapel so as to clear it of ash. Then he looked around, as if admiring the ruins.

"A queer place to be hidden in, eh?" he asked, flourishing the cigarette. "Romantic and all that. Haunted, they tell me. All the better. No one likely to interfere."

His voice was singularly tuneful. Had Clive or Bert met him elsewhere and seen him dressed in other raiment they would decidedly have proclaimed him to be a gentleman. But then, the times we live in are strange ones.

"The most honest, sometimes the most ragged," Bert murmured. "The more gentlemanly, sometimes the cleverer rascal. That chap's good looking."

Clive nodded. "Yes," he said. "I believe I've seen him somewhere else before this."

"Round about here?"

This time Clive shook his head. He could not recollect; but of this he was sure, he had seen this man, and under different circumstances.

"I'll swear he was well dressed then," he whispered. "But let's shut up. They're gassing."

"All the better," repeated the man out in the open, stretching his arms and yawning. "There's less chance of interference. But I'll tell you this. I'd rather we could work during the daytime than at night. I never was one for staying up. I'm a beggar to sleep. If only every other person would sleep during the hours of daylight, I for one would be contented."

"Listen to the selfish beggar," came an answer from directly beneath the listeners. "Here's Joe wishes to be left alone to do his work during the daytime, just because he likes to sleep at night. As if he weren't having his reward. Listen to this, Joe. Good things are not to be had without the expenditure of trouble, and without inconvenience to one's self. That's something worth remembering. Think what you get for a night's work. More than the average man makes in a whole year, perhaps. And if we're lucky, and things turn out as we hope, why, there's a fortune for each one of us. We're out for a big haul. The stuff's there, or should be. There don't seem a chance of our being interfered with, while here's Peter, who knows the inns and outs of every corner, able to advise us where to work, and, what's even better, able to keep watch when we're gone, and no doubt to throw dust in the eyes of those who might be inquisitive."

"For instance, the police," came from the third man, with a satirical laugh. "I'd just like to know what they'll make of this business we're after. But we've been too cute for 'em up to now, and I'm not afraid of running across them. This haul's bound to be either nothing or a real big un, and if it is, why, there'll be quite a little excitement in the neighbourhood."

Bert nudged Clive. "Hear that?" he asked, in a whisper. "They're going to attempt a haul."

"Here, too," answered Clive excitedly. "But exactly where?"

"Ah! That's what we've got to discover. They've evidently put the police off the scent, and we were quite right in thinking that the fellow who lives in this place picks up all local information for these fellows. Look out! They're at it again."

"Say, Joe," they heard from one of the men still invisible. "Let's look at that sketch again. I'm not sure where the window actually is, nor in what condition. But perhaps Peter will tell us. Now, lad, let's hear it."

There was a short pause, and then another voice chimed in, one less musical and far less cultured.

"The window. Oh, ah! Well, now, it's right away agin the very corner, and if there ever was a window that was strong, why, it's that there window. But the job can be done, particular by you gents that has had sich practice."

"Going to enter by a window," whispered Bert hoarsely. "But where?"

"And seein' as you've got the right sort o' tools, why it's jest as good as finished," went on the fellow known as Peter. "After that, why, it lies with yourselves. If you're careful I can't see as there's a chance of interference, and if the stuff's there, why, you has it. As for the police, they're safe. Why, bless you, when there's one of your night jobs on, and it ain't quite sort o' healthy for the police to be about, I jest manages to send 'em word somehow that there's a poachin' business comin' off, and that there poachin' business ain't never in the neighbourhood you're workin'. What's more, the news ain't never given by me, nor by the same man, never. Them police is jest little babies."

Evidently Peter had little opinion of the arm of the law. He held the local sergeant and his constable in open contempt, and now he was gloating over the clever means by which he had managed to hoodwink them. Clive heard him cackling. He slouched out into the open, crammed his pipe with tobacco which the man called Joe offered, and lit the weed by means of a piece of smouldering wood picked from the fire.

As for Clive and Bert, they withdrew a little later. They were still wanting precise information as to the part where this burglary was to be attempted, and they were not at all sure that the plan was to be carried out that night.

"But it's likely enough," reflected Bert. "Chaps like these don't come down to the country to hang about. They've chosen one of the large houses, and Peter will have thrown dust in the eyes of the police and sent 'em in the opposite direction. To-night'll be dark, for there's no moon just now. Now, what's to be done in the matter?"

That was a most difficult question. Gathered about the window by which they had entered, the three debated the point with hushed voice and eager gesture. Observation and the words they had overheard had been amply sufficient to convince them of the importance of their discovery. Only their own determination had gained admission to the ruined tower for them. But thanks to that they had unearthed a nest of burglars. The matter could not rest there.

"Impossible!" declared Bert resolutely, which sentiment Clive and Hugh echoed. "We'd have the neighbourhood shouting taunts at us and declaring we were funks. Those chaps below have brought this thing on themselves. They ought to have seen to it that no one could clamber into the tower. They didn't. That's their fault. But, as a result, we know that they're burglars."

"Yes. Regular rotters," Hugh agreed.

"And our duty's as plain as possible."

Clive pushed his hands deep into his pockets and looked decidedly stubborn.

"Yes, it is a duty," Bert admitted. "What's more, we're going to carry it through. Just you chaps shut up talking while I think a bit. You gas so much that you make a fellow's wits go wandering."

He had become quite spiteful. Hugh actually flinched under this reprimand and failed to retort. Clive coloured, looked indignant, and then turned to gaze out of the window. Each was therefore left to his thoughts, and though a method of procedure might not yet have been come at, this was quite certain: each one was fully determined that nothing should make him flinch from the task so unexpectedly set him. The arrest of those scheming burglars was decidedly a duty.

CHAPTER XII

ROUNDING UP THE BURGLARS

The predicament in which Bert and his friends found themselves after overhearing the discussion between the four men in the chapel of the tower was by no means lessened by an event which happened within five minutes of the return of Clive and Bert. They were grouped round the window through which they had gained entrance, debating the question. Bert, in the manner he favoured when addressing the members of that august assembly known as the Ranleigh School Debating Society, stood with his hands beneath his coat, firmly clenched at his back. He leaned slightly forward, wagged his head impressively when he wished to make a point, and silenced interruption with a keen and sometimes threatening glance.

"There you are," he was saying, as if summing up the whole position.

"We arrive here after a bit of a climb."

"Yes, we all know that," interjected Hugh impatiently. "If we hadn't arrived here, why—well, we shouldn't be here, should we?"

"Don't talk rot," came the rejoinder. "We arrive here after a climb; we discover four blackguards——"

"One moment," said Clive, gently enough, for he was positively fearful now of incurring the censure of the great Bert. "You must admit that they don't exactly appear to be blackguards. One, for instance——"

Bert tossed his head impatiently. He freed one hand from behind his back, and still leaving the other in its old position, holding his coat-tails in air, lifted the first, protruded a forefinger and held it out in a manner half appealing and certainly a little threatening.

"Do let's get on," he growled. "Who's such an ass not to know that modern burglars are often swells?"

"Agreed," cried Hugh, while Clive nodded.

"All the swell mobsmen of to-day cut a dash. Probably they've been to the best of schools, and if only you knew it, you rub shoulders with them when you go to dances and dinners and the theatre."

Bert was really terrific. Hugh blushed to think of his boldness. As if he and his brother were in the habit of going to dances, of being invited to dinners, and of accompanying friends to the theatre. Catch them being bored with one or the other! Why, Bert had only said on the previous day that dances were a nuisance. That he preferred cricket. That dinners didn't interest him, for people talked such rot. Besides, a chap couldn't get half enough to eat. As to theatres, well, there he had waxed quite indignant. Theatres indeed! Drivel! That had been his actual expression. And here he was holding forth! Hugh opened his mouth to protest.

"I say! Draw it mild. How can chaps rub shoulders with burglars at dances, dinners, and theatres if they never go, or hardly ever?"

Bert fixed him with a piercing glance. "Ass!" he hissed. "Who's meaning us? You means Dick and Tom and Harry. I wouldn't be bored with such things. But other folks are, and they rub shoulders with fine fellows, handsome chaps able to debate any question, and in the King's best English too, who are common robbers all the same. But you wouldn't be supposed to know all that, Hugh. You're too young."

There was pity in his tones. Hugh crumpled up instantly. His indignation a few hours ago would have been surprising. He might even have launched himself at Bert, for sometimes their breezes led to violence. But now? He wished the ground would open and swallow him. Bert's scorn and pity made him positively miserable.

"Sorry!" he managed to murmur.

"Oh, you can't help that, no more can Clive. You're both of you kids, and it's kindest to tell you. But do let us get ahead. We've discovered four blackguards down below, and we know the police are after them. We have heard of frequent burglaries in these parts of late, and we have overheard these fellows boasting of how they have put the police off the track. Now they're contemplating another. We've got to act, and——"

It was just at this precise moment that the event occurred which added to their difficulties, and, in fact, threw them into a condition of great excitement. A low, reverberating crash came bursting through the doorway of the room and reached their ears sharply. They looked at one another in dismay.

"A revolver shot," said Bert hoarsely.

"Perhaps they've had a row," suggested Clive after a minute's silence. "Perhaps they were dividing the stuff taken on former occasions and couldn't agree. There's another."

Five shots rang out in swift succession, and there was a half-smothered shout. Hugh looked doubtfully out of the window. He wondered if Bert would recommend a precipitate retirement, and sincerely hoped he would. Clive, too, followed the direction of his glance, and felt somewhat faint-hearted. But Bert rose to the occasion, just as he had done before.

"You stay here. I'll go and see what's happening," he said.

"I'll come too," cried Clive eagerly, while Hugh showed a decided inclination to follow. But their friend checked the impulse with a wave of his hand.

"Stay here," he said. "If there's shooting, better have only one hurt. If I don't get back within five minutes you'll know that something's happened. Then bolt for it. Hunt up the police, tell 'em the whole tale, and bring 'em along with you. Of course, they'd better come armed. Rather! Listen to that. There's more shooting. They must be hiding behind the pillars and potting at one another. Now, do as you're told. Just hop if I'm not back in five minutes."

He went off without another glance at them, and we must record the impression his courage created. Clive and Hugh were positively astounded.

"Never knew him like this before. What's happened to him?" asked the former.

Hugh shook his head dolefully. The whole thing was astounding and somewhat painful. Even in the midst of such excitement the thought was uppermost in his mind that Bert had shone brightly in this adventure, while he, Hugh, who as a rule thrust himself to the front as if he recognised his own superiority, was acting like a baby, and would willingly have bolted a moment ago if it hadn't been for his brother's example.

"I'm jiggered!" was all that he could exclaim, somewhat mournfully.

Afterwards they stood by the window listening eagerly, every little sound causing them to stir and start. And when the shots were repeated, which was every few moments, they positively jumped.

How slowly those fatal minutes passed too. Clive dragged a battered Waterbury from his waistcoat pocket, shook it violently to make sure that it was running, for, in spite of its general excellence, this same watch had of late struck work on occasion. What else could you expect? The ingenious Clive and Hugh had imagined that they had a startling improvement to add to the watch. It had surprised them that no watchmaker had ever hit upon such a simple invention. The thing was, in fact, brilliant and childishly simple, so much so that they burned to put it into practice. That meant that the cheap but reliable Waterbury possessed by Clive had promptly been laid on the operating table. Its vitals had been exposed. Its springs had been stirred with a canny instrument of Clive's own making, and then, the greatest triumph of all, the simple and brilliant improvement had been added.

"Simply ripping!" was Hugh's enthusiastic comment, as he watched his friend's dexterous fingers. "It'll go like a bird after this. You'll make a pot of money by selling the invention."

Alas! The stupid watch resented this unasked-for interference. There was something wrong with the invention added. Perhaps it didn't fit. Perhaps the vitals of the Waterbury had been slightly injured. Whatever the cause, the watch refused to go regularly after that experiment, even though Clive reluctantly withdrew his brilliant addition from the interior. It had a habit of stopping. Then it would plunge ahead without rhyme or reason. But it was going now.

"He left us two minutes twenty seconds ago," he said hoarsely.

"And gave us the limit of five. My eye! Ain't they shooting! It must be a regular battle."

The shots came frequently still to their ears, sharp and very distinct, while occasionally there was a shout. Hugh looked out of the window, wondering whether anyone passing on the road would hear the noise and come in their direction.

"We'd wave then," he told Clive.

"What?" asked that latter, giving his Waterbury a bang on the stone edge of the window. "Beastly thing's trying to stop. It gave a sort of whir. You know. You've heard it."

"I was wondering if anyone on the road would hear and come along. We'd wave," repeated Hugh.

"Of course. Any juggins would do that. But they won't hear. The sound breaks up in the building. You wouldn't hear it if you were down below in that old garden. How's time? I do wish Bert'd come back. Supposing he don't? What then?"

"We run for it."

"And leave him?"

"Those were his or—er, his wishes," said Hugh hurriedly.

"Oh! Then I suppose we must, though I don't like leaving him. But it's better than all being murdered. George! It's four minutes five seconds since he left us."

They counted the remaining seconds anxiously. They were breathless when the full five minutes had gone. Clive tucked the Waterbury sadly back into his pocket and looked enquiringly at his friend.

"Give him five minutes' grace," he said.

Hugh nodded. He noticed that the firing had become almost furious. Then there was a loud and startled shout, when it ceased all of a sudden.

There was blank despair on their faces now. What better evidence could they have of Bert's downfall?

"Those brutes have bagged him," groaned Hugh. "If—if only we had revolvers."

"I'm awfully sorry," said Clive lamely, for Hugh looked as if he would burst into tears.

"Awfully near blubbing," Clive told himself. And then, as if he felt that the responsibility of the situation had fallen on his own shoulders, he clutched Hugh by the arm and thrust him towards the window.

"Let's go," he said. "No use giving him longer grace. Let's get off to the police. We can then show them the way back and help in the capture."

Sadly and desperately did the two clamber down the ivy to the ground beneath. They sneaked away from the tower as if they were afraid that shots might follow them. Then they plunged into the copse in which their bicycles lay, and having found the latter, mounted their own and sprinted off to the village as fast as the wheels and their feet would allow. Two breathless lads at length threw themselves from their machines at the gate of the cottage which did duty as a police depot.

"What's amiss?" asked the police sergeant, coming to the door in his shirt sleeves to answer their loud and peremptory summons. "What! Mister Clive and Mister Hugh! You ain't been diggin' more pits fer Mr. Rawlings, have you?"

There was a stupid grin on his face. His insolence made the boys' blood boil. Were they never to hear the last of that business?

"I'm fairly sick of hearing of it," Hugh had grumbled on the previous day, for as is the case in the country, the tale had flown swiftly. Sly glances of amusement were cast after the retreating figure of Mr. Rawlings. That pompous individual now was far less patronising than on former occasions. He even nodded, instead of treating those who greeted him politely, as is the pleasant fashion in the country, to a lordly lifting of his stick. Mrs. Darrell's gardener chuckled perhaps half a dozen times a day when he thought of the occurrence.

"Of all the imps, them's they," he had often asserted down at the public which he frequented. "And mind you, I ain't so sure as some of their elders and their betters too, as you'd think, ain't mightily pleased at what happened. Bless you! The parson, he sent his boys away to school at once. Mister Hugh, he tells me that he and Mr. Bert come in fer a lickin'. But that don't prevent parson from bein' amused, do it? That don't prevent him thinking that it sarved Mr. Rawlings right. It's just this. You think of a man as you find him, and parson don't think much of him up at the Hall, if I'm a good un at guessing."

Whether the old fellow was a good un or not, the fact remained that the story was known far and wide, and the boyish escapade of our heroes condoned, if not actually approved of. Still, it was galling, to say the least, to call upon a police sergeant and to have the fellow casting the same old tale at them.

Clive lifted his head pompously. It was a way his father had had when in possession of the property, though he was an easy enough man to get on with. The sergeant recognised the movement. He remembered a reprimand he himself had received from Clive's father. Suddenly he lost his grin and became stern and attentive.

"Beggin' pardon," he said, "but what's happened? A fire? Or is it someone that's got killed? Or is it poachers?"

"Poachers?" asked Hugh in astonishment.

"Poachers, to be sure. Haven't I been worrited almost off my head of late with tales of 'em, and information that they was working? There's that farmer Stiggins. He comes ridin' in two weeks ago and says as there's going to be a raid by poachers up at Squire Green's covers way over by Pendleton Bottom. I gets on my bicycle, calls for Irwin, the constable, along by the cross roads, and we goes and hides with the keepers. But no poachers come along. Young gents, there was a burglary that night over in the opposite direction. There was three of 'em at it, we reckoned, and they got clear away with five diamond rings, silver forks and knives by the bushel, a box o' cigars, a bottle o' brandy and a self-filling pen. You ain't come to tell me of more poachers?"

Clive had recovered his breath by then. He was so impatient to tell his tale that he could positively have struck the sergeant.

"Poachers! Bother poachers!" he cried, though his eyes went to Hugh's with a significance there was no denying. Here, indeed, was corroboration of the story he had heard, and more proof, if any were needed, of the importance of their discovery. "We've come about burglars, your burglars," he cried. "Three of them, and a fourth who keeps watch when they're away and sends tales of poachers to the police. I heard them telling the story. They've been fooling you nicely, but we've got 'em now, sergeant."

It was the officer's turn to gasp. He pushed his untidy hair far back from his forehead, and stared hard at the boys.

"Just tell the tale straight through," he said eagerly. "You've bagged three burglars, you two has done that—never!"

"Ass! Who said we'd bagged them?" shouted Hugh angrily. "We've found out where they're hiding. We listened to their talk, and we know that they intend to make another attempt at burglary this very evening. They started shooting——"

"Ah!" The sergeant started and flushed. "Then they're armed?" he asked, with some show of anxiety.

"Rather! Huge revolvers. They started a row. Bert—you know my brother—well, he was awfully plucky. He went off to see what the row was about, and they shot him."

His lip trembled. Hugh had been too fully engaged up till now to realise the seriousness of his probable loss. But the mention of it to the sergeant unnerved and unmanned him for the moment. A second later he was watching the sergeant closely. The latter dived into the narrow opening of his cottage, reached for his coat and helmet and donned them swiftly, as much as to say that the very action made him into a real sergeant and showed that he was ready to do his duty. Then he produced a note-book, drew out a pencil and bit the lead. Having opened the book, he then looked at a watch as ponderous as Clive's Waterbury and noted the time down in his book with a business-like air which was most impressive. A few scribbled lines were hurriedly added.

"'At two fifty-two I was called by Mister Darrell and Mister Hugh Seymour,'" he read. "'They was on bicycles.'"

"Wrong," interrupted the latter. "We'd dismounted."

"But you come on bicycles," the sergeant reproved him severely. "'From information then received I learned that the said young gentlemen had discovered four burglars, the same as did a robbery two weeks ago, and the same most likely as has done others in these parts. From information received——'"

"You've said that once," said Clive impatiently.

"And I'll have to say it again. It's the law," declared the officer sternly. "It's the law, sir. 'Well, from information received, I learned that the said burglars were armed, and that Mister Bert Seymour had been shot.' Now, where's the place?"

"The old tower that's haunted."

"Ha! I suspected it. I've seed lights there of nights of late. People says it's haunted; but I'd made up my mind to see what them lights meant. It's lucky you went there first. I'd have been there to-night, perhaps, young gents. So it's at the tower? And there's four of the ruffians? That means that help's required. You young gentlemen come along with me at once. There's no time to be lost. I'll pick up the constable, and then get along to the Rector and Mr. Newdigate. They're magistrates."

Once more the officer dived into his cottage, to appear again armed with a bludgeon and wheeling his bicycle. In a trice they were all three mounted and racing away towards the cross roads, where the constable had his quarters. By the time the Rectory was reached their excitement had, if anything, increased, the more so since a dozen or more of the neighbours had joined them. Stevens, the village butcher, followed in his cart, a hay-fork gripped in one hand so as to be ready. There were a couple of young farm labourers, the local sweep, a big lusty fellow who might be expected to tackle at least two of the burglars. Ahead went the Rector, mounted on his tricycle, and very soon the second of the magistrates had joined him riding in his car, to which the Rector transferred his person, loaning his own machine to Tom, a youth employed about the village. By the time the cavalcade came in sight of Merton Tower there were at least twenty followers, while the brace of shot-guns resting in the back of the leading car showed that the band were bent on business, and were determined to meet violence with violence.

"If they shoots, why, of course, I shoot," the sergeant told Hugh hoarsely as they came nearer to the tower. "I don't like bloodshed—not me! But when there's desperate criminals to be dealt with, why, they has to have what they deserves. Where did you say you left the road to get at the tower?"

The two who had given the alarm, and had helped to discover the burglars, promptly pointed out the spot, and dismounted opposite the gap through which they had passed with their machines. The car was brought to a standstill instantly, and a boy who had attached himself to the gang a little time before was left in charge. Then, headed by Clive and Hugh, with the sergeant and the constable immediately behind them, and followed by the Rector and his fellow magistrate, the whole party thrust their way quietly through the cover of the wood which led to the base of the tower. Very soon they were halted at the edge of the copse, with the massive door within sight of them.

"That's where we got in," whispered Clive, pointing to the window above, and to the ivy growing thickly up to it.

"You clambered up by the ivy!" gasped the Rector, turning pale. "What recklessness! But we can't do that. Are the doors bolted?"

"Fast," said Hugh. "But there's a postern in one, which is padlocked."

"Then we'll soon make short work o' that," declared the sergeant, suddenly taking the lead. "Now, gentlemen, we've got to take precautions, or else we'll have these gaolbirds escaping. Constable, you just slip round to the far side, taking a few of these lads with you, and watch to see that no one breaks away. Take one of the guns, and shoot if one of the four we're after lifts a weapon or refuses to surrender."

There was determination written on the face of the officer. Some of the gaping rustics around turned pale beneath their tan. The Rector raised one hand as if to protest, and then, realising the situation, refrained from speaking.

"Now," went on the officer, "I take the other gun. Bill Watson, you've brought along that bar I asked for?"

A burly fellow with a smith's apron around his middle came forward. "I'm ready," he said. "If there's a padlock, it won't stand much from this thing. But supposing they shoot?"

"I'll be there beside you," said the sergeant at once. "Don't you fear. If there's going to be hanky-panky, I'll be first with it."

By now the constable had gone off to the far side of the tower, taking some of the gang with him. All was in readiness for the attack upon the stronghold of the burglars. The sergeant looked about him to make sure that every avenue of escape was closed, and then led the way forward from cover. The smith went with him, the Rector and his fellow magistrate followed, while the rustics came in rear, some rather timorously, some impelled merely by overweening curiosity, others because of their natural courage.

"Now, Bill Watson, do your duty," commanded the sergeant, when they had reached the doors. "In the name of the King, break open that lock."

Bill made short work of the matter. His bar was thrust at once into the hasp of the lock. He put his weight into the business. There was a dull snap, and at once the padlock fell from the door. Promptly the sergeant pushed it open and made ready to enter.

"Gentlemen," he said, turning to those who stood about him, "in the execution of my duty I am bound to enter. I can ask, but cannot demand your help."

Hugh almost cheered him. The fellow was so cool, and so dignified. One saw that he was ready if need be to enter alone, and brave the very worst. But that, of course, was out of the question. Hugh pressed forward and Clive with him. The Rector lifted his hat and stepped up to the door, and then one by one they entered. It was dark within, but a match which the officer struck showed that the way was clear. Guided by Clive, he went in the direction of the chapel. They crossed the floor of a huge room, passed through a wide passage, and then came to a doorway. Ah! the space beyond was flooded with light. It was clear that here the roof had fallen.

"The chapel," whispered Clive.

"And the burglars," said Hugh, beneath his breath, pointing to four figures in the distance.

"Forward!" ordered the sergeant sternly. "Rush 'em!"

"'FORWARD!' ORDERED THE SERGEANT STERNLY. 'RUSH 'EM!'"

They started out into the chapel at a run. With a shout of triumph they threw themselves upon the four men within, bowled them over before they had recovered from their astonishment or could use their weapons, and soon had them tethered in the corners. It was exciting work while it lasted. Clive and Hugh tackled Peter, and were almost killed by the frantic struggles of that burly ruffian. It took them quite three minutes to recover their breath. Then they went to one of the corners, where poor Bert lay huddled on the same iron bedstead which he and Clive had noticed.

"Merely stunned, not otherwise hurt," said the Rector, who was bending over him. "It seems that he must have fallen from the floor above. I will cross-question those ruffians."

The three fellows whom Bert and his friends had decided must be swell mobsmen stood at the far end of the chapel surrounded by a crowd of exultant rustics, and now with hands firmly bound. A great noise came from their direction, and going towards them Clive heard first one and then another of the dishevelled rascals expostulating.

"What's the meaning of this violence and of this extraordinary assault?" the man whom Clive knew as Joe was demanding. "Answer at once, sergeant. Why are peaceful people thus attacked and set upon by ruffians with an officer of the law to lead them?"

That officer might have been a mile away. He stood, note-book and pencil in hand, and once more took the time by his watch.

"I have to warn you that anything you say will be used in evidence against you," he said coolly, having noted the time.

"Humbug! Evidence indeed! You'll require that, my man," came the heated answer.

"I charge you with being notorious burglars, with lying here ready to commit another offence. My witnesses, who overheard you discussing your plans, are Mister Clive Darrell and Mister Hugh Seymour."

Very pompously did the sergeant give the information. The man called Joe looked as if he would explode, so great was his indignation. But though the mention of our two young friends' names may have meant nothing to him, they seemed to attract the attention of another of the three who stood in the background till that moment almost unobserved. He started forward, looked closely at Clive and Hugh, and then, to the amazement of his comrades and all present, broke into a fit of uncontrollable laughter. He almost grovelled in his ecstasy. The Rector was really alarmed for the man's reason, while Bill Watson, the smith, stepped farther away and raised his iron bar in readiness for self-protection. It was Joe and the sergeant who first noticed the curious change which had come over Clive and his young friend. They were backing away. They looked horribly frightened. Clive had gone a fiery red, while Hugh was almost purple. They looked, in fact, as if they had seen the ghost said to haunt this ancient tower, and as if the sight had scared them out of their wits.

"I—I think we'd better be going," Clive managed to blurt out at last.

"Er—yes," agreed Hugh huskily.

"One moment, young gents," said the sergeant. "Why, if that chap ain't still laughin'. See here, my man, you just cut it short, or——"

He was interrupted by another gust. The burglar immediately in front of the one so vastly amused joined him in his merriment. Then Joe saw the fun, wherever it existed, and presently there were all three shaking with mirth, while their captors looked on sternly. And then the one who had set the fashion stepped to the front, torn and dishevelled after his encounter. Clive and Hugh backed away, and would have bolted, but at a glance from him stood rooted to the spot. "Sergeant," said the man, "I'm Mr. Canning, a master at Ranleigh School. Ask those boys if they recognise me."

No need to ask. The faces of our two young friends supplied the answer. It was actually and decidedly Mr. Canning, the "Peach," as many called him, because of his blooming cheeks, the master so fond of giving "impots." Clive groaned aloud as he looked at him. Hugh wished the remaining roof of the chapel might fall in and bury him yards deep.

"Oh!" exclaimed the sergeant, looking glum of a sudden.

"And these are my friends. Mr. Oxon here, whom we call Joe, is the owner of Merton Tower. To proceed, there is a legend of buried treasure. He has lately come upon a clue hidden away in an ancient family manuscript. What more natural than that he should invite his friends to help him search for the missing valuables? What more natural than that the strictest secrecy should be employed? That these boys have discovered us is unfortunate. The fact that we have been taken for burglars is readily understood. It is a most excusable and humorous mistake. Allow me to assure you that we are the most harmless of individuals. As to the boy who fell into the chapel, he is merely stunned. We have been wondering how he managed to get into the tower. I suppose I should have recognised him. I didn't. As to the shots, we were merely amusing ourselves with a six-shooter. There. You have a full explanation."

Oh, the misery of it all! The stern looks of the Rector, the grins of the rustics, the smothered anger of the sergeant and constable. Never were Clive and Bert and Hugh more miserable than on the days which followed. People laughed aloud whenever they met them. At church half the congregation stared them out of face. While the thought that Mr. Canning had been one of their captures made all three turn almost yellow at the thought of the coming term at Ranleigh and the consequences of their late adventure. The worst of all undoubtedly was the fact that Masters managed to get wind of the business.

"How's burglars?" he asked, ungrammatically, immediately on encountering his old friends on their return to Ranleigh.

There was strife for the ten minutes which followed.

CHAPTER XIII

TRENDALL AND SOME OTHERS

After all, Masters had to have his joke, and knowing that inconsequential and extraordinary young gentleman as we do now, we can imagine that even the fierce ire of Hugh and of Bert and Clive had little terrors for him. He harped on that stale old joke of the burglars.

"How's burglars?" he fired off at the unfortunate heroes of that late adventure quite a dozen times within the first twenty-four hours of their return to Ranleigh, and was promptly hustled. Then, too, think of the bitterness of it all, the "Peach," the placid Mr. Canning, smiled at them and winked.

"Like his beastly cheek!" declared Clive indignantly, speaking in undertones to Bert and Hugh. "See the beggar smile and wink?"

"Grinned, the beast!" said Hugh, his lips pursed together. Hugh always did that when he was annoyed. He appeared to be endeavouring to muzzle himself, as if long experience of his temper warned him that an open mouth would result in some very bitter sayings. "Grinned, ugh!" he repeated.

"After all," began Bert, in those aggravatingly droning and dreamy tones of his, "you can't exactly blame the fellow, now can you?"

"Eh?" asked Hugh sharply. Here was an opportunity to be taken. A few more words from his respected brother would lead to a flare-up between them. Hugh rather wanted that. It would clear the air and get rid of some of his own irritability.

"Sticking up for the Canning beast, eh?" he demanded threateningly.

"No. Not quite, but—well, if you were in his shoes——"

"I'm not," snapped Hugh.

"But, if you were, you'd——"

"Wouldn't deign to wear 'em, ever," declared his brother haughtily.

"Oh, well, let's imagine someone else wearing them. He'd grin, wouldn't he? It was mighty funny, you know—er—for Canning."

"Oh, shut up!" shouted Hugh.

"Let's talk of something else," suggested Clive. "I say, the school's going to the dickens."

"Without Harvey, yes," assented Hugh, forgetting his irritation for the moment. "What'll we do? Who'll be captain of the school?"

They looked blankly at one another. To speak the truth, a bomb had fallen squarely into the middle of Ranleigh boys. Harvey, the head scholar and captain of the school, had left suddenly. He was not to have said good-bye for a couple of terms. But the Head had announced within a few hours of their return that Harvey had been called abroad suddenly to join his father in India. It was, without a shadow of doubt, a terrible blow.

"What'll we do?" asked Hugh blankly, appealing to the members of the Old Firm, now gathered about him. "The school'll go to the dogs."

"Not while the Old Firm's lively," said Masters.

"Try me as captain," suggested Susanne, with one of his quiet grins.

"Oh, do let's talk sense!" cried Clive pettishly. "It'd be ripping if Sturton got it. He's in the running, he's a scholar, and he's splendid at games. George! wouldn't he give some of the outside footer teams socks if he were captain."

But, till the point was cleared up, and the Upper Sixth had duly met together to discuss this momentous question and elect a captain, there was unusual despondency throughout the school. The Old Firm went about disconsolately that afternoon after their arrival.

"Nothing to do. Nowhere to go. Nothing decent," grumbled Hugh.

"Except impots," said Masters, with a scowl. "I've still some unfinished for that fellow Canning. A chap never gets clear of them at this school. I complained to the Governor."

"Ah. What happened?" asked Bert.

There was silence for a moment. Masters looked anything but pleased at the train of thought the question gave rise to.

"Let's do something pleasant," he said. "My Governor don't understand a fellow. To begin with, look at my allowance! A dog'd be disgusted. As for the impots, he laughed—laughed, I tell you."

Bert grinned. This question of impots was in the case of Masters quite an amusing affair. Besides, whenever the matter was mentioned Bert's mind always went back to the day when Clive's magic pen was brought into requisition, and when Masters had conducted his work so skilfully that he had contrived to ruin the tablecloth and drench himself in ink. But to grin at this point was dangerous. Bert straightened his features while Susanne changed the conversation.

"Hullo! Here's Trendall," he said. "He and Rawlings don't speak nowadays. I'm a bit sorry for that fellow."

"So am I," agreed Bert.

"Acted like an idiot. Might have belonged to the Old Firm if he'd behaved," remarked Hugh magnanimously.

"Let's invite him to feed," suggested Clive of a sudden.

"I say!" cried Masters, hearing the words. "You know—well, I don't mind, of course. In fact, glad to invite him. But Trendall's a fellow to eat; it'd be expensive."

"Hang expense! Hi, Trendall!" shouted Susanne, always the prince of good fellows.

The object of their regard was at that moment crossing the quad, looking forlorn and unhappy. The new term had begun badly for him, in fact. He was depressed like every other fellow at the thought of Ranleigh's loss. And then, slowly but surely, and in some few cases rapidly and with uncouth bluntness, he was being led to see that he was by no means a popular individual.

"Sit next one another in Hall?" he had asked Marsham, once quite a friend of his.

"Promised," came the surly answer.

"But there's another side. I'll sit there."

"Blandy's bagged it; you can't," Marsham told him sharply.

Thereat Trendall swallowed his annoyance and went elsewhere. But what a change it was to the commencement of the term before, when Clive had first made the acquaintance of Ranleigh! Then Rawlings and Trendall had grandly elected their table companions. No one had then been strong enough to refuse their invitation. Still, Trendall had not yet had his full lesson.

"I say, Wilkins," he began, accosting one of his own form fellows, "how'd it be if we went clubs with our grub this term? You know, I've had a bit of a turn up with Rawlings, and you and I have always been pals."

Wilkins was a thin, hook-nosed individual, with sandy hair already thinning at the temples, prominent cheek bones, a bent figure, and a pair of curious pink eyes which long ago had given him the soubriquet of the "Rabbit." He was one of those ill-developed youths who always appear anxious and hungry. But he had his good points, plenty of them, and was friendly with the majority.

"What say, Rabbit?" added Trendall, with all his old assurance.

"Thanks; not for me," came the chilling answer. "Try Parkin Tertius. He's new this term. He don't know too much about you."

"Look here!" ejaculated Trendall angrily. And then, recollecting the change in his circumstances, and deciding that he could not afford to be pugnacious, turned mildly upon Wilkins.

"Don't be funny, Rabbit," he said in tones almost of entreaty.

"Rabbit! Hang your cheek! I'm Wilkins to you, Trendall. Just see that you don't forget it."

His own particular friends would have smiled at Wilkins' fierceness. The Rabbit was the very last person to act in this manner. A little while ago he would never have dared speak to Trendall with such directness. Not that he was taking advantage now of the downfall of that young fellow. Wilkins was merely disgusted with him, just as were the majority of Ranleigh, and meant to let him know it. And after all, perhaps the Rabbit was doing Trendall a real service in thus dealing with him. For bluntness at school brings its lessons. It is never pleasant, perhaps, but it is more bearable there than in later life, when lessons are assimilated less easily.

Trendall turned sadly on his heel and went off dejectedly, his hands sunk deep in his pockets. At the corner of the corridor he came face to face with Rawlings, when the two passed one another without even nodding.

"Who funked after Guildford?" The gibe came floating down the corridor. "Who sat tight so as to let Susanne and his crowd get a whacking for you?" came with maddening distinctness.

Rawlings stopped abruptly. He felt almost impelled to return to Trendall's side as if to claim his support at such a moment. But Trendall was already moving rapidly away. With cheeks aflame and despair at his heart he raced from the corridor, leaving Rawlings to face the tormentors. Flushed to the roots of his hair, his hands in his jacket pockets, Rawlings strode majestically forward. He could see a bunch of small boys at the far end of the corridor, and made no doubt that they were the authors of those gibes.

"Come here, Jarvis," he commanded huskily, singling out a lad somewhat taller than the others. "What do you mean by shouting in the corridor?"

"Shan't!" was the answer flung at him. "You're not a prefect now, and I've as much right to shout in the corridor as you have."

Rawlings lifted his hand threateningly. Jarvis dived swiftly, twisted out of the grip of the bigger boy, kicked his legs from beneath him and then bolted.

"Who left Susanne's gang in the lurch?" came screaming down at Rawlings.

"Look out!" shouted Jarvis, hugely delighted at the success of his movements, and at seeing the bully sprawling. "Susanne's coming. Better hop, Rawlings. Susanne's promised to give you a hiding."

To return to Trendall, he dashed away from the corridor, hid his face in his class-room for a while, and then sauntered aimlessly across the quad, his chin sunk disconsolately on his chest, his hands once more buried deep in his pockets.

"Hi! Trendall!" he heard, and took no notice; doubtless it was those kids again.

"Little brutes," he growled. "All the same, we deserve it. Rawlings and I acted like low-down cowards. We left Susanne and his crowd to stand the whole trouble. We were found out, as I was sure would be the case. It'd have been better to have owned up. I would have done but for Rawlings. But there, we acted like hounds. Now they're making us pay for it."

"Hi! Trendall!" came floating once more across the quad. "Look sharp, there's a good fellow."

There was something kind about the voice. Trendall looked up and over at the far side. His cheeks flushed instantly, for there were Susanne and his friends beckoning to him. He hesitated. It was true that at the end of last term he had made amends to the Old Firm, and they had magnanimously shaken hands with him. But were they really inclined to be friendly? Had the intervening holiday swept away such good intentions?

"Well?" he asked doubtfully.

"Come over here," shouted Clive. "We want to speak to you."

"Rotten this about Harvey, eh?" began Susanne when at last Trendall had joined them, and was standing somewhat shamefacedly near the group. "Makes a chap feel like kicking the bucket. Let's have a feed, eh?"

"You know, over by the tuck-boxes," said Clive, nodding vigorously.

"Bert's got some ripping sardines," Masters informed the company. "And there's a whole loaf of new bread in my box. At least, it was new two days ago. Expect it'll be a bit hard now. But there's heaps of butter. I sneaked a whole heap from the kitchen. You see, our cook's a perfect ripper."

"This way," pointed Hugh, leading the party off to the huge room wherein tuck-boxes were stored. "We've fixed the whole business you know, Trendall. It's to be a sort of feast of peace. Something after the style of Red Indians smoking the pipe of peace. Susanne wanted it to be that really, using a pipe he's brought from home with him. But eating's better. Besides, there's a heap of stuff that must be tackled soon or it won't be fit for consumption. Here, take a pew."

Trendall was breathless. When one came to look at him now it appeared as if he had lost a good deal of his usual flabbiness. His cheeks seemed no longer fat and jowly. His whole aspect was more alert and pleasing. And now there was positively a smile on his lips, a glad smile, a smile almost of gratitude.

"Awfully decent of you chaps," he said.

"Rot! Try a sardine," cried Susanne, stripping the lid off and handing the tin. "Sorry there ain't forks, Trendall, but then, fingers first, eh? Hook one out with your penknife if you like. But it's easy enough to get hold of a tail. They are splendid like that. You just eat them like the Italians eat macaroni. Only look out. Sometimes the tail breaks away, and an oily sardine makes a beast of a mess on a fellow's breeches."

"Ripping!" ejaculated Trendall, swallowing his second sardine. "But, I say, I'm having more than my fair share."

"There's heaps more," declared Clive instantly. "We want you to have a real solid feed. Like those biscuits?"

"Look here, you fellows," said Trendall, and then paused, as if he had not the courage to continue.

The Old Firm became silent for the moment, Masters because he could hardly be expected to answer, seeing that his mouth was stuffed with bread liberally coated with butter and jam. They looked at their old enemy in a manner which showed their friendship. In fact, it was obvious to anyone who cared to look, and to Trendall certainly, that this was undoubtedly the Old Firm's method of showing their feelings.

"Ham, eh?" asked Susanne, breaking a somewhat trying silence, and offering their guest a huge slice hacked from a joint by means of Clive's penknife.

"Thanks. It's mighty kind of you chaps, but, really, I feel an awful brute to take your things and enjoy your hospitality. I——"

"Oh, that's all right," smiled Bert, looking straight at him. "Bygones are bygones, Trendall. We're burying the hatchet."

They were burying a good deal more to look at Hugh and Masters. The enormous masses of food those two healthy youngsters were causing to disappear threatened them with apoplexy.

"And, you know," said Susanne, "we're jolly glad to have you with us. The Old Firm don't like having enemies. This feast's to celebrate the loss of one of 'em, and to offer him friendship."

"Friendship! You—you don't mean——" began Trendall almost breathlessly, and then, remembering the painful experience he had already had, stopped abruptly. But Susanne's happy, open smile reassured him. Clive improved the occasion by offering their guest an enormous apple, while Masters bashed a hole in the lid of a tin of sweetened milk and held it out invitingly.

"You have first go," he said. "I daren't offer it to Hugh. He's such a thirsty beggar, and Clive's no better. Better have the first shot, Trendall. Then you're sure to get plenty."

But their guest declined the invitation with a shake of the head. For the moment his thoughts choked him. He gulped. Looking at him, Susanne felt sorry for their late enemy, for he was so obviously overcome by this cordial welcome.

"We understand all about it, don't you know, Trendall," he ventured, as if to save Trendall. "They're all bygones. We begin afresh here. You're one of us."

"You don't mean that you—want me to join you? That you would be glad to have me with you?" gulped Trendall, perspiration now on his forehead, the huge slice of ham on the lid of a tin box, serving as a plate, now neglected. "I—I——"

"That is, we'd like it, if you would," cried Bert, who had a knack of always saying the right thing at the right moment.

"You see," reflected Clive, "the Old Firm ain't a limited company. We've powers always to add to our numbers. We go on the principle of 'the more the merrier'—in reason, of course. Well, there's the invitation. Join the Board. Become one of the unlimited."

There were positively tears in Trendall's eyes. He pitched the tin lid to the floor and stood up. Clive could see that his knees were actually shaking. His face had gone a deadly pale colour. His breath came fast and deep and in jerks. Bert was terribly afraid lest he should faint and fall at the feet of those who were doing him this honour. Then a flush came to the sallow cheeks. Those who had known Trendall in the old days, the bad days when Rawlings dominated his thoughts and actions, would, had they seen him at this moment, have declared without hesitation that now they saw a vast improvement. The old sly, sneaking air was gone. This young fellow was no longer filled with arrogance. And when he smiled at Susanne and Clive and the others, genuine friendship looked out of his eyes, even if the latter were somewhat blurred by the mist which had risen so suddenly to cloud them.

"I'll join gladly," he said, with a catch in his voice. "If only you fellows knew how gladly! I've been a pig in the past."

"Hush!" interrupted Bert. "Bygones, you know, Trendall."

"Are bygones, and not to be remembered," cried Masters, having now got rid of the huge hunch of bread which had obstructed his vocal organs.

"Then let's shake hands again," said Trendall. "You can't tell how decent I think it of you fellows."

It was decent. When the Old Firm—that is to say, its first members—came later on to discuss the matter, they agreed that they had behaved nobly.

"Of course, we might have kept the enmity up for a long while," said Masters. "That'd have made Trendall sit up a trifle. But it's better to be friends. And think how useful."

"Useful. How's that?" asked Bert.

"Well, to commence with, Trendall's a slogging good chap at classics. If I'm in a hole ever——"

"You're always in one," laughed Bert, interrupting him.

"There's Trendall to help me," continued Masters, scowling at the interrupter.

"A nice way to look at a friendship!" jeered Susanne. "What next?"

"Well, you know," said Masters lamely, "I used to sit within sight of Trendall."

"That's why you warned us that he was such an eater," cried Clive. "He didn't do much this time, anyway."

"It wasn't that I meant. But Trendall's a lucky beggar," said Masters, his eyes opening at the thought of what he'd seen. "Talk about a spread at table! Why, his people sent him a whole turkey last term, a turkey ready cooked, with sausages. I just wanted that turkey. Wish my people'd think sometimes that turkey's good for fellows at Ranleigh."

Everyone, no doubt, have their own way of looking at the same matter. Masters at the moment viewed the addition of Trendall to the Old Firm from the point of view of what he personally would gain. Not that he was really serious. It may be said, in fact, that Masters was above such pettishness. Still, it was true enough that Trendall was first rate at classics, while Masters was an utter duffer. A little help now and again would certainly be an advantage. As for the turkey, well, it was known that Trendall had ripping hampers. Why shouldn't the Old Firm rejoice at their coming?

It may be imagined, too, that this sudden accession of Trendall to the ranks of Susanne and Clive and Company created quite a storm at Ranleigh. That very afternoon they were seen for the first time strolling arm in arm across the ground sloping down in front of the school. They were laughing and chatting as if there had never been such a thing as a disagreement between them. Then they turned into the tuck-shop, and casual visitors there saw and marvelled at Trendall treating fellows to apple tarts and cups of tea or coffee to whom, a couple of months before, they could imagine his administering something far less pleasant. That evening, in Hall, Rawlings saw the members of the Firm gaily signalling to one another, while, as if to make matters worse, there was Trendall seated comfortably between Hugh and Bert Seymour. Rawlings scowled behind his cup. He kicked savagely at the boy opposite when he remarked on this singular friendship which had arisen so unexpectedly. And then he found his attention caught by the entry of the members of the Upper Sixth. They came in in single file. There was Sturton, tall and cool and unconcerned. Stebbins, the fellow next behind him, a strong candidate for the captaincy, looked bored and sullen. Fellows liked him at Ranleigh; but not as they liked Sturton. Then came Bagshaw, "the oyster" as some called him, the poet, the leader writer, pale of face, stooping and delicate, but with flashing eye and jovial smile which were always captivating. You could knock poor Bagshaw down with the greatest ease. A fellow in Middle School could defeat him without the need to remove a coat. And yet Bagshaw was a power in the school, a force there was no denying. The most muscular boy had been known to tremble before him. It was said of Bagshaw that even Mr. Canning felt less assurance when "the oyster" was his opponent at the weekly meetings of the Debating Society.

Slowly, one by one, they filed to their places, while the heads of all at Ranleigh were turned to watch them. And then the figure of the Head suddenly appeared on the dais, with the master of the week beside him.

"Sturton is elected Captain of Ranleigh," he declared, and then disappeared with a discretion there was no denying.

"Hooray! Three cheers for Sturton!" bellowed one of his supporters.

The boys shouted till they were hoarse. Bert and Hugh and Trendall did their best to drown the shouts of those beside them. Susanne beat the table with a knife till the noise was deafening.

"Speech! Speech! Speech!" came thundering through the Hall; and—who would have thought it?—it was Bagshaw the delicate who possessed that enormously deep voice. Then Sturton popped up on the dais, and waited there for silence.

"You fellows," he began, his hands deep in his pockets, a habit at Ranleigh as elsewhere, "I'm awfully sorry about Harvey——"

Cheers. Counter cheers from opposite sides of the Hall. "For he's a jolly good fellow," started by Masters, and dropped with suddenness when that young gentleman found himself the only one chanting.

"He was a rattling good fellow"—more cheers. "One of the very best"—a perfect tornado—"and we all loved him. I say that he was one of the best captains this school has ever seen"—more cheers. "You'll do as well," was shouted from the far end of the Hall. "Hooray for Sturton!"

"I'll do my level best, be sure of that," went on Sturton. "I want to thank the Upper Sixth for choosing me, and you fellows for applauding their selection. I'm going to work hard. I'm going to make you fellows work hard too, I can tell you." "Shame!" from the end of the Hall. Laughter throughout. "Not me," from the irrepressible Masters.

"Yes, and Masters too," continued Sturton, at which there was another outburst of merriment. "We're all going to work hard. We're going to train steadily, and at the end of the term we're going to pull off that footer cup we've been so long after. You fellows, three cheers for Harvey!"

They gave them with a vigour there was no denying. Ranleighans shouted themselves hoarse in their exuberance. And then they filed out of the Hall where many busy tongues commenced wagging.

"Don't seem so bad after all," observed Clive. "This afternoon everything was at sixes and sevens, and a fellow could have sworn that we were in for a sickening term. Now it's A1. Sturton's Captain."

It was a fine thing for Ranleigh too. Harvey had been a fine fellow and a first-class leader. Sturton was to be as good. We shall see what he did with the material he had to handle, and how he made ready for the great day when Ranleigh was to fail or triumph.

CHAPTER XIV

THE STRENUOUS LIFE

Sturton was as good as his word when he said he meant to work and to make the rest of the school work with him.

"A regular nigger-driver," grumbled Masters, his face as long as a fiddle as he read the announcement on the board in the corridor close to the quad. "Listen to this. Here's a oner."

Very slowly, for he was not an expert at reading aloud, Masters gave the crowd about him the contents of the notice. There was no doubt about it either, bold though the innovation was. Sturton had put it down in big black letters which there was no mistaking.

"Notice!" it read. "In future, with a view to bringing those at Ranleigh to a condition of fitness, there will be compulsory exercise for all daily. The head prefect of each dormitory will present a list to the Captain at the end of each week, setting out against the name of each boy what exercise he has taken daily. It will be left to the honour of individual boys to make a truthful return. Exercise may take the form of football, fives, running, or gymnastics. At least an hour and a half must be spent at one of these. For football boys may join their own dormitory scratch games. For fives they may make up a four as formerly. In the Gym. they will be under the direction of the sergeant. On Saturdays there will be dormitory football, save when there is a school match. Once a week there will be a school run.

"E. Sturton."

There it was in cold letters.

"When do we breathe and sleep?" gasped Masters, when he had assimilated the whole of this momentous notice. "This means slavery."

"Rot!" ejaculated Bert, who happened to be near him. "It'll mean a deal less loafing, less guzzling at the tuck, or round where the tuck-boxes are kept, and a deal more fitness about the fellows."

"Hooray for Sturton! He means business."

It may be imagined that the innovation was discussed from every point of view. There were plenty of fellows at Ranleigh who eagerly welcomed the change.

"It's the best way of dealing with slackers without a doubt," said Bagshaw. "Wish I could take part in the thing myself. By the way, of course Sturton ought to put something about boys being excused who are ill, and so on."

A second notice was pinned beneath the first without delay, which made the position perfectly clear, while it showed that the Captain had no idea of altering his decision.

"Those in the 'sick-room' will be shown as so in dormitory lists," it ran. "Those permanently excused active exercise by doctor's orders will, if fit for the same, carry goal-posts, referee, or otherwise make themselves useful and interested in the games of their fellows. Absence from the school will be the only other excuse taken."

"And what if we kick and decline to be run about by this fellow Sturton?" asked Rawlings, who had now managed to chum up with one named Norman, head prefect of West Dormitory, a somewhat sulky, nerveless individual. It was a matter for wonder, in fact, how he had contrived to ascend to the post of head prefect of West. Certainly his own ambitions and efforts had not carried him to that exalted station. But he happened to be a brilliant mathematician, and by no means backward in other branches of his studies, and had therefore soon arrived at the Sixth Form. Force of custom rather than anything else had made a prefect of him. As a consequence, West, once noted for its brilliance in games, had not improved under his leadership. If Norman could have his own way he would have allowed matters to go on much as they were before Harvey took the lead. He had grumbled then at the added energy required. He positively growled when he had read Sturton's notice.

"What if we kick?" he repeated, for in Rawlings he found a ready and sympathetic listener. "What'll he do? Can't kick the whole lot of us, can he?"

"Then he'd have to grin and bear it," smiled Rawlings sardonically. "One would think we'd come to Ranleigh to be at Sturton's beck and call. Supposing a chap hates games; he's got to play 'em simply because of this idiot. What will you do? Cave in?"

The question was artfully put. Rawlings made Norman believe that he thought that such a course was only natural. In effect, he very strongly hinted that Norman had no alternative, that he was too weak, and that he was afraid of incurring Sturton's displeasure. And as may be imagined with a sulky individual like Norman, opposed to active exercise of any sort, sulkiness became swiftly stubbornness. From that instant Norman made up his mind to oppose the captain of the school to the utmost extent, in which decision he was secretly and actively encouraged and helped by Rawlings.

"Of course, I'll have to send in this bothering weekly return," said Norman, after a while, when the matter came up again for discussion. "But that doesn't say that I'm going to bother whether the fellows have actually been playing footer or fives or—what's the other, there's such a heap of 'em?"

"Gym. Wonder it isn't skittles."

"Well, I shan't bother, and you can let the fellows know that."

West soon gathered the meaning of their prefect. For the benefit of that dormitory, and to the credit of the majority of its members, it may be stated that few availed themselves of the dark hints thrown out by Rawlings. Sturton was a general favourite, and Ranleigh boys were wise enough to see that a certain amount of exercise was good for everyone, while it certainly helped to make them efficient in games and gave added chances in school matches. *Esprit de corps* was by no means dead in West, and much to Norman's annoyance a goodly proportion of the boys there followed Sturton's wishes to the very letter. A few did not. They banded themselves on the side of Norman and Rawlings. At the Saturday matches played between teams selected from individual dormitories the play of the boys of West was marked by slovenliness on the part of some, by desperate eagerness on the part of others. Even Sturton couldn't help noticing the matter.

"It's that fellow Norman, with Rawlings behind him," said Bagshaw, who was the Captain's right-hand man, just as he had been in the case of Harvey. Bagshaw was, indeed, a born organiser and leader. Had he been possessed of health and strength there was not the smallest doubt that he would have been Ranleigh's Captain. But none but an active leader is understood of schoolboys. Ranleigh liked and admired Bagshaw. Often enough he was feared. But he was never admired as were Harvey and Sturton.

"Pity, too," added Bagshaw. "Norman's a queer fellow, and wants understanding. He can be as nice as possible if properly handled, and as sulky as a bear if crossed. There's no doubt that he's made up his mind to break this scheme you've started."

"Then he must stand by the consequences. But I'd be sorry to have an upset. Look here, Bagshaw," said Sturton, "take an opportunity to speak to him. Persuade him in a friendly way, and not as if I wished it, to play the game and help the scheme. Everywhere else it has been swallowed. Fellows are as keen as mustard, and what is more, I'm sure they are happier. For there's always something to do now. It's too early to speak yet, but the Head says he thinks the boys look better. You have a chat with Norman."

No better envoy could have been selected. Bagshaw was a master of tact and discretion, and it followed, therefore, that he allowed several days to pass before accosting Norman, and even then it appeared to be a purely accidental meeting. Moreover, the result of his tactful discussion was, for the moment, excellent. Norman saw the error of his ways. A strong character such as Bagshaw's easily appealed to and swayed him. But there was Rawlings to reckon with, and that immaculate and scheming gentleman rapidly set himself to work to upset all the good Bagshaw had accomplished.

"So you're going to work in with Sturton?" he asked, with a sneering smile, when Norman had confided in him. "Congratulations!"

"What else can a fellow do? He asked me," answered Norman lamely, half apologetically, for Rawlings' sneers and gibes made him flinch.

"What else? Oh, nothing. Of course he asked you," said Rawlings meaningly.

"Eh? Why?"

"Well, he couldn't do anything else, could he? Sturton can't compel. This is a free country. Supposing you kicked? Why, we then come back to the very question you asked when this tomfoolery was first started. Supposing you kick? What can Sturton do?"

"Yes, I see; so we have. It's the same question over again," admitted Norman.

"Well, and what can he do?"

Norman was floored. Rawlings had the peculiar power of always making him feel as if he were a weakling and a fool, and as if others were getting the best of him. He only wished that Bagshaw had had that discussion with Rawlings, or when he was present. He felt angry with himself, and, of a sudden, angry with Rawlings for his asserted superiority.

"Look here! You always know best what to do. Or think you do," he stated bluntly. "What'd you do if you were in my place?"

"Not be led by the nose, that's one thing. Not allow the wind to blow me both ways. Not give in as soon as I found out that a fellow was afraid of me."

"Afraid of me! Sturton? Not he."

"Sturton, yes," said Rawlings, with another of those satirical smiles. "Else why did he send Bagshaw to interview you? He knows you're kicking. What can he do? He's floored. He's bound to send round and ask you to be a good boy and help him."

"But—but Bagshaw didn't say that," replied Norman desperately. "He pointed out that it was a pity that I should be the exception. He asked me to think of the school."

"School be hanged!" declared Rawlings. "It's Sturton, Bagshaw's asked you to think of. This is his pet scheme. Chaps have swallowed it because they couldn't help. You hate it. Then why be a mug and let him win you round with tales of the school and its honour, and so forth?"

All the good that Bagshaw had effected was destroyed in a few moments. Norman was, as we have said, one of those vacillating fellows whose opinions a breath will change. And here was Rawlings persuading him against his better feelings, and persuading him, too, without much difficulty. It may be said, indeed, that Rawlings had a perfect mastery in that direction. It was a pity that he did not use his powers to better purpose, while for the one he so easily twisted round his fingers, it may be said that it was a pity in his case that Sturton did not at once deal severely with him. For discipline and force are also persuasive powers. There are many youths and men also who, when left to their own devices, pursue a crooked line, their course marked by tempers, perverseness, and ill-feeling. But, if compelled by a strong hand, one they recognise as strong, run a course marked by its directness, and distinguished by eagerness for their task, enthusiasm for their leader, and the very best of tempers. Norman had it in him to behave like that. As a leader, even in a small way, he was worse almost than useless. Driven if need be, or led if he were wise, he could be a most excellent ally.

However, for the moment he had been persuaded into opposing Sturton's excellent scheme, and we must leave him and West Dormitory to their devices.

Discussion in the ranks of the Old Firm waxed furious when first Sturton posted his notice. But a few hours' contemplation, and some heated arguments, soon made converts of them. Even Masters grumblingly assented to the scheme.

"Awful nuisance, of course," he said. "But there's one thing."

"What's that?" demanded Bert.

"Exercise don't give time for impots. That beast Canning'll have to do without 'em."

But, strangely enough, Masters began to escape impots. Seeing the energy with which his friends threw themselves into the Captain's scheme, he had perforce to do likewise, and to his own astonishment he found the inclination to work in form time greater, the temptation to misbehave less, while he was distinctly less inattentive. But there was something more. He and Clive were deadly in earnest where football was concerned. They played respectively inside and outside right in the forward line, and but a few days from the beginning of the term had been lucky enough to attract Sturton's attention.

"George!" he remarked to Bagshaw, always his close attendant. "Didn't know those youngsters had it in them. At any rate, I didn't think Masters could be half as fast. He stuffs so much one would think it impossible. Look at 'em now. They've got the ball between them. Pretty!" he shouted. "Well done, Masters and Darrell."

You could have dug a pin in deep without Clive flinching. So greatly was he elated that he would easily have borne any suffering; while, as to the pain of a pin prick, that was nothing. It was part of the entrance rites of the Old Firm that a member must bear the thrust of a pin till it was buried to the head, and that without flinching.

"Worth watching, those two youngsters. Good fellows," said Bagshaw, who knew the inner history of every boy. "Might, one day, do for the team."

Sturton looked the two youngsters carefully up and down.

"Might," he agreed. "Two years hence, perhaps. They're real nippy forwards, and ain't selfish. Just look at Susanne!"

The latter attracted and held their attention for some while, for the Frenchman was a promising player. Slow, but strong, he played an excellent game at back, and had the weight and size for kicking.

"In a year he'd be big enough and know enough of the game," said Sturton. "Put him down, Bagshaw."

That day, in fact, saw the names of four of the Old Firm entered in Bagshaw's list of promising Ranleighans. For in the Gym they came across Hugh disporting himself on the horizontal bar, where he performed cleverly.

"Yes, sir. Make a good gymnast. Been trained badly or not at all," the sergeant told them. "But I'm watching him. This Mister Seymour'll be good to watch and bring along. Ranleigh could do with another of those challenge shields from Aldershot."

He nodded across to the wall of the Gym, whereon hung the shield won outright at the Aldershot public schools competition.

A month made an indisputable difference to Ranleighans. Steady, daily exercise told its tale without a doubt. The health of the school was decidedly better. True, the Head had at first been astounded and almost alarmed at the increased amount consumed at meal time. But then, the tuck was less often visited. Boys who in past times had lolled the afternoons away because there was nothing to do, now had no time to slack over their tuck-boxes and gorge. It was becoming almost bad form to gorge, though due allowance was, of course, made for the natural capacity of growing boys. And then, throughout the school there had arisen a friendly rivalry. The Head, with that discretion which marked him, came forward with a dormitory cup for runs, and this was to be won by the dormitory receiving the greater number of marks at the end of the term for the prowess of its individuals. Another dormitory cup was put up by a friend for football, and a third for gymnastics.

But the chief inducement of all, the aim and object of the whole school without exception, for even here Rawlings and Norman were in agreement, was the great annual football match with Parkland School, on this occasion to be played at Ranleigh.

"Harvey did his best to win, so did others before him," asserted Sturton, when six weeks of the term had gone and already a marked improvement in the playing of football had been apparent. "We'll do our utmost too, and choose our men carefully. I'm going to make a change this time."

"What's that?" demanded Bagshaw.

"Choose my men early, play them constantly, and fill up gaps and the places of those who go back in their play with reserves on my list. The most important thing is to get our team playing together, so as to know one another. Of course, we've a match against Ringham boys, and one or two others. But we've always beaten them in past years, and will do so again easily. So I mean to raise a team of masters and boys. Fortunately there are a number of the masters who play keenly, and they with selected boys will put up a game which will test the fellows we choose for the big match. How's that?"

The scheme, added to Sturton's other one, was, in fact, good, and, we must add, one practised at many schools. By carefully watching the dormitory games, and checking the playing of boys whose names had been recommended by their prefects, Sturton soon had a list of likely players. Two elevens were chosen from these, and a fine game played between them, when the Head himself helped in the selection of the final eleven. Then, once every week, and rather oftener as the great day approached, this eleven played a strenuous game against another composed of masters and boys, while Bagshaw coached them and refereed at one and the same moment. A looker on at that game could not have helped admit that one and all were in fine condition. After all, boys cannot take part in a weekly run, the length of which was gradually extended, in daily exercise of some energetic nature, in gymnastics and fives and what not, without becoming wonderfully fit. There was also the regular morning dip, which, though not compulsory, had now become a regular habit with the entire school. So popular was the notion indeed, that boys now descended by dormitories, times being arranged, and a limited period being given for the bathing.

Even West Dormitory had come up to scratch, while Norman, at first grudgingly, and now with generous openness, expressed his approval of Sturton's scheme, and applauded its success. But then, Bagshaw had had something to say to that. There had been a discussion between himself and Sturton and the Head, and as a result Rawlings had been promoted to another dormitory.

"On probation, you will please understand," said the Head, kindly but seriously, when informing that lordly gentleman. "Last term I had the painful task of degrading you. Now I am advised that it would be as well to give you another trial. You will go to East, where I hope you will remain next term as a prefect."

As it happened, there was a sterling fellow in charge of East, a tall, burly youth from Australia; one, too, in the habit of calling a spade a spade, and intensely loyal to his school.

"Just the fellow to sit on Rawlings if he wishes to belittle the new scheme," Bagshaw had advised. "At any rate, he's not likely to come under his influence. If the Head would move Rawlings there, on probation, and say nothing to Harper, in East, why, no one'll be the wiser, and Norman, left to himself, will see that he's been acting like a fool, and will come into line with the others."

The wise Bagshaw was of huge value to Sturton and to the school generally. The plan he proposed, and which the Head adopted, worked wonderfully. Norman regained his keenness of a sudden, while Rawlings found himself in strange quarters. He despised this big Australian Harper. But he took good care not to let him see that he did so, for Harper was not the one to put up with nonsense. Rawlings was even wise enough to keep his sneers and gibes to himself for a while, till he knew exactly what his senior's feelings were. And on the first occasion, when, imagining Harper to have cause for displeasure with Sturton, he ventured to disparage that fine fellow, and belittle his scheme, Harper turned upon him like a tiger.

"That's your sort, is it?" he asked grimly. "Don't you let me hear you say another word against Sturton or this scheme he's started. And look here, Rawlings. I noticed you skulking last dormitory run. You'll lead our fellows to-morrow, and I'll be with you."

Thereafter Rawlings kept very much to himself. He hated Harper, hated the exercise he was bound to take, and loathed Ranleigh. But, then, that was because he was too arrogant and selfish for his fellows. If he were disgusted, and if Harper's open contempt of him galled, there were plenty of others at Ranleigh who loved the place, who gloried in the improvement which Sturton had wrought, and who awaited the final test with eagerness and no little assurance.

"We'll lick those Parkland fellows hollow," declared Masters, as he lay in bed one evening.

"If we can," ejaculated Susanne, with caution.

"If we can!" cried Masters indignantly, sitting up promptly. "There's a thing to say! Why, even Sturton says we've a chance, and that's something."

It was a great deal, in fact. Sturton had taken pains to ascertain the fighting strength of Parkland. Against that he weighed the prowess of his own team. And, though unusually reserved in such matters, the admission had been dragged from him that Ranleigh had a chance. That chance the following Saturday was to see made absolutely certain or dashed aside. Ranleigh awaited the day with a curious mixture of fear and eagerness.

CHAPTER XV

STURTON'S POLICY IS VINDICATED

The great day at length arrived, the day on which Ranleigh was to rise to the giddy heights of success, or to fall once more beneath the hitherto superior attack of Parkland boys. A cold wintry sun peeped in at the dormer windows of the dormitories as the boys were rising, and set them cheering. They started the noise in West, actually in West Dormitory, where Norman, in place of scowling severely upon the delinquents, even encouraged them. The cheering was taken up in all the four South Dormitories, so loudly too, that the Head, still abed in his own house close adjacent, turned out in a violent hurry.

"What's that?" he demanded, appearing on the landing in dressing-gown and slippers, a somewhat dishevelled object it must be admitted, and one at the moment hardly likely to have awed the school had he come before them. "What's that, Jarvis?"

The latter was a youth employed about the house, at that moment on his knees and supposed to be scrubbing the hall floor. But Jarvis was not at work. He was listening intently, and just before the eager question was flung at him he actually raised his scrubbing brush, waved it violently overhead and gave vent to a cheer of his own.

"Stop that nonsense!" commanded the Head. "What's this stupid noise for?"

Jarvis, still brush in air, gaped at him in horror. Then he grinned. After all, those who knew the Head knew him to be a very human individual, with an overpowering love for Ranleigh and all that went to make the school a success. "Please, sir," he began, and then grinned again, while a thunderous burst of cheering came through the open hall windows and swelled past the ears of the waiting Head. "Please, sir, it's the day," grinned Jarvis. "You've forgotten, sir."

"Day! Of course it's day. It isn't night, stupid!"

"But *the* day, sir," came the answer.

The Head stamped impatiently. No one was more anxious that Ranleigh should win the coming match. But, for all that, he had other worries and anxieties, those common to all headmasters, and for the moment he had forgotten that this was the day of trial. Then he remembered and gasped.

"To be sure! To be sure, Jarvis! But this noise is most unseemly. I—er——"

He paused for a moment and then disappeared. "Leave 'em to it," he told himself, with a smile. "Boys will be boys. A little noise means encouragement. Let 'em continue."

Ranleigh boys did, with a vengeance. The fellows in North had taken the matter up long ago. Any other morning they would have still been abed, snuggled down till the very last moment, till they must rush to the indoor bath there to take their dip. Now they were up, with towels waving overhead, shouting to drown the cheers from South. As to East, the lusty Harper himself set an example, which all followed, even Rawlings, though somewhat feebly. And then, having had their dip, the School dressed with unwonted care and elaboration.

"Of course, you fellows will have to sport the School colours," said Masters to the few smaller boys near him in the dormitory, boys with whom his reputation was certainly enlarged since his addition to the ranks of the Old Firm. "You haven't got any, Tompkins. Then you'll jolly well have to find 'em. Sneak someone else's if you can."

"Can't," declared the youthful Tompkins, looking about him helplessly. "I've tried. Carter caught me in the act and swore he'd report me for prigging."

"Can't! There ain't no such word," said Masters severely, though he had used it often enough himself. "Ah! Bright idea! Look here, young un. I've two sets. I'll sell you one. Here we are. Dirt cheap! Two bob, money down."

That caused Tompkins to look askance at the great Masters. He had a very shrewd idea that, whatever the condition of the tie he was asked to purchase, he would certainly not be getting the best of the bargain. He was sure of it a few seconds later, when the article was produced. It was one which Masters had himself bought second, or more likely third or fourth hand, and it bore unmistakable evidence of hard and long wear. Tompkins turned his nose up.

"That!" he exclaimed. "Two bob! Not me!"

"Look here," said Masters. "None of your cheek, kid. It's a bargain; and you'll be jolly well kicked if you don't sport colours."

The end of the matter was that the seller deigned to take sixpence, the same to be paid by weekly instalments of one penny, Tompkins being by no means flush. Their dressing was hastily completed, when they rushed down for call-over and Chapel. Later, at breakfast, heads were turned from all directions to watch the various members of the team on whom the honour of Ranleigh was to depend. Those lucky gentlemen were eating stolidly and with satisfaction. It was clear that, whatever the ordeal before them, their appetites were not impaired. As for Sturton, he was positively boisterous.

"We'll put up a game, at any rate," he told Bagshaw across the scholars' table. "We'll give those Parkland fellows the game of their lives."

"And don't forget," cautioned his friend, "steady does it. Training is everything. If Parkland fellows are as fit as ours, why, then the tussle'll be all the harder. But if they're not, then we should come along well after half's called. That'll be the time to break up their defence and run through 'em. So keep our chaps in hand at first. Let 'em break out hard once the match is half finished."

There was anxiety even on the faces of the masters. And why not? They were every bit as keen as any of the boys. The Old Firm, usually so truculent and full of spirits, was quite subdued during morning school. The fate of the great day hung like a load upon their shoulders.

"What'd we do if we were beaten?" asked Clive desperately. "Ranleigh'd go clean to the dogs."

"Rot!" came Bert's characteristic answer. "We'd just grind away again, and beat 'em next time, certain. But Ranleigh's going to win. I've put my bat against Masters' tennis shoes, and must have 'em. You'll see. Sturton'll pull us through, and those tennis shoes fit me to a T."

Susanne, the friendly Susanne, actually nodded to Rawlings on this great day, while Trendall failed to scowl at him as had been his custom. As for Rawlings himself, he was in a fever. He wasn't such a cur that he didn't wish to see Ranleigh victorious. But, then, victory meant even greater popularity for Sturton, for Norman, and for Harper and other members of the school, and Rawlings was intensely jealous of anyone's popularity. He would have been king of Ranleigh could he have ordered it. He would have been the highest and the noblest, and then, what a life he would lead some of the fellows! Susanne, for instance—yes, he hadn't forgotten Susanne's behaviour, and how he had worsted him at their first meeting. Norman, too, for he hated Norman now that he no longer could control him, and Clive Darrell. He sneered as he thought of the latter, but the sneer became a frown. Rawlings was not quite sure what his own particular feelings were as regards our hero. In his heart of hearts he rather feared him. And the secret knowledge he had, knowledge unsuspected by Clive and his mother, but vaguely suspected and hinted at by their old gardener, gave him added cause for fear. Still, Clive had nothing to gain by this match against Parkland, and therefore Rawlings betook himself to the playing-field with as cheerful a face as he could assume, arm in arm with Soper, one of his own kidney, a slacker—one, in fact, of Ranleigh's bad bargains.

By two o'clock the field was crammed. Ranleigh boys wandered round and round the touch line, cheering madly now and again when they met a crowd of opponents. For Parkland was near at hand, and had sent every boy and master to watch the historic contest. There was a terrific burst of cheering when at length the Parkland eleven put in an appearance. Big, hefty fellows, they came down to the field in a group, and, arrived at the outskirts, Barlow, their Captain, a fine fellow, even when compared with Sturton, took the practice ball and punted it.

"My word!" groaned Masters, watching it soar. "He's a kicker! If they're all like him what chance do we stand?"

The question was answered within the minute. For having gone back and forth, the ball was finally kicked again toward the entrance to the field, for another group of players had suddenly put in an appearance. It was Sturton and his eleven. The Captain caught the punted ball in mid-air, stepped a couple of paces forward and sent it hurtling toward the sky. A terrific cheer greeted the performance and the arrival of the home team. Not that Ranleigh had stood still and silent when Barlow and the Parkland team came on to the field. They gave them a lusty and noisy greeting, while Parkland fellows, naturally enough, yelled at the top of their voices. Ranleigh fellows were sportsmen ever, and could afford such a welcome. Still, they had their own duties to perform, and they let Sturton and his team know well, and Parkland fellows also, that their undivided favour went in one direction.

And now the touch-line was black with figures. Already Barlow and his men were on the field, while Sturton was just entering the touch-line. Clive felt a little cold thrill run down his spine as he watched their Captain. Sturton, his head a little in the air, a cool smile on his handsome face, led the way direct towards Barlow, and shook that fine fellow's hand eagerly. Then followed Robson, a little shorter than Sturton, but nicely built, with particularly well-made legs and thighs. The back of his head supported his football colours, while issuing from beneath the cap was an abundance of fair hair. Robson also sported on his upper lip a line of similar-coloured fluff, much to Susanne's envy.

There was Norman close behind, Harper, the big Australian, and Purdey arm in arm, laughing heartily at some joke passing between them, Jenkins Primus immediately behind them and the remainder of the eleven. There was Bagshaw, too, dressed in a new suit of knicker-bockers, with a muffler round his neck, a flag in one hand and whistle in his pocket.

"Hooray for Ranleigh!" Masters started the shouting. The boys took it up all round the field with a vengeance, while the players arranged themselves.

"Parkland! Parkland for ever!" the enemy retorted with tremendous cheers, and then broke into the weirdest chant, something particular to Parkland.

"Hear 'em singing, or groaning, which is it?" said Masters, with huge disdain. "We'll make 'em sing, I can tell you fellows! Hullo, Tompkins, where's those colours?"

His grammar was not always too correct, but his meaning was at any rate evident. He pounced on Tompkins, tore his coat open and exposed his tie.

"A beastly red thing!" he shouted, seizing it and pulling at it till half the unfortunate Tompkins' shirt was dragged about his neck. "Here, what's the meaning of this? Treachery, eh?"

He eyed the delinquent fiercely. The wearing of this red tie was not only an insult to Ranleigh on such a day, but it was clear disobedience of orders. Had he not himself, the great Masters, commanded all the small boys of One South to don the School colours?

"Just you hop right off to the school, kid," he commanded severely. "If you ain't back here in double quick time with that tie, why—well, you'll see. Just fancy a Ranleigh fellow sporting a red tie on a day like this! Here, hook it, my beauty."

"But—but," expostulated the unhappy Tompkins—"but, Masters, I say——"

"Don't you say it then," declared that young gentleman fiercely. "Just hook it, quick."

"But it's no good going to the school," said Tompkins, determined to have a hearing. "You see——"

"I don't. Now, look here," began Masters, getting red in the face, for it began to look as if Tompkins would defy him, and already Bert was grinning that nasty satirical grin of his which angered other members of the Old Firm besides Masters. "I'm not going to stand your gas. You——"

"I tell you it's no good," cried his victim stubbornly. "What's the good of going to the school for a thing that isn't there?"

"Not there? Here, you're kidding."

"I'm not. Franklin's got the tie. He's wearing it now. He's got something to say to you."

Tompkins was beginning to regain confidence. Masters was as red as any beetroot. The mention of Franklin brought something unpleasant to his memory. If he could he would have closed this discussion promptly. But his victim meant him to have the whole story.

"You see, Masters," he said, "Franklin says he sold you the tie at the beginning of the term. You were to pay ninepence for it. You never did. Franklin says you gave him a fives ball, and that isn't anything like worth the tie. So he's taken it. He wanted one, you see. He's wearing it now. If you want me to have it you'd better ask him for it."

Masters growled. He recollected the transaction. "Why, that beast Franklin has got the tie and fives ball as well," he shouted.

"And says you owe him ninepence still," grinned Tompkins, while Bert and Clive and Hugh joined in the merriment.

"Owe him ninepence still!" their unfortunate comrade exclaimed, with every sign of righteous indignation.

"Yes, for hire," grinned Tompkins. "And, of course, our bargain's off. Franklin says he means to have his money, too, without waiting. He's bigger than you, Masters. I'd pay it if I were in your shoes."

Whereat the worthy Tompkins took himself off, secretly grinning, while the great Masters nursed his wrath and put up with the gibes and fun of his fellows. Not that he was ragged for long, for the two teams were now in position. Bagshaw brought the new match-ball and placed it in the middle of the circle marked in the very centre of the ground. Then he retired towards the touch-line, inspected his watch, pulled his whistle from his pocket, nodded to each Captain in turn, and then blew a shrill blast upon it.

They were off. Norman, playing centre-forward, kicked the ball across to Sturton, next on his left. The latter dribbled it neatly past a couple of the opponents and sent it on to Harper, on the outside left. The latter, seeing a crowd converging on him, kicked it right across to Bell, on the right of the field. But the enemy's half was down upon him in a moment. The ball hurtled back towards the Ranleigh goal, was headed by Jones Tertius, Ranleigh's half-back, so celebrated for his tactics, was jogged on a little by Harper, and was then taken in hand by Riseau, inside right, a quick and clever player. The watching crowds held their breath as the leather was rushed up toward the Parkland posts. Riseau passed neatly to his left, and well within the Parkland line Harper centred. But there the rush ended. A huge fellow, one of the enemy's backs, pounced upon the ball, lifted it a couple of yards high with a neat movement of his foot, and punted it over the heads of the players.

"Down on it, Parkland. Now's your chance!" bellowed the visitors, while Ranleigh fellows looked on in terror. The rush in the opposite direction was, in fact, swifter even than had been the previous one undertaken by Ranleigh fellows. Barlow shouted to his outside left. The man centred, and at once the Captain of the visiting team sent a shot at the goal which, but for Moon, would have succeeded. But Moon was a treasure. Ranleigh chaps shouted his name till they were hoarse. To this day, and for many a day to come, his prowess in goal will be remembered at the school. For Moon was a huge fellow, an ox in size and weight and muscular development. His arms were of the size of the average fellow's legs, and when he hit out his blows were terrific. See him then waiting for that shot between the posts of Ranleigh's goal. Not flurried, not at all, for Moon was an old hand. Watching eagerly and keenly, balanced on his toes, ready to spring to the rescue. And see what followed. Moon's right fist swung out, clad in its leather glove. Even Sturton could not have kicked the ball harder. Moon's terrific blow sent it soaring away over the heads of the players to the centre of the field, thus saving the goal for Ranleigh. Ah! They know at Ranleigh how to encourage a man, how to show their approval. The groan which went up from the lips of the visitors, their grumbles at their want of fortune, were drowned out of hearing by the shrill yells of Ranleigh boys, by their mad cheers and cries of delight. It was magnificent! Clive felt quite overcome. Masters declared that a testimonial must be given to Moon to mark this noble occasion, and would, in fact, have commenced a collection at once had not Susanne, knowing him somewhat thoroughly, declined to part with even a penny.

But the ball was being dealt with actively again. Ranleigh swept it well out of their own ground and sent it over the touch-line within easy distance of the enemy's goal. A moment later "Hands" was given against the home team, while the rush which followed the free kick carried the ball within the circle directly in front of Ranleigh goal. Then Moon pounced upon the leather, slipped, and fell in the mire. The greasy ball squeezed out of his hands as a pip shoots from an orange, there was frantic kicking for some few seconds, and then, to the bellows of the Parkland boys and groans of the Ranleigh fellows, it was kicked between the posts by Barlow.

Clive looked desperately at his fellows. "One to Parkland," he said. "They're awful hot. Think we'll be able to stop 'em?"

Susanne nodded his head cheerily. He was feeling just as anxious as the rest. But cheerfulness was half the battle with the Frenchman.

"You wait," he said, chewing a pencil. If he had been away from the school and its surroundings he would have had a cigarette between his lips. For the weed, he often asserted, consoled him wonderfully. "You wait till after half. Sturton'll give 'em socks then. Our chaps haven't started."

It was evident enough that Ranleigh had on this occasion been taken by surprise. The sudden rush of the enemy and the unfortunate slip of Moon had resulted in their undoing. But Sturton showed no signs of dismay as he led the men back into their own ground.

"Go steady," he whispered to them. "No rushing after this. Of course, push 'em for all you know, but keep well in hand. I'm going to stake everything on the last half of the game. By then they'll be cooked if they're not as fit as fiddles."

When at length Bagshaw's whistle went for half-time, and slices of lemon were brought out to the players, the score stood at three to one, Ranleigh having secured but a single goal.

"But you'll run up the score when we get going again," declared Bagshaw hopefully, as he chatted with the men during the interval. "I'll swear their chaps aren't as fit as we are. They've been going hammer and tongs all the while, and have only two more goals than we have. You chaps must push them hard. Make the running from the very commencement."

If Bagshaw was hopeful, others of Ranleigh School were not. There was now an air of depression about the fellows. The cheering of late had hardly been so loud or so enthusiastic. Clive wrapped his overcoat a little closer round him, for he felt positively chilly, while even Susanne looked less cheerful. As for Masters, it was a bitter day. He had hoped to be able to look down on Parkland fellows. If he were to be hoarse for a week after, it would have been fine to shout them down, to answer cheer for cheer. And now it looked as if they would do all the cheering. Also, to add to his depression, Franklin found him at half-time and became disgustingly insistent.

"You'll just jolly well pay up that ninepence or get kicked, young Masters," he said. "It's bad enough to have to lose a match like this, for I suppose that that's what's going to happen. I ain't going to lose money as well."

"But—but I swapped a fives ball," pleaded Masters feebly. "That's worth sixpence."

"Most are; yours wasn't. It went to pieces first game; it was a rotter," declared Franklin harshly. "None of your bunkum. That ninepence or a kicking."

It was no wonder that Masters welcomed the renewal of the game; though, to be sure, he was now silent. But in a little while he had almost regained his cheerfulness. For Sturton and his men were making the pace. Instead of playing on the defensive, they were carrying the war into the enemy's country. Within five minutes, in fact, they had scored a goal, whereat Ranleigh applauded vociferously.

"Just watch them closely, you fellows," Barlow cautioned his Parkland eleven, as they went back into their own ground for the kick off. "That was simply a rush. We got our first from them in the same way. Hold together and keep the ball always in their half."

"Well done," commented Sturton. "Don't let 'em rest. We're fit enough to keep at it hard till the whistle goes. So push 'em, boys."

How magnificently Moon used his fists! The shots which the Parkland team made at the home goal might easily have succeeded. But Moon made light of them. He always seemed to be in the right place and at the very right moment, while his ponderous blows sent the ball flying far from the goal. But if he had his work to do, so also had the keeper of the Parkland goal. Within ten minutes of the recommencement of play, Harper sent in a shot which struck one of the posts with a thud and scared the visitors. It brought a howl of delight and encouragement from the Ranleigh fellows.

"Pitch 'em in hard," Clive found himself shouting frantically. "Bravo, Sturton! Well done, Norman! Hooray for Ranleigh!"

But time went on swiftly. In spite of every effort, and in spite also of the almost obvious fact that Parkland men were hard pressed and none too fit, Sturton and his team had not yet equalled the score of the enemy. Ranleigh's score still stood at two, against three by Parkland, and time was terribly short.

"Play up, Ranleigh!" screamed the boys. "Stick to it, Parkland!" shouted the visitors. Sturton looked about him coolly, though there was anxiety in his eyes. He called to his men curtly. "Now, Ranleigh," he said. "Time's almost up. Let's do something."

They backed him up manfully. That brilliant little half who had nursed his forwards assiduously all through the game got the ball when all alone and dribbled it swiftly toward Parkland's goal. Ranleigh forwards were then well in advance, and a well-placed kick sent the leather neatly amongst them. Sturton passed with the rapidity of lightning to Harper, at the same time stepping aside to evade the frantic rush of one of the visitors' backs. Harper rushed the ball still closer to the goal, passed it to his nearest man, had it sent back within the instant and lost it. But that little half was there to support. He jogged the leather upward. A Parkland man got in a punt, sending the ball to a great height. There the wind caught it. Sturton, watching its flight, rushed in to meet its fall. A man charged him. He slid aside, and just in the nick of time headed the leather. A roar of cheering told him that he had been successful.

"A drawn game. Well, that's better than last time, when it was six to two," said Clive. "But it's rotten luck. Our chaps are heaps the better. Play up, you fellows!" he yelled, almost angrily.

And Ranleigh did play up. The eleven had seen Bagshaw consulting his watch with some anxiety and knew that there could now be but a couple of minutes left in which to finish the game. Parkland fellows knew it also, and were as keen to win as Ranleigh. Off went the ball again. Visitors and Ranleighan spectators of the game kept up a continuous roar, which might have been heard right down in the village. Scarves were waved aloft. Fellows tore up and down the field at the back of the spectators. Even masters were stirred out of their usual calm. But it seemed to no purpose. The ball oscillated round about the centre of the field for what seemed ages. Then the visiting team took it triumphantly along with them, and sent a long shot at Ranleigh goal which plumped straight for the centre.

"Done!" groaned Clive, hardly daring to look.

"Good old Moon!" shouted Susanne and Hugh together. "Moon's done for 'em. He's sent the ball back to our fellows."

It was an old trick of the Ranleigh goalkeeper. It may be doubted whether there are many goalkeepers who could put up a similar performance, for, as we have said, the Goliath in Ranleigh goal could strike with his fists harder almost than the average fellow could kick. In any case, he gave the ball a terrific buffet, sending it spinning back to the Ranleigh forwards. It was then that the fellows stood on their toes in their anxiety. Harper had the leather and muffed it. Sturton somehow managed to gain possession. It shot across to the far left a moment later, was rushed forward by the outside left, dribbled across to the inside man, and then sent flying between the Parkland posts. Perhaps ten seconds later, while yells of delight still filled the air, the whistle of the referee was heard blowing.

"Look here, Franklin," said Masters, meeting him some few minutes later. "Blow those colours. I don't care whether I owe you ninepence or nine bob. Come to the tuck for a blow-out. Ranleigh's won, my boy. A chap can't afford to quarrel about mere pennies on such a glorious occasion."

They chaired Sturton from the field. A pack of juniors endeavoured to do the same for Moon, but broke down under the ponderous burden. Even Parkland fellows cheered, for they were sportsmen.

"You played us a fine game and beat us handsomely," said Barlow, taking Sturton's proffered hand with a smile of friendship. "I hope you chaps will give us a return. My word, the improvement is an eye-opener!"

"And due to the new method," said the Head of Ranleigh that evening, when Sturton and the eleven took dinner with him. "This historic match is an answer to all critics. The School has much to thank our Captain for. The improvement in tone and fitness is wonderful."

Well, the day was done, the battle was fought and won, and Ranleigh was weary of triumph and happiness.

"Good night," whispered Susanne to Clive.

"Good night," came the answer. "Er—I say, Susanne."

"Eh?"

"There's one thing."

"Heaps," was the sleepy response.

"Yes, but I'm serious. I'm going to stick to footer till I get into the team. Hear that?"

"Mighty interesting," yawned Susanne. "Wake me up when you've got there, and, by the way, don't forget to speak when you are Captain."

Clive grew red with vexation. For he was serious, very serious indeed. In his own secret mind he registered that night a resolve to grow up as fine a fellow as Sturton, to fight his way into the football eleven, and—the biggest resolve of all—to even ascend to the glories of Captain of Ranleigh.

"I'll do it," he mumbled as he fell asleep.

CHAPTER XVI

A GREAT DISTURBANCE

Time waits for no one, and that statement was as true of Ranleigh boys as of any others. Clive Darrell, in a mere twinkling as it seemed, had become quite an old stager at the school. Since that momentous match when Sturton had led his eleven to victory, thereby stimulating Clive to declare the most ambitious of sentiments, two and a half years had slipped by, two and half years which had seen great changes at Ranleigh.

"But always the Old Firm hangs on and exists," reflected Bert, as he sat on the table in Upper Sixth and stared into the fire. "I remember the term when Harvey left."

"One of the best," interjected Susanne, now no longer a gawky, ill-dressed youth, given to smoking cigarettes on every occasion, but spick-and-span, as immaculate as Rawlings, very English in appearance, and looking quite twenty-one years of age, for the great Susanne sported a moustache, and could, had he wished it, as he often declared, have grown a beard even.

"Better than any of the masters, too," he had said. "Awful bore, don't you know, you fellows. A chap has to shave regularly now every day. That means getting up half an hour earlier——"

"Draw it mild," Hugh had cried. "Half an hour. That's enough for a dozen shaves."

Whereat Susanne had crushed his friend with a withering glance and an air of superiority which made Hugh blush.

"What do you know of shaving?" he had asked satirically, closely inspecting his friend's smooth chin. "Not much. You're a baby."

But the subject under discussion was the change which had come to Ranleigh. Harvey had swayed the destinies of the school. Then Sturton had come upon the scene with his new ideas of exercise for all every day. Clive remembered the success of that innovation. Then Lawton, an Upper Sixth fellow, had followed, and held the post for more than a year. Later Franklin had ascended to the giddy height to which Clive ventured to aim. As to the Old Firm, as Bert had said, it still clung tenaciously together.

"As big friends as ever," reflected Susanne. "That's something. Of course, there have been rows, eh?"

"Some. That one between Masters and Clive was a bad un. Remember it?"

Susanne did. It was back in a past age. It had taken place long ago. But in those days it had appeared excessively severe, and had threatened the break-up of the partnership. And the cause was really so very simple.

"All about a cricket ball," laughed Bert. "Masters had lost one."

"Yes, Masters always does lose something," agreed Susanne. "Of course, he discovered the exact article in Clive's locker."

"Of course! And claimed it."

"Refused all explanations. Almost went to the extreme of accusing Clive of theft. In the end said he must have put the ball there himself in mistake. They fought it out."

That was where the seriousness of the thing came in. And yet, looking back upon the event, there was little doubt that the tussle which had resulted cleared the air wonderfully. For Clive and Masters went at one another with their fists, and having struggled through half a dozen rounds were declared to have made a drawn battle of it. Of course they shook hands. In fact, within ten minutes of the finish of the contest they were chatting in the old amicable manner and demolishing a cake which had arrived at the school for one of them that very morning.

"And the funny thing about it all was that the cricket ball—the one Masters had lost—was discovered tucked away in a corner of his own locker, where, no doubt, he himself had placed it," laughed Susanne. "That's Masters all over. Flares out in an instant. Licks the dust afterwards when he knows he's wrong, and makes the most ample apologies. By the way, Bert, I wish that fellow Rawlings would take himself off. He spoils our happy family here. No one wants him, and precious few trust him. Besides, he's too old to be at the school any longer. He ought to have gone up to the 'Varsity long ago."

It may be said with truth and fairness that Susanne was by no means prejudiced. He didn't like Rawlings, and never had done so. More than that, Rawlings was decidedly unpopular, and had been so from the day when the ranks of the Old Firm had been recruited. Had he been different, more friendly and less underhanded, he would most certainly have been captain of the school. As it was the Sixth voted *en masse* against him, a fact which Rawlings did not fail to perceive. It made him furious. He hated his fellow prefects, detested the masters, and was stupidly and outrageously jealous of them all. And the presence of this unpopular fellow, older than any of the others in Upper Sixth, was a damper to their enjoyment. He was a damper elsewhere. In East he was head prefect, and a martinet. He seemed to air there all the high-handed manners he loved so much, and which were forbidden in his class-room. Why he remained on at the school was a problem which none could solve. But there he was, barred by the Sixth, detested by the juniors in his dormitory, and disliked by not a few of the masters.

Clive, too, had ascended to the Upper Sixth. It may be said, indeed, that his rise had been meteoric. Of a sudden he had taken most seriously to work, had developed an acuteness hitherto unsuspected, and much to the delight of Old B., who coached him, had rushed his way up the school till now he was the youngest fellow in his form. A prefect also, he was senior in his old dormitory, reigning where Sturton had once held sway.

Masters had managed to crawl to the Lower Sixth, and was noted in the school more for games than for lessons. His sturdy, genial figure attracted the admiring eye of many a junior as he tramped the corridor, and when we admit that he was still as much a boy as ever, we do no harm to his reputation. Trendall, now an excellent fellow, was with Susanne and Bert in the Upper Sixth, while Hugh, now Ranleigh's chief exponent of gymnastics, was in the Upper Fifth.

It seemed, in fact, that nothing more could be wanted by the Old Firm and their fellows at Ranleigh to complete their happiness, and that something approaching an earthquake would be needed to upset their equanimity. However, it is the unexpected which always happens, and one night Ranleigh was stirred to the very depths of its foundations.

"Darrell—I say, Darrell," whispered a tremulous voice somewhere near the hour of midnight, while a ghost-like figure bent over him. "Darrell, please, are you awake?"

Clive wasn't. He stirred uneasily at the touch of this junior's hand, for Parfit, the boy who had stolen across from his bed to wake him, was hardly eleven years of age. Naturally timid at the thought of disturbing so august a person as the head prefect of his dormitory, Parfit quaked as Clive rolled over on to his other side and snored. Then, as if forced on by desperation, the lad shook him with a heavy hand.

"Darrell, please," he called. "I—I——"

"Hullo!" Clive sat up, gaping and rubbing his eyes. "Bell gone! Eh? Then what the dickens——! Why, it's Parfit."

"Please, Darrell," said the youth, "I'm awfully sorry for waking you, but——"

"You'll need your sorrow, young un," came the none too friendly interruption, for Clive, like others, objected to be roused in the middle of the night without due reason. Not that he was hard with his juniors. Indeed, he was always jovial with them.

"Well, what is it?" he asked, hearing the boy's teeth chattering, and at once speaking to him kindly. "Been scared, eh? Been dreaming something that's disturbed you? Well, cut along, young un, you'll be all right."

But Parfit had no intention of cutting. "It's not dreaming, Darrell," he said eagerly. "It's fire."

"Fire!"

"Yes, I—I think. I'm next to the door, and I feel sure I can smell smoke. Please, Darrell, I hope you won't be angry, but I felt bound to come and wake you."

Clive was out of his bed like a shot, and getting into his dressing-gown and slippers before Parfit could believe it.

"You get back to bed, young un. I'll go and see. And don't talk of being sorry. If you smelled smoke, or thought you did, why, of course, the thing to do was to wake me. I'd have licked you if it had been a piece of foolery. But, right or wrong, you can expect only thanks for what you've done. So cut, there's a sensible fellow. I'll hop downstairs and see whether there's anything in it."

He slipped down the length of the dormitory while Parfit was thanking him, and swiftly pulled the door open.

"Yes, smoke," he told himself, sniffing. "And thick. I can see it coming up the stairway."

There was a gas jet on the stairs, kept burning all night, and sure enough, by the light it gave, smoke could be seen filtering up the stairs and whirling in thin wisps over the banisters. Clive shut the door behind him, gathered his dressing-gown about his body, and ran downstairs.

"I can hear crackling," he told himself, stopping for a second or more to listen. "That means a fire. George! This is serious!"

It was more, as he discovered when he reached the foot of the stairs. For there the smoke was dense and suffocating. It was swirling from the opposite side of the wide corridor passing between the two staircases leading to the South Dormitories, while beneath the one giving access to Two and Three South the flash of flames could be seen through the dense haze.

"A fire under the stairs. Spreading fast, by the look of it," Clive thought. "It'll reach the gallery above, perhaps, and then the fellows in South Dormitories would be cut off and would have to clear out through the door to West landing. What ought a fellow to do?"

His inclination was to go tearing off up the stairs to his own dormitory, there to awaken the boys, while he rapped hard at the door of the room leading out of One South, occupied by Mr. Branson. And then he thought of the excitement which would result once the alarm was sounded.

"Make sure that it's a bad thing first of all," he said. "I'm going to squint in through that door and see what's happening."

His eyes were shedding streams of tears by now, for the pungent smoke attacked them remorselessly. Then, too, he was choking violently. To cross the wide corridor below and open the door beneath the far stairway, behind which the fire lay without a doubt, meant encountering denser and still more choking fumes. But Clive did not think of the discomfort or of the danger of the act. He thought of the welfare of Ranleigh, of the commotion there would be were he to give an alarm, and of the fact that action on the part of himself and others of the prefects in South Dormitories might put an end to the fire, and that without disturbing others. Wrapping the tail of his dressing-gown round his mouth, therefore, he darted to the bottom of the stairs and raced across the corridor, diving into a swirling cloud of choking vapour through which he could not see. But the reflection of the flames within the door he aimed for caught his eye. He felt for the handle and pushed the door open. Instantly flames blazed out at him, while hot smoke poured into his face, enveloped him completely, and went swirling up to the roof. There was a perfect furnace beneath those stairs. He could hear the woodwork all around crackling. It was clear that the conflagration was of a serious nature and most threatening. Instantly he banged the hot door to, and raced across for his own stairway. And in the short time it took him to ascend he had made up his mind how to act.

"Wake Susanne first. Let him do the same for the other prefects. Then take towels, blankets, and water. If the thing can't be beaten out, we'll wake Mr. Branson, and turn every fellow out of the dormitories. Here goes for Susanne."

But a violent fit of coughing doubled him up at the top of the stairs, and for a while he was helpless. "Please, Darrell," he heard in the midst of the attack, while Parfit's voice came feebly to him, "is—is it smoke? Is there a fire?"

Clive did not deign to answer. He shook off the fit of coughing with an effort and raced into Two South. He knew exactly where Susanne slept, and soon had that worthy along with him. In fact, in less than two minutes every prefect in South was mustered. Taking their bath towels with them and bearing cans of water they dashed down the stairs, while Clive himself reached for the extinguisher kept on every landing.

"We'll give it a trial," he said to Susanne. "If we don't make any sort of effect on the fire we'll sound an alarm, collect all prefects, and man the hoses. In fact, as only three or four of us can work below, I'll get Slater and Gregory to mount the nearest there is. Come on, you fellows."

A word to the two junior prefects, Slater and Gregory, sent them off post-haste to the nearest stand-pipe, near which a hose was coiled, while Clive led the way down the stairs to the site of the fire.

"Tie your towels round your faces," he gasped, for the smoke was even more irritating now, and was denser even. "Now, we've half a dozen cans of water between us. I'll open the door. Let my extinguisher play on the flames for a while, and then finish the business with water."

But though an extinguisher may be an excellent invention, and will extinguish a fire swiftly, its successful action depends entirely on one point. The contents must be delivered on the fire direct, and to that end the one who grips it must approach sufficiently close to the flames. Here, as it happened, that was almost impossible. For when the staircase door was thrown open the improvised brigade was swept back by an appalling gush of flame and smoke. Clive ducked his head, turned his face away, and set the extinguisher going. But the effect was *nil*, for the actual fire was situated round the angle of the door. Clive forced his way nearer till he was within two feet of the entrance, and endeavoured to direct the jet round the corner. And then Susanne dragged him backward.

"THE IMPROVISED BRIGADE WAS SWEPT BACK BY AN APPALLING GUSH OF FLAME AND SMOKE."

"You can't do it," he said peremptorily. "Your clothes are on fire already. Here, you chaps, help to beat them out."

The effort to say as much set him coughing violently. But the words were heard distinctly, and Martin and Fellows, two of the helpers, at once attacked the flames which had taken hold of Clive's dressing-gown. A moment later the whole party was forced into the outer corridor by an even fiercer blast of flame, accompanied by pungent smoke.

They gasped for breath, and then looked desperately at one another.

"We must rouse the school," declared Clive.

"Certain," came from Susanne.

"Then let's do it. I'll take South. Susanne, will you go to North? Martin can take East and Fellows West. Don't shout. Wake the chaps quietly. I'm going to shut that door first, though, and see what Gregory is doing."

There was no time for discussion, for it was clear that they had a serious fire to contend with. And though Ranleigh, like every other well-managed school, where thought is taken for such a happening, was equipped with extinguishers and hoses, while the boys were given fire drill at regular intervals, it looked as if this outbreak might prove too serious for them. Clive looked grave when he thought of what might happen.

"Couldn't expect much help from the village," he told himself. "The whole place would be on fire before they could possibly get here. We've got to fight this thing out ourselves. Ah, there's Gregory. Got it fixed?" he asked, as that youth came panting through the smoke towards him.

"Nearly," came the answer. "We shall want another length of hose. I'm going for the one at the end of the corridor. We'll have it ready in two minutes."

"Then I'll get up to the fellows in South. Look here, Gregory, I'm going to shut that door now. When you've got the hose going, break the place open and play direct on the flames."

He dived through the smoke, his towel pulled up to his eyes, and, led by the red glare of the flames, was soon near the door. But the heat was now overpowering. Though Clive tried twice, he could not get near that handle, while at the end of the second attempt his gown was again in flames and he had to beat hard with his hands to extinguish them. Meanwhile, the peace and tranquillity of Ranleigh's night was swiftly being disturbed. A hum was coming from the dormitories. Clive found One South in a condition of animation.

"Turn out, you fellows," he said, as if this was the most natural thing to expect them to do, and as if it were the usual time for rising. "Stay here till I give you permission to move. I'm going into the other South Dormitories. I shall want Peart and Godfrey and Offord when I get back. You other fellows had better make a bundle of your things. There's a fire below. I'll kick the first fellow who makes a shindy."

One by one he awoke the dormitories, commanding the boys in Two and Three South to gather their belongings at once and pass out through Four South. By the time he reached his own dormitory again every boy was ready, while those he had called for were standing in the gloom by the door.

"You others skip," said Clive, still in his ordinary tones. "Peart, go along to the Head's house and ring till he answers. Tell him what's happening. Godfrey, you get off to the Matron, and knock at her door. Tell her not to be alarmed, but merely to make ready and warn the maids. Offord, your job is to rouse the butler and the beakies, and tell old Sant to cut the gas off at the meter. There, off you bundle."

He seemed to have been giving directions for an age, whereas from the commencement, when Parfit had wakened him, till this moment, but very few minutes had elapsed. But those few minutes had made all the difference to the conflagration. When Clive dashed out of the dormitory, having wakened Mr. Branson, and descended the stairs, the opposite staircase was blazing, the flames sweeping right up to the roof of the corridor. The crackle of flames could now be distinctly heard, mingled with a curious sizzling. In the far background, through the doors leading to the quad, as a rule kept firmly fastened, he imagined he could make out a group. Then thick volumes of smoke hid everything. He felt someone step down beside him, and then heard Mr. Branson speak.

"It's serious," he said. "You've called the Head?"

"Everyone, sir," said Clive. "Gregory's out there, I think, with one of the hoses. Fancy we could do something from here. I'll see."

Unceremonious at such a time, he bolted up the stairs again and so to the West landing. Five minutes later he and Susanne held the nozzle of a second hose, and from the point of vantage which the stairs gave them poured a torrent of water into the blazing mass on the opposite side of the corridor.

Meanwhile, it may be imagined that Ranleigh was in a condition of disturbance, though thanks to the example which Clive had set in the first place, and which Susanne and the others had so naturally copied, there was no panic, nor even shouting. Perhaps five minutes after the first alarm, when it had become obvious that the whole school must be roused, every Ranleigh boy was assembled in the quadrangle, where, pressing as close as possible, they watched Gregory and his friends directing water upon the flames. They would have hampered the workers even had not Masters and Trendall promptly taken a grip of the situation.

"Look here, you fellows," cried the former, "you'll all get back to this line here. That'll give the brigade every chance to do their work. Trendall, send along anyone who breaks the rule. I'll deal with 'em."

There was something sinister in the speech, and hearing his voice Ranleigh obeyed on the instant. For Masters was accustomed to speak in jovial tones. With him an order came always as a request, such as, "Oh, I say, Parker, just cut along like a good chap and bring down my cricket togs," or, "You fellows here in Middle, there's a beastly noise. Go on with your prep., do."

And his requests were obeyed with promptness as a general rule. If not, on rare occasions, Masters could become very insistent. But he was seldom threatening, and hearing the threat in his voice now small boys slunk back to the quad steps and, with bulging eyes, watched the fire over the heads of their seniors. Fellows in the Upper School shuffled backwards, eyeing Masters askance, while even those in Upper Fifth, fellows soon to be prefects and perhaps a trifle jealous of the Sixth and of those in authority, quelled their inclination to push to the front.

At this moment the familiar figure of the Head arrived on the scene.

"Who's directing matters?" he asked of Mr. Branson, who stood beside the group of boys plying their hose from the entrance to the quad.

"Well, I am partly, and Darrell is mostly," came the answer. "Of course, I haven't had time yet to learn how the thing was discovered. But when I was awakened Darrell had made all arrangements. He and those with him, Feofé and others, have behaved splendidly. There hasn't been a sign of panic. Boys in South have cleared out with all their belongings."

"Good. Where is he? What other directions has he given?" asked the Head.

A gust of wind at that moment went swirling through the centre corridor past the fire, sucking long tongues of flame along with it and carrying them toward the chapel. But it also had the effect of sweeping the smoke away, enabling those in the quad to see their comrades grouped on the staircase opposite the one beneath which the fire raged. There they were, sheltering behind the blistering woodwork which formed the closed banisters, the heads of three of them, wrapped in towels saturated with water, just appearing above the rail. A nozzle between two of the heads gripped by a pair of hands sent a jet of water sizzling across the corridor into the centre of the fire. The Head thought he could recognise in one of those towelled faces the features of Clive Darrell.

"Can I get through?" he asked, stepping toward the entrance of the corridor.

"Too hot, sir," Mr. Branson told him. "You must go round by West. I'll stay here and direct matters. I think we are getting the better of the flames."

At once the Head of Ranleigh turned and hurried away, the boys collected in the quad making way for him. And we must state it now with no small degree of pride that he set as fine an example as had any of the prefects.

"Might easily have been a panic, with all the boys rushing here and there shouting and shrieking," he told himself. "Everything is wonderfully orderly. I must back these boys up. Coolness is what is wanted. But I must also learn what steps Darrell and his helpers have taken in other directions. That's essential. One has to consider what to do supposing the flames beat us."

It was therefore, in spite of his hurry, with measured tread and an appearance of unconcern that Ranleigh's Head stalked through the assembled boys and reached West landing. A minute later he was amongst the prefects on the South staircase, watching that descending jet of water pouring into the flames.

"Which is Darrell?" he asked coolly, and at the sound of his voice one of the group turned. Clive, for he it was, tore the towel from his face at once and smiled at the master.

"Getting it down, sir," he said.

"Ah! You could leave for a moment? The smoke here makes one cough."

Clive handed the nozzle to his friends and went up the stairs two at a time. At the top the two stopped to discuss matters.

"Now, tell me how the thing was discovered and what steps you have taken to warn people," asked the Head.

"Parfit smelled smoke," said Clive hurriedly, anxious to get back to his task. "I came down and found the fire. Then I turned Susanne—er—Feofé, you know, sir."

"Yes, I know as well as anyone," smiled the Head.

"I turned him and all the South prefects out. We tried to stop the fire with an extinguisher and cans of water. But the thing had got too firm a hold. It was really serious. Then we decided to call up the school and man the hoses. Gregory and Martin did the last. I sent prefects round to the various dormitories. Fellows from One South were told to call you, the Matron and the butler and his men. Er—that's all, I think."

"All? Then you haven't——?"

"Oh, I forgot," said Clive hurriedly. "Of course, I told 'em to turn off the gas, so as to save an explosion, and I sent for the butler. One of the men got on to his bicycle at once and went off to call the village brigade. But we'll be able to do without them, sir. Can I return now, sir?"

He was eager to get back, and the Head dismissed him with a hearty shake of the hand.

"You've done splendidly, Darrell," he said. "There really was no need to call me. I shan't interfere. I shall watch, and if you get the fire down, it will be all of your own doing. I'm proud to have such prefects."

Well might he be proud too. The seeds which Harvey and Sturton had sown two and more years ago were now bearing fruit with a vengeance. Perhaps at no previous period had Ranleigh been blessed with such a set of prefects, and here was proof of it. The orderliness of the school under trying circumstances was extraordinary. The coolness of those who had taken the fire in hand, and their measures to warn all and sundry, were really remarkable. No wonder the Head was filled with a glow of pride. No wonder Ranleigh boys went mad with delight as they saw the flames extinguished. And then how they cheered the fellows who had been conducting the fight!

The early morning found the Hall filled to overflowing. Masters were there in full strength. Ranleigh was present without exception, some of the smaller boys yawning widely. Even the village fire brigade had been invited to partake of refreshments. And then they slowly filed off to their beds, a whole holiday with late breakfast having been proclaimed from the dais. But that holiday was one only in name for Clive and Susanne and a few others. They collected in the Upper Sixth when the school was almost empty, and Susanne shut the door and turned the key.

"Now, Clive," he said, "you tell the fellows."

At once eager glances were cast at our hero. Masters sat up abruptly. Bert stood looking almost fiercely at his old friend, while Trendall was obviously puzzled. Clive went to the fireplace, leaned against it, and slowly glanced at each of his comrades in succession.

"It's a beastly thing to have to say," he began, somewhat awkwardly. "But I'm bound to tell you. That fire was started on purpose. Someone wanted to burn the school down. I'm positive."

"What! Positive! Surely there's a mistake," gasped Bert.

"None. Susanne will tell you. I'm going to show the proofs to everyone present, but only on a pledge of secrecy. You give it?"

They nodded at him one by one.

"You can trust us to a man," said Masters.

"Then come. Ourselves and the village sergeant are the only people aware of the business."

"And, of course, the beggar who carried out the job," said Susanne bitterly.

Never before perhaps had a group of the school seniors looked so serious. Jones Quartus, happening to meet them as they issued from the Sixth and passed along the corridor, positively shrank away from them. The group of curious youngsters gathered near the site of the fire shuffled backwards.

"Here, cut!" commanded Masters abruptly, and at the word they bolted, as if only too eager to escape from the presence of their seniors. Then Clive led the way. When he and his friends returned to the Sixth some five minutes later, accompanied by the police sergeant, not the smallest doubt existed in their minds that some miscreant had successfully attempted arson, and that the fire had been started for some sinister reason.

"We've got to get to the bottom of the mystery," said Clive.

"Yes," agreed Susanne. "But how? That's the difficulty."

It was, in fact, an absolute necessity, for the two weeks which followed saw no fewer than three other outbreaks of fire on the school premises, all, however, happily extinguished after causing little damage. It was no wonder, then, that the prefects of Ranleigh set themselves seriously to work to discover the incendiary.

CHAPTER XVII

WHO IS THE SCOUNDREL?

It was a saint's day, and Ranleigh made holiday once Chapel was ended. Outside in the playing-fields the shouts and laughter of the boys could be heard distinctly from the Sixth Form room. Occasionally there was a clatter in the tiled corridors over which the feet of so many Ranleighans had passed in the years gone by. Otherwise there was peace and quietness in the school and the time was propitious for discussion. And in the Upper Sixth Form room voices subdued and smooth exchanged the views of various of the prefects. Trendall was there, watching Clive and Susanne with a friendly smile of approval. How different from the glances which he had once cast at them! Bert, cool and dreaming as of yore, apt to indulge on every opportunity in satire, sat upon the corner of the table staring thoughtfully into the fire. Masters stood propped in one corner, nibbling the end of a pencil and glancing first at one of his friends and then at another. By common consent Clive had been voted to the chair.

"We've got to do something, and at once," he said, commencing the proceedings as soon as he had occupied the only chair in the room. "It is up to us to act."

"Hear, hear!" from Masters. He stopped nibbling for a moment. "Hear, hear!" he repeated, and then went rather pink seeing the eyes of all on him.

"And at once," asserted Clive again.

"Without delay, certainly," agreed Bert crisply.

"That is, once we've come to a decision what shall be done. No use acting without a plan," said the wise Susanne, an opinion which Trendall applauded.

"Then, it being agreed that something must be done, and at once, we come to the crux of the situation."

Clive looked at each in turn invitingly. "We want ideas," he went on. "We've reached a crisis here. Has any fellow any plan to put before us?"

There was silence. Masters took to nibbling his pencil violently. It was obvious that he was very much disturbed in his mind. Susanne kicked the worn floor boards impatiently, while Trendall and Bert seemed to have all their attention centred on the fire. But no one accepted Clive's invitation to speak. To tell the truth, no one had so much as an idea. The situation with which Ranleigh was face to face was unique.

"I'll recapitulate events," said Clive, for he was wont in these days to use some terribly long words. The slang so common to his speech in bygone days was now almost forgotten. Indeed, the manners and the ideas of the Old Firm had changed wonderfully and very much for the better.

"There was a fire two weeks ago."

"Hear, hear!" cried Masters, whereat everyone glared at him.

"Glad?" asked Bert, with cutting sharpness. "Perhaps you'd have liked to see us all consumed!"

It was Masters' turn to become scathing.

"A fine thing to suggest," he cried. "You'll say I made the fire," he retorted. "Go on, Clive. Bert's out of sorts this morning. There was a fire. Right. Hear, hear! Let's get along with it. I've a right to say hear, hear! Didn't the fire give us a chance of seeing what Clive's made of, and the sort of chaps we have at Ranleigh?"

He wore an air of triumph. The others present at this meeting applauded loudly.

"It was fine," said Trendall, his eyes sparkling. "The Ranleighan'll have a fine tale to tell. Though I'm one of the prefects I'm bound to admit Ranleigh did well. The Head said so; so did the 'Surrey Liar.'"

It was the name given to a certain county paper which had come out with a fine description of the fire at Ranleigh, and had eulogised the behaviour of the boys. However, this was not getting along with the discussion, and Clive therefore took the matter up again.

"There was a fire; we checked it. It was put out," he said. "Of course, there was an investigation, as a result of which we discovered that paraffin had been thrown about in the big cupboard under the stairs. There were some unconsumed shavings there, as well as a tin which had once held paraffin. That tin came from the boot-room where the beakies work."

"Proving that one of the beakies was responsible for the business," cried Trendall.

"Not at all. The boot-room's open always. You or I could easily enter. Still, it doesn't say that a beaky did not start the fire. This is clear, however, that fire was maliciously set going by someone, and that someone belongs to Ranleigh."

"Either as boy or servant," said Susanne. "Of course, we rule masters out. Such a thing is impossible with any one of them."

"And boys too," suggested Bert. "Whoever heard of a fellow wanting to make a blaze of his school? It's preposterous! So we come to the conclusion that the miscreant is a worker here. In fact, one of the many servants."

There were enquiring glances between the debaters. In the end all turned to stare at their chairman. But Clive's young face was inscrutable. He neither supported nor opposed the statement for which Bert was responsible.

"What's the use of trying to narrow our suspicions down to a single group?" he asked. "On the face of it, I admit that a servant may very well have been responsible for that fire. But then, it might have been anyone. There was a fire. That's good enough for us, and we know that it was purposely set going. We know also that there have been others, and that in every case there is clear evidence that an incendiary was at work. Well, there's the position. You chaps have got to tackle it."

There was, in fact, no need to add to his description. Somewhere about Ranleigh there existed an incendiary. Who was he? Boy, master, or servant?

"Or lunatic," suddenly asked Susanne, as if he imagined that others were following his train of thought. "That's it. Is the fellow who's doing this caddish business merely a lunatic, and so irresponsible?"

"Mighty likely," agreed Masters, coming closer and looking very earnest. "But what if he is? Where's the difference? There's an incendiary all the same, and wondering whether he's boy, master, or servant, and in any case sane or mad, helps us not an atom. Let's stop jawing about things that don't help and get to real business. I'm for watching."

"Watching what?" asked Bert sharply.

"The school, of course. Parading the corridors."

"When? At night?" asked Trendall at once.

"When have the fires broken out? Always at night time. Always between the hours of eleven and one a.m. Then that's the time for watching."

"And you suggest that the prefects do this watching?" asked Clive. "The scheme is one that promises finely. As you say, every fire has occurred in the hours you mention. If the place had been patrolled, then the fellow responsible would have been discovered. So you suggest that the prefects take it turn and turn about to watch? Isn't that it, Masters?"

"Not a bit. I'll ask a question. Has any fellow here any doubt about the others in this room? No? I can see you haven't. You needn't stare at me as if I'd accused you, Bert. I merely asked a straight question. Well then."

"Yes, well then," repeated Susanne encouragingly.

"Can any fellow here say that he's absolutely sure that the culprit isn't to be found somewhere amongst the prefects?"

They shook their heads slowly at him.

"Masters is talking sense," asserted Bert, after a few seconds' silence; whereat the great Masters flushed a beautiful red. It wasn't often that Bert praised. And if he did, there was often enough a sharp sting underneath his compliment. "He's talking sense," repeated Bert, "for once in his life. I'm glad."

"Ah!" gasped Masters. He would gladly have set upon Bert at that instant. But then, everyone knew that Bert was always quizzing. He was grinning even then. Why on earth couldn't he be serious sometimes and forget his quizzing and his satire?

"A fellow can't get along when he's interrupted by an idiot," growled Masters. "Where was I? Oh, I remember. Well, you can't swear that this lunatic isn't to be found amongst the prefects. All the same, I'm open to stand treat to everyone here if a Ranleigh prefect proves to be the fellow. Ranleigh prefects ain't that sort."

He puffed his chest out and flushed red as he spoke. Masters took a tremendous pride in his school and his fellows. "There's not one who'd be such a cad," he declared. "Don't you deny it, Bert."

"Certainly not. I'm in agreement. I'm only smiling at my thoughts. I was just remembering the time when Masters wasn't a prefect. A bigger set of cads and bullys then didn't exist, er—according to Masters. Of course, I agree with what he says now. Ranleigh prefects are fine fellows. Ain't we amongst the numbers?"

There was a general tapping of feet on the floor. The men present were getting impatient, and really it wasn't the time for wit. They glared at Bert.

"Shut up!" commanded Susanne. "Let Masters get along. Well?"

"Well, there you are," said that worthy. "You ain't certain of all the prefects. But you are of the lot here. Supposing we decide to watch. Here are the watchers. We keep the thing to ourselves. Not a word to the others."

"And watch all night. A tough proposition," reflected Trendall. "There are five of us."

"Call it six," said Bert. "There's Hugh. He's not much good; but he'll do."

"Then six," Clive told them. "Two every night. That means one night's patrolling in three. A fellow could manage that easily, and we can always put in a sleep during the day. Then I suggest that we divide ourselves into three parties, each consisting of two. Those two will each take half the school premises, and will meet on their rounds every few minutes. It'll help to keep 'em awake."

"Awake! As if a fellow would care to sleep and so fail in his job," cried Masters indignantly.

"You wait," said Bert. "A chap gets awfully drowsy about midnight, particularly if there's nothing doing. The suggestion Clive has made is good. Get along, Mr. Chairman."

"Then we divide into twos and patrol, each man meeting his fellow every few minutes. Of course, we shall want rubber shoes and a dark lantern apiece."

"And a revolver?" asked Trendall eagerly.

"No. Nothing. If a Ranleigh chap can't use his fists if there's occasion, why——"

"Better chuck the business now," said Susanne. "Clive's right. No weapon is wanted. Once we catch sight of this chap we shall know how to deal with him. So mum's the word. Not a whisper to the other fellows."

"Tell no one, not even the Head," cried Bert. "Secrecy is of the greatest importance. I suppose we start to-night?"

"At once," agreed Clive. "Let's put the six names on strips of paper and draw them from a cap. That'll give us our couples. We can toss to decide who's to take the first patrol."

They carried out this suggestion promptly, and within a little while had the matter settled.

"Susanne and Hugh together," said Clive, reading out the result. "Then Trendall and Bert. Masters and I go together also. Now for first turn. Up with your pennies."

It happened that Bert and Trendall were to be the first to patrol, and it may be imagined that there was a considerable amount of suppressed excitement about those two worthies, as also amongst their companions in the adventure, as the evening approached. But the Old Firm had had an excellent training in smothering their feelings. To look at them that evening as they took prep. in their several form rooms you would have thought that they had no such thing as a secret. In Chapel Bert's face was serene as he went to the lectern to read the lesson. And how well he read! Sitting back in his place amidst the men of the choir, Clive could not help but admire. His memory carried him back to that day now it seemed so long ago when he himself, then small and puny, had for the first time entered this handsome building. He recollected how he had watched Harvey ascend to the lectern, with what awe he had regarded him, and how he had trembled at the thought that some day he might be called upon to carry out the same duty. And here he was, destined to read the second lesson of the evening, cool and calm, nevertheless, admiring, as admire he must, the smooth, even reading of his old friend Bert.

Then they trooped out to the dormitories. There was the customary ten minutes' silence, and then the hum of many tongues wagging. But gradually the sounds died down, till there came the heavy-footed thud of the beaky. Out went the lights. From many a bed came the snores of sleepers. Clive lay with wide-open eyes listening and thinking. He wondered what Trendall and Bert were doing, for it must be remembered that the rise of the Old Firm in the school had resulted in a partial severance. As prefects they were divided, Clive ruling it in One South, his old dormitory.

Ah! he heard someone stirring! A door opened. It was not in One South. Where was it?

"Old B. coming to bed," Clive told himself. "Then it's about eleven. Those two will be slipping downstairs in a few minutes."

Yes, it was nearly eleven. The big clock began to chime the quarters as the door of One South was noiselessly pushed open. Clive lifted his head and looked in that direction. The well-known and popular figure of Mr. Branson entered the dormitory. On tip-toe, for he was ever thoughtful, bearing a lighted candle in one hand, he gently closed the door and slid across to his own room opposite. And in the years that he had been at Ranleigh, how many boys had seen him going to bed? Not many, we trow. Not because of the late hour, for Old B. did not hold with them. But simply for the reason that boys sleep well, while Old B.'s steps were of the lightest, in spite of his burly figure. The door closed after him, the last stroke of eleven sounded. Silence fell upon Ranleigh school and its surroundings. And then Clive's eyelids drooped. Like the other fellows in the dormitory, he fell asleep and forgot for the moment all about the task which he and his friends had set themselves.

"Well? What happened? See anyone? Hear anything?"

The questions were rained upon Trendall and Bert as soon as the Old Firm were gathered on the following morning.

"Not a soul. But Clive was right about a fellow getting drowsy," said Trendall at once. "If it hadn't been for the movement and the need to meet Bert I'd have dropped off on many an occasion. I met him five minutes after the hour of eleven had struck. We went off to bed at two o'clock precisely."

"Then Bert? Well?" asked Clive of that young fellow. Bert grinned. Evidently he had contrived to gather some fun out of the adventure.

"Jolly nearly made an awful ass of myself," he grinned.

"Where's the difficulty?" asked Masters, with unaccustomed satire. "Ain't it pretty usual?"

"Shut up!" cried Clive. "You chaps are always sparring. Now, Bert."

"Masters would have landed us finely in the soup if he'd been there," continued the one addressed. "You see—well, is it necessary to explain why he'd have done the usual? No. Well, then, I started with Trendall, and just ten minutes after twelve heard someone moving."

"Ah! Go on," gasped his listeners.

"Someone moving! Who?" asked Hugh eagerly.

"I'm coming to it," said Bert coolly. "It was somewhere close to the spot where the fire first took place. I crept in that direction."

Clive felt a queer little sensation about his spine. Bert's narratives were always a little uncanny. He could imagine him creeping like a snake towards the point where he had heard someone moving. "Do get on!" he cried impatiently. "You do take such a time to tell what happened."

"And you're always in such a violent hurry. Well, I crept there. I was in the quad, of course, and as all the corridor windows are open I could easily look in. There was a step in the corridor. Some fellow was creeping along. But he wasn't silent altogether. Now and again his boots made quite a noise. I slid along parallel with him."

The faces of the listeners grew eager. They pressed a trifle closer to Bert, wondering what was coming.

"At the corner of the quad, where the corridor turns, the fellow came to a sudden stop," said Bert. "Things looked fishy. I could hear him rummaging in the boot lockers standing there. I wondered whether I ought to open my lamp and take a squint at him. You see, I wasn't at all sure who it might be."

"Of course," agreed Susanne. "You wanted to get some idea. You didn't want this beggar to know that you were there till you were fairly sure what he was up to. You see, we're watching for an incendiary. We ain't out for any other purpose."

"I'd have collared the chap at once," declared Masters, who was nothing if not impetuous.

"Ah, yes, *you* would," Bert told him, smiling pityingly on him. "That's just my point. Here was a splendid chance for a fellow to make an utter hash of the business and an ass of himself into the bargain. Masters would have collared the beggar. I didn't. That's the difference. You see, it wasn't an incendiary."

"Then who was it? Tell us," demanded Clive.

"Only Raleigh, stinks master," grinned Bert, whereat there was a roar of laughter. Masters even grinned, though he felt really angry with Bert. Then, suddenly remembering the episode of the burglars, he smiled sweetly at him. It would do for next time, he thought. When compliments were flying around again, and there was need for gentle repartee or a stinging retort, he had it ready. Asses indeed! Bert needn't talk after such a business.

"You see," went on Bert, "he'd been out to supper with some people, I suppose. Ain't he rather gone on that Miss Daisy?"

There were nods from the circle. It was a well-known fact that the science master was paying his addresses at a house in the village. Miss Daisy often took part in Ranleigh concerts, and was decidedly popular. So that, if it were any relief to Mr. Raleigh, he had the good wishes of all at the school.

"They're engaged," Trendall told the company. "They'll be married in the summer."

"Then good luck to 'em!" cried Bert. "Well, there he was, and all the fumbling was for a candle. He found it after a while, just when I thought he must have laid his train and splashed the petroleum about in preparation for a fire. In fact, I was within an ace of flashing my lamp on him when there was the scrape of a match. It made me feel quite funny, I can tell you. I thought he must be about to start the fire. And then, when the flame burned up I saw Raleigh's features plainly. He lit his candle, stamped on the match, and went up the stairs to his room whistling quietly. There, you've got my report. I was getting a bit sick of watching when the time came along to give up. Masters, just you take warning by what happened. It's lucky we're not going to take revolvers. You'd have shot poor Raleigh at once, and then Miss Daisy'd have been a widow before she was married."

Bert was perfectly right in repeating the warning, and perhaps it was stupid of Masters to listen to it so unkindly. But then, had he been impetuous, Mr. Raleigh would have become aware of the watching, and, no doubt, every one of the masters as a consequence. However, no mischief had been done, and the secrecy so important to the success of the business was still maintained. That second night Susanne and Hugh took their posts in the corridor, prepared to watch the security of Ranleigh. Nor had they much to report when again the Old Firm was assembled to hear them.

"But it's a bit of a joke, all the same," laughed Susanne. "Wonder what the masters would say if they knew how we were watching? One generally supposes them to be abed at a respectable hour. But they ain't always. It was Raleigh's turn last time. Hugh and I saw two of them creep in between twelve and one while we were watching. Who knows? Perhaps Clive and Masters'll have the pleasure of welcoming the return of the Head from a supper party."

That made them grin. Bert jogged Masters' elbow. "What a lark it'd be!" he said. "Of course, you'd collar him. My word! The scene would be worth watching."

Perhaps it was as well that the members of the Old Firm saw every atom of fun that was going, for the task they had set themselves was destined to prove monotonous. After all, once the novelty of patrolling a huge place wears off, it has few attractions. Then, too, a cosy bed pulls hard after a long day's exercise. A whole fortnight passed, in fact, without anything unusual happening.

"Someone's twigged what we're doing, eh?" asked Susanne.

"No," said Clive. "I'm certain. But whoever set those fires going is too canny to be caught easily. They say that lunatics are awfully artful. This chap's stopped for a while. We've just got to be patient."

And so for a few more days they continued watching, shadowing many a late-returning master. It was almost three weeks from the date of the commencement of this duty that Clive heard sounds that roused his strong suspicions. Someone was moving in the corridor, someone who had not entered the school through the front door as had been the case with masters. A figure glided past him as silently as a ghost. This was something entirely different from what he had experienced in the whole course of his watching.

CHAPTER XVIII

TRACKED DOWN

Clive stood as still as a post, watching and listening. Overhead there was a small crescent of the moon floating over the school and partially illuminating the quad. But the corridors were plunged in stygian darkness. Had he actually heard anything? Had someone really passed him?

"Well, I'm jiggered," he observed to himself, clinging doubtfully to one of the cross-bars placed across the usually open windows of the corridor by a thoughtful directorate, and with a view to keeping small boys from clambering through them. For it was the custom at Ranleigh to indulge in an ample measure of fresh air, and those corridor windows remained free of glass until the depths of winter.

"Feel certain someone went by," thought Clive. "Felt rather than heard him. But—but where's he gone? Is he just opposite me. Ah!"

No wonder he was puzzled, for as we have intimated, whoever had gone down the corridor had made not the smallest sound. Recollect that it was a little past midnight, that the school was plunged in slumber, and that, to the best of Clive's belief, he and Masters were the only two about the premises. Remember that the circumstances provided an intense stillness, and that at such times sounds usually inaudible come to the ear with certainty. He had heard something, he was sure.

"As if a fellow had a dressing-gown on and the gown were trailing on the ground," he told himself. "The merest whisper. It may have been a man's deep breathing. But there's not a sound now. Not a single sound."

But there was something else. There came the flicker of a light away to his right, a mere flicker, and then the same all-pervading darkness. Clive slid off in that direction at once, halted when he judged he had reached the correct position, and strained his ears and eyes to detect the author of that sudden glimmer. And what a job he had to be sure to drown the sound of his own breathing and his own thudding heart beats! That was the worst of such intense stillness, and of excitement, for he was excited.

"The chap took me by surprise," he muttered beneath his breath, as if by way of excuse. He struggled against the feeling of excitement, but failed hopelessly. His heart still thudded against his ribs, beating with unusual rapidity. And then, worse than all, a sudden tickling sensation at the back of his throat assailed him. He was going to cough. He was——

No. He beat the feeling down, and of a sudden once more had all his attention engaged elsewhere. For from a spot some ten feet to his right, from the centre of the inky darkness of the corridor, a jet of light swept across to the far wall. He could see the actual point from which it arose. There the beam glowed brightly, perhaps an inch and a half in depth. It spread itself gradually through the darkness, till it obtained much greater dimensions and finally settled on the brick and stone inner wall of the corridor in a wide ellipse of light. Silently it stole along the brickwork till it fell upon a door.

"The Head's entrance to his house. This is queer," Clive thought, while his excitement rose. Let us be brutally frank about this young fellow. He was no coward. He was noted for dash and courage at Ranleigh School. But, like every other fellow there, he was susceptible to outside influences. And here was one decidedly uncanny and out of the ordinary, one which affected him most strangely. Clive felt positive pain in his scalp. His hair bristled beneath the school cap which he had donned for this adventure. He felt almost scared. Raising his hand he thrust the fingers beneath his cap, and instantly the beam of light vanished. It was there one instant. It was gone the next. There was merely dense blackness, and silence.

"Phew!" Perspiration trickled over his brows. His palms were moist and clammy. He began to wish that Masters would turn up, only that would be awkward.

"Give the whole show away," he told himself. "This is beastly ghostly and uncanny, but I ain't going to be funked. There's something mighty suspicious here, and that beam comes from an electric hand light. Then there is someone operating it. Ghosts don't have such things. Don't need 'em."

The very thought tickled him vastly. It was queer at such a moment to be struck by the utter absurdity of the suggestion that a ghost should require a lamp, and should be so up-to-date as to have adopted an electric one. Still, the deathly silence gave a most undoubted ghostly appearance to the whole transaction, and we must excuse Clive if he was impressed by it.

"He ain't moved. Shall I show him up with my lamp?" he asked himself. "No, I'll wait. Ten to one this is the beggar we're after. But he's done nothing yet. I'm out to catch an incendiary, and if this is he, why, I sit tight till he's got to the business."

Ah! The beam flashed again, alighting on the tiled floor of the corridor, and stealing along it to the foot of the Head's door. It slowly climbed it till it reached the keyhole, concentrated itself upon that orifice, and then gradually grew smaller and more brilliant, while the point from which it originated approached the door ever so slowly, the beam shortening in proportion. Click! There was the faintest of sounds in the distance. The beam disappeared, strangled by the hand which operated the lamp.

"Masters making his round and coming along to meet me. He'll alarm this beggar," thought Clive. "Better get off and warn him. I'll get him to watch the far end of the corridor."

He went off like a ghost himself across the quad, entered the corridor by the open doorway below the entrance to East Dormitory, and halted outside the Bursar's office. Yes, there was the gentle slither of an almost noiseless footfall. Clive whistled gently.

"That you, Masters?" he asked in a hoarse whisper.

"Yes. What's up? You've seen something?"

"Just now. The fellow's got an electric lamp, and he's along there in the corridor. I'm not sure that he's our man, and I came back here to warn you not to make a sound. Look here, watch along there by the steps leading to the washing rooms. I've just thought this beggar may be an outsider who breaks in, or makes his way into the school by the back doors. You'd catch him at the turn of the corridor, and in any case you'd be within hearing and I could call you. That right?"

"I'm off. Yell if you want me," answered Masters. "Look out in case the fellow's armed. George! I never thought of that possibility of a man getting into the school from outside and doing this firing business. Hope it'll turn out so. Ranleigh don't want such scum about the school."

He went off without another word, while Clive slid into the quad again and stole along by the corridor windows. In a little while, having used the greatest caution, he had reached the spot he had stood in before, and straightway leaned against one of the barred windows and stared in. There was not a sound. No beam of light helped him to discover the whereabouts of the ghostly stranger parading the corridor.

"Gone! Slipped off on hearing that sound," Clive told himself. "Bad luck to it! He's beaten us again."

He fingered his own electric lamp, with which Masters was also provided.

"Shall I, or shall I not?" he wondered, his finger on the sliding trigger. "Supposing he's over there, still waiting and listening? Supposing he's slid off and is at work elsewhere?"

It was a dilemma. There are very many placed in the same position of responsibility and under the self-same circumstances who would have hesitated, and rightly so, who would have determined to do nothing that savoured of rashness, and who would have decided to curb their impatience, risking everything lest by premature action they should wreck the whole enterprise. Still Clive swung badly between the two decisions. He brought his electric lamp out of his pocket, presented it across the corridor, and then tucked it back in his pocket again, just as he had done a few moments before. It gave him a start, a minute later, when he again had his lamp in position, though the trigger was not yet moved, suddenly to perceive a ray of light opposite.

"Why, he's opened the Head's door," he told himself. "That light's shining from the inside. The beggar's managed to get into the house. What's his business?"

It was something dishonest and underhand, in any case, else why such silence? why this flitting in the depths of night, when the school and its residents were sunk in slumber?

"Frightfully fishy," Clive told himself. "Either a burglar or the incendiary we're after. I'm going across to that door to take a look in. No, I'm not."

He bobbed down like lightning, his head below the window frame through which he had been staring. For the light within the half-open door increased. It swung across to the opposite side of the corridor, and then, through the surrounding darkness, Clive saw the bull's-eye orifice through which the beam was projected. Nothing more was visible. The hand which operated the lamp, the man behind might not have been in existence. He was invisible. It looked, indeed, as if the torch were supporting itself, and swaying from side to side by its own efforts. And then, of a sudden, the beam died out.

"Beggar felt it necessary to come out of the house into the corridor so as to make sure no one was about," Clive whispered to himself. "Now, is he still outside the door, listening and waiting, or has he gone in again? I'm not going to wait much longer. This cad means business, and if he's up to the old game, why, the sooner I nab him the better. Supposing he's already made a fire!"

That caused his heart to increase its exertions again, for his excitement had abated a little after his first discovery. But as he thought of this serious possibility, his pulses stirred with a vengeance. Why, the whole fate of the school might be in his hands! Delay and hesitation at this moment might see old Ranleigh, the place which he and hundreds like him loved, some young, some growing to manhood, some already arrived at that stage in life's progression, and getting rather on the seamy side, might see it burned to ashes. The thought sent a chill through his sweating frame. Clive moved quickly in the direction of the open door at the west end of the quad and crept into the corridor. Was that a flash of light he saw from beneath the door?

"Jolly like it. Believe he's gone in again. I'm going to chance matters."

He touched the trigger of his lamp and sent a flood of light on the half-open door. The corridor was empty. There was no figure beside the door. Clive darted over to it, and stood at its edge, peeping round into the passage leading to the Head's own study. It was a dismal place at any time, badly lighted in the most brilliant day, and now sunk in the depths of impenetrable darkness. It was a heart-breaking sort of passage, with uncompromising and unsatisfactory walls, which gave not the smallest encouragement to a malefactor. And here it was that malefactors gathered. Not the class of malefactor that Clive was now after, but wretched Ranleighans, haled before the Head, sent there often enough with the politest of notes by one or other of the masters—notes, too, which the wretched victims had themselves to bear. They were almost like death warrants. Clive had experienced the dreadful feeling of bearing one. He had waited in that depressing passage while another sinner preceded him. He had listened to the drone of voices behind the Head's door. And then had come the sound of tribulation. Staring into this dark pit brought his early days at Ranleigh back to his mind. What a thrashing he had had on that occasion when he and Masters had broken bounds and contrived to stampede two of Squire Studholme's finest horses!

Then his thoughts were just as suddenly switched from old recollections to present events. He was on the point of flashing his own lamp into the passage when the darkness was illuminated from the direction of the Head's door. That, too, was half open. The miscreant was inside. Now was the time to lay hands on him.

"Catch him nicely in a trap. That'll do," thought Clive. "He's coming out, though. What's he up to?"

The reflection from the walls of the passage threw into relief the figure of a man, gowned in something loose.

"Overcoat," said Clive. "Hat crammed on his head and rubbers on his feet. He's—he's pouring something along the sides of the passage. Paraffin. I can smell it! Jingo! Then this is the beggar! I've got him right in the middle of the act. This is what we've been waiting and watching for."

Yes, there could be no doubt now, for the penetrating odour of the oil was already filling his nostrils. But how silently the rascal worked! But for the faint whisper the tail of his coat made now and again as he stepped along the side of the passage there was not another sound. Clive watched the fluid pouring from the spout of the fellow's kettle as if he were fascinated. It spread slowly and greasily, as paraffin does invariably, across the woodwork and matting of the floor. It ran freely from the receptacle in which this rascal had brought it, and then slowly became less in quantity, till it merely dribbled from the spout. And all the while an elliptical, bright ray of light fell on the particular spot upon which the fluid was falling, the mere outline of the bending figure of the man being visible to the watcher. Suddenly the light went out. There was a faint scraping noise, as if the kettle had hit against the wall. Then the light flashed for a second again, and once more disappeared.

"Gone back into the Head's room. Now I have him," said Clive, whetting his lips. "It'll be a business, but I ain't going to be funked. This is a matter concerning the whole school, and I don't shirk it. All the same, I wish Masters were closer."

He rounded the door, flashed his own lamp for one instant so as to give him a view of the passage, and then went noiselessly onward. Outside the study door he waited and listened. Yes, someone was moving inside. He heard the faint rustle of papers. The fellow no doubt was piling them upon the pool of paraffin he had poured on to the floor. Or perhaps he was scattering the fluid broadcast. It was the moment to nab him. Clive stepped into the doorway and——

A blinding flash of light blazed right into his eyes. The bull's-eye of this ruffian's lamp was within ten inches of his face and suddenly opened upon him. There came a startled cry, a sudden movement, and the clatter of a kettle falling to the floor. Then Clive was dashed backward into the passage with terrific violence, and stumbling on the mat outside the study door, fell heavily on his back, his own electric torch clattering away into a corner. He felt the sweep of the fellow's gown or overcoat across his face and gripped swiftly for his legs. His hand closed on something, trousers perhaps, though the material seemed extraordinarily thin. Then he was kicked savagely, though the softness of his assailant's soles caused but little damage. But it threw his grip off, and in a moment the fellow was fleeing.

"Beaten me after all," thought Clive as he sprang to his feet and groped for his torch. "Ah, here's the thing. Now, which way did he bolt?"

He was out of the passage like a flash of lightning, and turned into the corridor. At once his finger went to the trigger of his torch and sent a beam ahead of him. Yes, there was a flying figure in advance, going at full speed down the corridor, and without making even the smallest sound. Clive gave chase instantly, first with the help of the light given him by his torch, and then in total darkness, for his finger had slipped from the trigger. But he had it on again in a moment. There the fellow was, plainly visible, his clothing blowing out behind him.

"I'm gaining on him," thought Clive. "We're bound to have him nicely, for he's going straight for the corner. He'll be round in a jiffy, and I shall be after him. Masters will see my lamp from the post he's taken and will be in splendid position to stop him. Bother the torch. My finger's slipped again."

A second earlier the flying figure had arrived within three feet of the end of the corridor, where it turned abruptly to the left. Clive reached the spot perhaps ten seconds later. He flashed his light round the corner and along the other corridor. There was nothing visible. Not a soul was in sight. Even Masters was not present, and was doubtless waiting round the corner at the far end. But where had this fugitive gone? Into the archway leading to the Bursar's room and to East Dormitory, or through the opening to the quad? Clive flashed his torch through the latter. No. There was no one in the quad. Then elsewhere? He sent the beam against the banisters of East Dormitory. No. There was no one. This fugitive seemed to have been actually swallowed by the surrounding walls. Clive was sorely puzzled and perplexed. He retraced his steps to the corner of the corridor, and peeped into a boot-room there. That, too, was empty. The man had been too clever for him. He had gone.

"Dived into that boot-room, without a doubt. Waited for me to pass and then went off back along the same route towards the Head's door. I'll go along there after him. Wonder whether he fired that paraffin? Must find that out. Why, even now a fire may be blazing. My word! To think that a chap could go in for such a caddish business."

But who was the man? Did Clive know? Had he recognised that fleeting figure?

There was a deep furrow across our hero's face. Even as he raced back along the corridor he was conscious of a feeling of unusual distress, of sadness almost, of despair at the thought of what must inevitably follow his discovery. For the miscreant was without question a Ranleigh boy. Clive had not seen his face—had seen little else, in fact, but legs rapidly moving and a flowing gown, above which was a head hidden beneath a hat pressed closely down upon it. But even figures have their own special features. Every individual almost has his own particular movements, something, however small, which differentiates them from others. And Clive knew the special run of this fugitive well. In a court of law, perhaps, his evidence was useless. Here, at Ranleigh, perhaps it was little better. Were he asked at that moment to say who the miscreant was he could merely shake his head.

"Couldn't actually dare to declare the fellow's name," he told himself as he raced up the corridor. "I feel sure. But others would doubt. They'd doubt naturally, and considering the circumstances, the excitement, the intermittent light, why, I may easily be mistaken. I daren't wreck a fellow's future on such flimsy evidence. Perhaps I'll nobble him yet. At any rate, I'll try my best. My word, what a slippery beggar!"

He was back at the Head's door now, to find it wide open, where no doubt he had flung it as he raced after this mysterious incendiary. The passage within was empty. He searched every corner with his torch. The corridor outside the Hall was equally vacant, and there was no one on the stairs leading to West and certain of the masters' rooms, nor on those giving access to North Dormitory.

"Then the beggar's back in the Head's room," he thought. "I'll go right in this time, close the door so that he can't try the same sort of business, and then nail him. George! The place smells of paraffin. He meant to have a proper flare while he was about it. Now, is he in the Head's study or not?"

No, he wasn't. At least, the place seemed empty. But a combination of misfortunes was pursuing Clive on this adventurous evening. To commence with, he had been taken by surprise by the crafty fellow he was watching, and had been tripped up nicely. And now, perhaps because the fall had injured it, his torch failed all of a sudden. Clive groped for a match-box, upset some ornament on the mantelpiece, felt his fingers light upon something remarkably like a match-box, and gripped the latter. Then he rapidly withdrew one of the matches and struck it against the box. A candlestick was within easy reach, and in a second he had the wick burning. It was giving off a good light, and he was holding it above his head so as the better to see his surroundings, when the door was pushed swiftly open, a figure bounced into the room, and in a twinkling our hero found himself gripped by the collar.

CHAPTER XIX

A MONSTROUS ACCUSATION

It was a terrible moment for Clive. In the midst of his own vexation and chagrin at the failure he had made, and at the knowledge that he had just missed laying hands on the criminal who had been setting fire to the school, to be pounced upon of a sudden, gripped with suffocating firmness and shaken like a dog, was disconcerting, to say the least of it. It was positively maddening.

"Let go, you fool! Clear off, and let me go on with the business," he cried in tones of anger. "Do you hear? Let go."

Clive was no saint. He had as many faults as the average fellow, and perhaps more than some. But they were honest faults, faults seen in the light of open day. Not the low, mean ones affected by some fellows behind the scenes, to their own shame and the abhorrence of all right-thinking people. Clive had never been one of those fellows who sadly upset the discipline and more of a school. He was a rock to lean on where questions of principle and honour were concerned. The Head knew it. Old B. knew it better still perhaps. The masters and the school thought quite well of our hero. But he had a temper, and showed it now. He struggled and fought like a madman. But still those iron fingers gripped his neck.

"At last!" he heard in the deep, cross tones of Mr. Axim. "At last the wretch who has troubled us so long is run to earth. Stir an inch, sir, and I'll deal sternly with you. There'll be no trifling, I can assure you. Though you are a Ranleigh prefect, and not yet a man, you can expect the roughest handling."

That was Mr. Axim all over. He was, perhaps, the most unpopular of all the masters. In fact, we may state that Ranleigh had seldom been so unlucky. Mr. Axim seemed indeed to have been born with a natural antipathy for boys, and it was ill luck that he should have come to Ranleigh, or, for the matter of that, to any school. To him boys were unnatural animals. He was ever suspicious of them. Their overflowing fun and humour he could not understand, while boyish forgetfulness and want of care were, in his eyes, unpardonable offences. Was it fate, too, which had made him Clive's one particular *bête noire*, almost a persecutor? For friendship between them had never existed. The merry, light-hearted Clive, so serious when it came to mechanics, so studious when he was interested, was with this Mr. Axim a sulky dunce, unable to grip even simple rudiments. But then driving never agreed with our hero. A little sympathy, a little human friendship, and he was your best supporter, ready to "swat," as the boys termed it, ready to work his fingers almost to the bone so that he might give satisfaction. With Mr. Axim he had, in his earlier days at Ranleigh, been for ever in trouble, and since then the two had avoided one another as far as possible, each unmistakably disliking the other.

"At last, and the Head's pet prefect!" said Mr. Axim, laughing satirically, and with an air of triumph in his voice. "Let us see what he has to say to this capture. Pet prefect indeed! Pet hypocrite, I think. And to think that I warned him of you! To think that the one who did so nobly in putting out our first fire should have set it going. Ha! ha! I suspected the game. You should have thought of me, Darrell, when you went into this scoundrelly business."

Clive was too astounded to make any reply, and if he had wished, the grip compressing his neck behind made speaking almost impossible. His wits were whirling. He felt inclined to shout, or to break out into hysterical laughter. It was bad enough to have missed the man he was after, when he and his friends had taken so much trouble. And now, to be accused of the deed himself, to be told that he had been caught red-handed, was half maddening, half ludicrous. Had it been anyone else but Mr. Axim, Clive would have explained. But this master's obvious triumph, his satire and biting sarcasm kept our hero's lips silent.

"So," said Mr. Axim, as if gathering his ideas and thinking the matter out, "so, returning from a pleasant evening in the village we accidently discover Darrell as the much-wanted incendiary. Good! We now proceed to disillusionise the Head. We will ring this bell and awake him."

He tugged at the cord promptly, and somewhere far away in the depths of the house Clive heard an answering clang, repeated some five or six times. Mr. Axim went to the door and closed it, standing afterwards with his back to it.

"I'll not soil my fingers any longer," he said. "You can stand over there in the opposite corner. No. Leave the candle. A desperate young ruffian such as you are might easily complete the job I managed fortunately to disturb. Now, a clean breast of the whole business will be the only course for you to follow."

Clive scowled at him, and then closely inspected his surroundings. As he had suspected, there was a pile of papers in one corner, from which came the strong odour of paraffin. Everything, in fact, was ready for the conflagration. It merely wanted the match, and that at least he had been instrumental in preventing. Suddenly there was a tap at the door. The Head of Ranleigh entered. Slowly his eyes passed from the figure of Mr. Axim to that of Clive. He sniffed heavily, turning his head in all directions. Then, as if he had more than half gripped the situation, his pale and impassive face became suddenly paler in the candle light, while he wore an unusually stern expression. Crossing to the wide table on which his papers were neatly arranged and ticketed, he drew his writing chair nearer and sat down, resting his forehead on his hands. And thus he remained for a few moments, as if anxious to put his thoughts from him. It was with a fierce "Well?" that he finally addressed Mr. Axim.

"This is the end of the trouble," said the latter. "You have had fires at the school. The matter has been a mystery. There is the culprit. Clive Darrell."

"And you?" asked the Head severely, turning upon our hero. "You admit this fact? You agree that Mr. Axim discovered you in the act of setting fire to these premises? Answer at once. Are you responsible for the whole of this wicked business?"

"Decidedly not. There has been a mistake, sir," said Clive, hardly knowing where to commence his story.

"A mistake! Of course," laughed Mr. Axim hoarsely. "There always is an error in these affairs, no matter whether the culprit be discovered candle in hand, in the midst of heaped-up papers saturated with paraffin!"

"You were found like that, Darrell?" asked the Head, sadly enough.

Clive nodded. He glared across at Mr. Axim defiantly. "I admit the fact," he said curtly. "But I am not the culprit. Mr. Axim has been too clever, for he has merely come upon the scene after I had discovered what was happening. I followed someone here. I wasn't sure what was happening, though I had my suspicions. I came down the passage and was about to enter the room when this fellow suddenly put his electric torch on me. There was darkness a second later. He knocked me over, and sent my torch flying. I chased him down the corridor and then lost sight of him. Thinking that he might have returned here, I came back again. That was the moment when Mr. Axim proved so clever."

The latter gasped. Clive's effrontery made him positively giddy.

"A pack of lies," he cried. "If there had been a struggle you would have heard it. Of course he lost sight of this fellow in the corridor, simply because he never existed."

"Silence, please," commanded the Head, lifting a shaking finger. "Clive Darrell, you state that you discovered an incendiary at work. You had a torch. You chased this man. You no doubt saw him. Then give the name. Was it one of my Ranleighans?"

"Yes," came the prompt answer. "I feel sure it was one, though I'm sorry to have to admit it. But who, that's another question."

Mr. Axim sniggered. Clive could willingly have kicked him. The Head's pale face took on a sterner appearance.

"You saw and followed, and admit that this miscreant was a Ranleighan," he said icily. "Then you can also give the name of the individual."

"No. I refuse. In my own mind my suspicions are so strong that I feel certain. But I never saw his face. I'll condemn no one on such evidence. I regret I am unable to give you the name of the fellow."

Mr. Axim laughed again, causing the Head to frown. Clive crossed his arms over his chest and confronted his questioners. And then the master who had come upon him stepped up to his side, took the candle and slowly inspected him.

"Rubber shoes, for silence of course," he reported. "Got a sweater on, for warmth, ditto a dressing-gown. Smells strongly of paraffin, and has a box of matches in his pocket."

His elevated eyebrows were more than expressive. He looked at his senior as much as to say, "The evidence is conclusive. This boy is a liar."

But Ranleigh's Head was not the one to condemn without a searching investigation. He had thrown himself back in his chair, and was staring now at the candle. He was terribly grieved, if the truth be known, most terribly disappointed. For Clive was an especial favourite. He could have sworn that the young fellow was honest and upright. Besides, this was the act of a fanatic. Clive wasn't that. He was a decidedly level-headed fellow.

"You refuse that name?" he asked after a while.

"Yes, sir."

"You have no other explanation to offer?"

"Most certainly!"

"Ah!" smiled Mr. Axim, and then, *sotto voce*, "More lies, I suppose. Hear him!"

"Then let me hear it."

"These fires have naturally upset Ranleigh fellows. We felt it a duty to discover the culprit. We decided to watch the premises during the night. Masters and I were on duty at eleven to-night. You will find him down in the far corridor."

Mr. Axim's face fell. The Head's took on a happier expression.

"Fetch him here, please," he said, turning to the master. "We will wait for your return. Be quick, please."

He aimlessly turned over the papers on his table while Mr. Axim was absent. But very soon the latter was back, bringing a very startled young fellow with him.

"You were watching with Darrell, then?" asked the Head.

"Certainly. We decided to see into this jolly business and catch the cad—er— the fellow that was doing it. Er—Clive and I were for duty to-night."

"Together?"

"No, sir. Separate. We were to meet every few minutes."

"You met then?"

"Often. At last Clive crept along and told me there was someone about. He asked me to watch at the far end of the corridor."

The Head nodded. Mr. Axim gave vent to a malicious chuckle.

"Well out of the way there, I think?" he asked. "Did you see anything of this chase which we are told followed?"

"What chase?" asked Masters, looking across at his friend. "I don't understand. I've been waiting there ever since in case Clive's man bolted. What's happened?"

There was an impressive silence for one whole minute.

"Only I'm accused of preparing a fire here," said Clive. "Mr. Axim caught me."

"Red-handed," cried the latter. "Matches in pocket and candle in hand. Now he has the impudence to declare that he himself disturbed a fellow here. He chased him down the corridor, when the culprit disappeared. But you neither saw nor heard them! That's significant. More than that, Darrell saw this wretch, recognised him, he believes, but will give us no name. Queer, a little, don't you think, Masters? But let us go a little deeper into the question. That first fire commenced close to One South. Darrell was the one to discover and quench it. It was marvellous how he had managed to think out all the details of the business."

"Wait! Parfit woke him first. He gave the warning," cried Masters, his face flushed with anger and distress at the accusation aimed at his friend. "When you begin to dig deep, Mr. Axim, we'll have all the details, please. Just remember what I've mentioned."

"I do," came the cutting and sharp answer. "Parfit announced smoke. The smell had awakened him. Agreed. But there's no fire without smoke. Darrell had ample time to do his work and get back to the dormitory. My argument begins to tell, I think."

He looked searchingly at the Head, while Masters stared at Clive as if he were stricken speechless.

"We go further now," said Mr. Axim, a note of exultation in his voice. "The post of School Captain falls vacant next term. Darrell is a candidate."

"Yes," nodded Masters.

"That fire and his management of the boys made him first favourite. It gave his popularity a tremendous fillip. But who was chiefly instrumental in discovering and controlling the fires which followed? Clive Darrell!" cried Mr. Axim, pointing a condemning finger at our hero. "Who would have had all the kudos here to-night, once this fire had started? The wretch stands there. Clive Darrell, being conveniently on watch, and having thoughtfully got rid of his companion, prepares for a flare, makes ready to set it going, with the one idea of waiting for the flames to become sufficiently serious. Then he makes the discovery. Wakes the school, oh so gently, and descends to-morrow morning even a greater hero than he was before. In fact, he becomes certain King of Ranleigh. There, sir, you have the case clearly. There is clear motive for such conduct. Clive Darrell is the one you are after."

Very carefully had the Head followed this argument. He didn't like Mr. Axim overmuch, but he knew him to be a shrewd fellow. For the life of him he could see no fault in this argument. It was a terrible indictment. Everything seemed to argue against the truth of Clive's story. Everything? No. Let him declare the name of this fellow he had chased. Then let them confront him. That would clear his name absolutely.

"Clive Darrell," said the Head sternly, though kindly, "you have followed Mr. Axim? The evidence looks black against you. As to the motive, I find it harder to believe that you would play to the gallery for any post than I do to conceive of any reason for your firing these buildings. One thing alone can clear you. Give me the name of this person you followed. Let us bring him face to face with you."

There was dead silence. Mr. Axim actually smiled. Masters looked terribly distressed, while the Head seemed thoroughly miserable.

"You refuse?" he asked.

"Yes."

"Then go to your dormitory. You will be expelled in the morning."

It was a disastrous ending to the ambitions of our hero.

CHAPTER XX

THE OLD FIRM HANGS TOGETHER

There were white faces amongst the members of the Old Firm on the morning following Clive's arrest by Mr. Axim, and the sentence which the Head had passed on him. The school itself was agog with the news.

"Darrell's bunked! Heard it? What's he done?" was passing on every side.

The prefects discussed the matter for the most part sorrowfully and a little shamefacedly. It was a terrible blow to them to find that amongst their number there was such a criminal.

"It's more than a bunking business," said Roper. "It's a case for the criminal courts. Darrell'll get years of imprisonment. Arson is a most serious offence. I wouldn't have thought it of him."

"I don't believe it. There's some mistake, I'm positive," declared Jenkins, one of Clive's particular friends. "Hear what the Old Firm have to say."

But that the Sixth were not likely to have an opportunity of hearing, for Bert and Hugh and the others were collected together at that moment in the Gym, whither they had departed so as to have peace, and so as to be able to discuss matters in private. Hugh, as if habit were too strong for him, sat across the horse. Bert, his face unusually stern, leaned against the same apparatus. Susanne stood close at hand, his broad shoulders stooping to a marked degree on this fatal morning. As for Trendall, there was grief written unmistakably on his decidedly pleasant features. Then Masters joined them. They were awaiting his coming, and gave vent to sighs of relief as he came through the Gym doorway and walked toward them. But it was a weary, despondent Masters. There was not the usual elasticity about his step. This fellow, apt to see fun in almost anything, and very seldom down-hearted, might have been at this instant preparing to attend his own funeral.

Susanne beckoned him forward.

"Now, tell us all," he said. "Everything, so that we may judge."

"Then I'll start at eleven last night, when we met in the corridor and commenced our patrolling."

Very rapidly he narrated the events of the night, unimportant in his own case till the latter part. Still, he missed nothing, giving them the closest details. Each one of the Firm stretched a trifle closer when he came to that portion of the narrative when Mr. Axim called him, and he discovered Clive face to face with the Head. He even told them what words had passed, how Mr. Axim had summed up the matter, how Clive had refused to give the name of the boy he more than strongly suspected.

"There's the whole case," he said at last. "I grant you it's black. Things somehow seemed to have worked round to incriminate Clive. It's an awful business. I hate that fellow Axim. He's a howling bounder."

They agreed with him at once.

"And we all trust Clive," said Susanne impressively. "He's the victim of circumstances."

"Anyone could sum up the case blackly against him," cried Bert. "Listen to this. Because a fire breaks out in the neighbourhood of South Dormitory Clive must be the culprit. That's Axim's argument. Why not Susanne, then? Because Clive is a candidate for Captain of the School. But so am I. So's Susanne, so's Masters and plenty of others. But listen again to Axim's reasoning. Clive must be the culprit not only because he's a candidate for Captain, but because he engineered the brigade which stopped the fire, and because he managed to think of all sorts of issues, sent to have the gas cut off, sent for the fire brigade, etc. Pshaw!"

He stamped his foot. Looked at quietly one could see the fallacy of such reasoning. Why because Clive had done his best should he necessarily have had an eye to his chances of being elected as Captain of Ranleigh?

"The suggestion's preposterous. I wonder the Head hasn't seen it!" said Trendall. "Because a chap does well, is he therefore necessarily to have an ulterior motive? The argument's rotten. If persisted in it would soon kill initiative in an institution. A chap would be afraid of being accused of all sorts of things. Of course, what clinches a bad argument is Clive's admission that he saw this chap, believes he knows the fellow in spite of not seeing his face, and yet won't give the name. He refused."

"Bluntly," said Susanne, almost with a sob. "We interviewed him early this morning, Masters and Bert and I. Refused curtly. We asked him why."

"And what's the answer?" demanded Hugh. "Mind you, Clive's a queer beggar. He loathes Axim. Axim tried to drive him, and that's quite enough to make Clive shut up. Then he's got queer ideas of honour and all that. What did he say?"

"Refused to discuss the matter. Simply said he wasn't sufficiently sure of his man to launch such an accusation against him. Then shut up and got quite angry."

"School's summoned in Hall for eleven," said Bert. "I propose we go again and see Clive. He must give way; we'll compel him."

The idea was one which appealed strongly to them, and since if all went numbers might defeat their object, Hugh and Susanne were selected for the interview, and at once went off to the Bursar's office where Clive was incarcerated pending his departure from Ranleigh for the railway station. Ten minutes later they were back, their faces almost haggard.

"He's gone—hooked it!" cried Susanne, looking round at his friends with anxious eyes.

"Gone! Bolted?" asked Bert, bewildered. "Why?"

"Wouldn't stand to be bullied any longer. Wouldn't have the Head and others constantly coming to demand the name of the fellow he'd seen. Said that since they openly disbelieved his story they'd better sack him—in fact, that he'd sack himself. He left a note to tell 'em what he was doing."

Clive had indeed launched a thunderbolt at all at Ranleigh. The anxious and harassed Head found his troubles vastly added to by this unforeseen event. For days past his had been an unenviable existence, and had the Old Firm but known it, he had taken steps to have the outside of the school closely patrolled every night, while various of the servants had been watched. In fact, the Head had scorned the idea that this incendiary was one of his own community. Advised by the village sergeant of police, he had come to the conclusion that it must be some madman living in the neighbourhood, or someone outside with a grudge against the school, someone probably with an intimate knowledge of the buildings. Strong suspicion, in fact, fell upon one of the men employed about the place a few weeks before, and summarily dismissed for misconduct.

And now he knew it to be a Ranleigh boy. One had been taken actually red-handed. But that boy was Clive Darrell. Even now, with the evidence so strong against him, the Head could not believe it. And yet, after full discussion, he could see no room for error. It seemed certain that not only had Clive done this thing and thrown dust in the eyes of the police and the school officials, but he had also hoodwinked his own special companions. That system of patrolling was but a ruse to disarm suspicion. It was strange, more than strange, that Clive should always be at hand on these occasions when fire broke out, while, if he were the guilty person, as Mr. Axim proved so easily and conclusively, then the motive was plain if despicable.

It may be imagined, too, that this train of argument cut the ground from beneath the feet of Susanne and his friends. What could the Old Firm bring to controvert such evidence? Merely the stubborn refusal to believe Clive guilty. Merely to scoff at the idea that he had made fools of them.

And now he was gone. If his tale were true, one event and one only could clear his name and bring him back to Ranleigh. That boy whom Clive refused to name could come forward and declare the true facts of the case, and so clear his comrade.

"Axim don't believe there is another fellow in it," said Bert bitterly, when the news of Clive's going was brought to them. "The Head would like to, but the evidence is too strong for him. But I'm still positive that Clive's straight and honest. He'd never dirty his fingers with such a business."

"And I'm going to find him and this other beggar," declared Hugh.

"Bravo! We'll all help," came from Susanne. "Now, look here, you fellows, I've a proposition. We don't want to worry the Head or break regulations, do we?"

"Certainly not," from Trendall.

"Regulations, no. I'd break that fellow Axim's head," growled Masters.

"At the same time, we believe our biggest and best friend to have been wrongfully accused of this crime of arson."

"Yes," said Bert emphatically. "He is a victim of circumstances."

"And since his future and his fair name concerns us more than school regulations, I'm going to break 'em. I'm going off at once to find Clive. Hugh'll come with me, also Masters and Trendall, if they like."

Each one mentioned eagerly accepted. "It's the least we can do," said Masters. "How'll you set about it?"

"One moment," cried Susanne, lifting a hand.

"What about me, then?" asked Bert.

"You will have just as important work. You will read our manifesto. We'll draw it up now, put the full facts in it, and declare our intention of searching for Clive. At eleven, when the school meets, and the Head comes in to announce Clive's expulsion, you'll stand out and demand that this decision be delayed for a while, till we've investigated the matter. He won't refuse. He's far too decent a fellow. Meanwhile, we shall move off. I'll hire that new car they've got at the 'Green Man' down in the village, that is, as soon as we've made sure he hasn't taken the train. Then we'll run round in all directions asking for information. It's nine now. Let's get the manifesto written and signed, and then slip off. Bert will see what can be done here to pick up some crumbs of evidence."

Without discussion, without further thought indeed, the Old Firm adopted this proposition. They may not have been right. It would have been better, perhaps, had they started on their own ground by seeking further evidence in the school, instead of delegating that task to Bert. But then, the Old Firm was notorious for its impetuosity and also for warm-heartedness. They were true friends ever, and here they meant to prove it. If Clive were innocent, then he should be found and brought back to the school. If he were guilty, why, not one of the Old Firm would believe it till he himself had admitted it.

And so that manifesto was drawn up by Bert, when all signed it. Then he watched them depart from the school, and went off himself to sift the matter to the bottom. It may be imagined what a sensation his presence caused some two hours later, when, the Head having come before the assembled school and mounted the dais to make his painful announcement, Bert walked from amongst his fellows and coolly—for he had braced himself for this trying ordeal—stepped up beside him.

"Boys of Ranleigh," began the Head, not having noticed Bert, "I have a most painful announcement to make. You are aware that fires have occurred in the school of late, fires caused by an incendiary. The culprit has now been found. I regret to say that it is Clive Darrell."

There was dead silence in the Hall. The Head stood with his shoulders thrown back, his eyes firmly closed as was his wont, looking positively miserable. It was, in fact, a miserable business. Here was a promising boy's future ruined. The only little solace, and it was likely enough only a temporary one, was the fact that Clive had bolted. There was a warrant out already for his arrest, and to see him in the police court, to witness his trial and condemnation would be the very last straw. Ranleigh's unhappy Head would have given thousands could he have undone the whole matter, thousands to save Clive Darrell, for he liked the young fellow, and thousands also to save the honour of the School. He opened his eyes then, heard a step beside him, and saw Bert for the first time. Mr. Axim had seen him a minute earlier, for all the masters were present, as was the custom on such occasions, and had officiously attempted to arrest him. But Bert shook his hand off peremptorily, and now advanced to the Head's side.

"I have to ask pardon, sir," he began. "Clive Darrell is an old friend of mine, and I come here to support him in his absence. I have here a paper recapitulating the evidence against him, which I and Clive's best friends have drawn up. We feel sure that you are too fair not to allow us to put it before the School. May I read it?"

There was surprise on the Head's face. Mr. Axim was openly scoffing. But a partisan of Clive's down at the end of the school boldly set up a cheer. Feeling was indeed running high. Ranleigh still could not believe Clive Darrell guilty, and now by their cheers they openly demanded to hear the evidence in full. It was, indeed, a novel situation. The Head grappled with it magnificently. He stood aside, and then held up his hand.

"We pride ourselves on fair play at Ranleigh," he said. "Let Seymour Primus and his friends prove Clive Darrell innocent, and I shall be the first to thank them. Read the paper."

Bert did, slowly and impressively. Perhaps Susanne could not have chosen a better man to put those facts before Ranleigh. The boys seemed to grip the situation instantly. There were cheers as he reached the end of his manifesto, and then dead silence. Bert had still something to say.

"Sir," he said, turning to the Head, "there is a Ranleighan here who is the really guilty party. Who set fire to the school? I beg that you ask him to come forward, and I ask also that you defer Clive Darrell's expulsion till we have had time to sift certain evidence. We have a clue. Fair play, sir, is all that we ask of you."

You could have heard the smallest pin drop on the tiled paving of the Hall. Even the smaller boys failed on this momentous occasion to shuffle their feet, an irritating habit they often acquire, while the seniors of Ranleigh School moved not a muscle. There were none of those sharp, barking coughs so noticeable in class-rooms, or in Chapel, which distract the attention of the reader and make his voice almost inaudible. There was a deep and impressive silence. As for the faces of those collected in Hall, they wore a hundred different expressions. The Head's fine, impassive features were heavily lined. He seemed to have actually aged. Mr. Branson, that genial giant so deservedly popular, showed utter misery on his somewhat heavy face. For Old B. had a tender spot in his heart for Clive Darrell, just as he had for many another boy. He had seen him arrive at the school, a mere mischievous chicken. He had watched him grow up, had coached him in his work and in cricket, where Clive did not shine as Bert did. Often had a smile or a word from Old B. encouraged our hero. And here was the end of it all—disgrace, dismissal; perhaps imprisonment.

"A better fellow never came to Ranleigh," he was muttering. "I don't believe this tale. There's a fault somewhere. Clive's a stickler for honour. Why should he give the name of a boy whom he believes he saw, but whose back was always towards him? Then, too, the only light he possessed was an electric torch, and that went out when his finger slipped off the trigger. I grant that many would have given the name. It's just the sort of occasion when Clive would refuse, partly because it's a point of honour with him to protect the name of all Ranleighans, mostly because there is just a doubt in his mind as to whether he can have been mistaken, and he will not therefore fling an accusation of such a serious nature at anyone on such evidence."

Old B. went scarlet in the face. His eyes flashed. He lifted a hand in protest, and stepped forward. "I——" he began, but the Head waved him back peremptorily.

"Wait," he asked a second later. Then his eyes closed. He threw himself into his characteristic attitude, while a deep frown furrowed his brow. From his position on the dais Bert slowly watched the expressions on the faces of those assembled, watched and waited. There was positive fear and alarm in the case of many of the youngsters. Middle School fellows were obviously stirred, though the presence of so many masters, and of the Head in particular, quelled any outburst. But the seniors were not so vastly impressed. There was resolution on some of the faces, indignation on others, and nowhere could he detect a sign of triumph at Clive's downfall. Nowhere. Jenkins stood with clenched fists, biting his lips and deep in thought. Roper appeared to be on the point of bursting into speech. His cheeks were puffed out and reddened, while his breast was absolutely swelling at the thought of the injustice which he considered had been done. Even Rawlings, the oldest boy present, looked sorry. There was none of the old truculence, the open scorn of his rival, for Clive had now become in every way his rival. More than once in the last year had Rawlings aspired to take the post of Captain of Ranleigh, but, as we have said, his unpopularity was too pronounced. And now that an election was imminent, it was certain that Clive, were he at the school, would have gained the coveted honour. That was Rawlings' fault. He should long ago have cultivated the friendship of his fellows. Now he had lost it for good, and without doubt should have left the school long ago. Why he remained on was never quite understood, though it was rumoured that some family trouble had caused him to stay. Be that as it might, he was still a Ranleighan, still unpopular, while of late, perhaps because his own bosom friends had left, he had become silent and taciturn, given to long fits of brooding, and sometimes to outbursts of passion.

No, there was merely sorrow on Rawlings' features, sorrow and a curiously dazed expression. And elsewhere only on the face of one was there any expression hostile to our hero. Mr. Axim scowled. He felt that he himself now stood as prisoner in the dock. For he it was who had caught Clive, he it was who had scoffed at his declaration of innocence, had summed up the evidence, had produced a motive for the acts, and had thus impressed the Head. And here was open rejection of his decision, of his arguments and of Clive's sentence. The position was, in fact, unique in Ranleigh's annals, unique perhaps in the annals of almost every school in existence.

"Monstrous!" he was muttering. "The evidence is clear. These people will be accusing me of the crime next. As if I were swayed by animus! As if it were not absolutely clear that Darrell is the guilty party.

"I—I protest," he cried, and then was silenced just as had been the case with Mr. Branson. The Head actually scowled at his assistant master.

"Allow me, if you please," he said, with acrid emphasis. And then he faced the School. Slowly he allowed his gaze to pass down the lines of boys assembled at their tables. He seemed to look closely into every face, seemed almost to ask the question on every occasion. Then he threw his head back and closed his eyes. But they were open a second later when he addressed the School in tones more solemn than any had ever known him to employ before.

"Ranleighans," he said, "I beg of you to listen to what I have to say. One of your old comrades has been declared to be guilty of the most dastardly conduct. I need not say more on that point, for the particulars are thoroughly known. Last night the evidence against him seemed to my mind to be conclusive. There was no fault that I could discover, and though Darrell himself denied the acts he still declined to give the name of one he suggested was the author of those fires. Now Seymour Primus demands a respite. I give it freely, willingly. If there be a doubt in this case, if delay may produce some evidence to clear Clive Darrell, then, in Heaven's name, let us delay. But let us also search our own consciences. That one whom Clive Darrell suggests is guilty, whose name he refused to give, is a Ranleigh boy. I beg of that boy to come boldly forward for his conscience' sake, for the sake of Clive Darrell."

The silence was positively trying. Bert felt almost as if he would explode if something did not soon happen to lessen the tension. Boys stood at their places absolutely pale and over-strung, unmanned almost by this ordeal. But none spoke. Not a boy came forward to proclaim his guilt and Clive's innocence. There was not so much as a sound for one full minute. And then there came a startling crash from the far end of the Hall. The clatter of feet was heard, the double doors were burst open, and there entered a small procession.

Susanne led the way, with Masters close behind him. Then came Hugh arm in arm with Trendall. The village sergeant of police followed closely, looking wonderfully important and just a little nonplussed at finding himself for a few brief moments the observed of all observers. But interest passed almost at once from him and those who led the procession. A solitary figure marching behind became the target for all observers.

"Clive Darrell!" shouted Bert. "Hooray for Clive Darrell!"

CHAPTER XXI

KING OF RANLEIGH

Such a scene had never before been witnessed at Ranleigh. Boys positively became frantic. They cheered and cheered as if they would keep on for ever. As for Bert Seymour, he waved his arms overhead and danced in his excitement, surely an unusual state of affairs with one so noted for sedateness.

And through the noise and the lanes of Ranleighans processed Susanne and his followers. There was a curious air of suppressed excitement and determination about them all. They turned neither to left nor to right, and acknowledged none of the frantic greetings thrown at them. Clive himself marched to the dais hands in pockets, not even deigning to glance at Mr. Axim. The latter's face was indeed a study.

"What's this?" he had asked himself at the commencement of the commotion which had ushered in this strange procession. "Feofé? Ah! One of Darrell's special chums, and, of course, the others close in tow. Members of the Old Firm. Can't help admiring the way they stick to a friend, but it's wasted labour."

The distraction was, in any case, at the very commencement welcome to him. We must be absolutely fair in our dealings with this master, and declare that indignation at the doubt cast on his own shrewdness and at Bert's open criticism of his method of summing up the evidence against Clive Darrell was beginning to give way to something approaching doubt of himself. Had he been absolutely impartial? Had he flown to conclusions, and taken too little heed of Clive's persistent denials and dogged refusal to discuss matters with him?

"Ought to have taken the fellow's nature into account," Mr. Axim was telling himself, for he wasn't at heart an unkindly master, nor even unfair. He was hasty, no doubt, and apt to allow prejudice to control his thoughts and actions. But when all was said and done, Mr. Axim was a Ranleighan, and at Ranleigh they go in for a fine stamp of master. And to the credit of this particular one, let it be stated that he was already discounting the wisdom of his late efforts.

"Supposing I'm wrong, and Clive's innocent? Supposing I've been hasty?" he asked himself. "Pshaw! We never got on well together. Didn't understand one another, I suppose. But that shouldn't make me unfair in my dealings with him. I—I——"

"You've acted like a hasty fool!" Old B. told him bluntly, for Mr. Axim in his agitation was speaking in a loud whisper. "You've been hard on the boy. He's innocent. I'll—hang it, man! I'll back him yet to be King of Ranleigh."

"But—but——"

"There isn't one. Did ever you see a guilty boy return to face his school after committing a crime of this nature? Never! Does that police sergeant look as if he had a possible prisoner behind him? Humbug, Axim! Susanne's face is sufficient to inform you that he has a tale of his own to tell us."

And Susanne had. The tall, broad-shouldered Frenchman looked positively brimming over with happiness, though there was an air of seriousness about him which showed that he also had some trouble. The same might be said of Trendall. But Masters was ever notorious for the openness of his feelings and opinions. He was absolutely truculent at this instant when the procession had arrived at the dais. He transfixed Mr. Axim with a glance which made that unfortunate and ill-advised gentleman wish that he had never had any dealings with this matter. Then all eyes were turned on the Head.

"With your permission, sir," said Susanne, halting at the edge of the dais and addressing the master with becoming respect, "with your permission we will mount the dais. We have information to give you. But first it would be as well to tell us what has been passing here in our absence."

The Head waved him up with a quick gesture. The lines were still drawn deep across his forehead, but there was, nevertheless, something approaching a look of relief. "You've arrived in the nick of time," he said. "Let me explain what has happened. I have made an announcement as to Clive Darrell. Seymour Primus, applauded by the School without exception, has traversed the evidence against him and has demanded delay in this unfortunate matter. To that I have agreed. Then, but a few seconds before your arrival, I begged that if any boy were present here who knew himself guilty he should for his conscience' sake and for Clive Darrell's honour at once come forward. Not a boy has stirred. That is the position."

Susanne mounted the dais slowly and deliberately. Those who knew him would have sworn that he was reluctant to speak, and yet he had information to give which would clear Clive's character entirely. He glanced down those expectant lines thoughtfully.

"Er—you fellows," he said, "I've—that is, we went in search of Clive. We were dead certain he was innocent."

Someone started a cheer just to encourage Susanne, for he was but a poor speaker.

"He was supposed to have bolted from the school with the idea of hiding himself. He hadn't. He went direct to the police station."

There was silence. Boys looked at one another. Some of the seniors wagged their heads.

"Bravo, Clive!" cried Mr. Branson, unable longer to contain himself, and then subsided, for the Head had fixed an indignant gaze on him. The police sergeant at once stepped forward. "Fact, gentlemen," he said. "At eight fifty-two he turns up. Of course I had heard of the night's happening. 'Arrest me, sergeant,' he says. 'I've been expelled for setting fire to Ranleigh.' Gentlemen, I didn't believe him."

Ranleigh howled its appreciation of the magnanimous conduct of this officer, Mr. Axim positively squirmed, while the Head looked more than uncomfortable. However, the sergeant had not yet finished.

"I arrested Mr. Darrell," he said. "On talking the matter over with him I suggested investigation. Mr. Darrell stoutly denied the crime for which he had handed himself over to my keeping."

"Ah! Investigation," gasped Mr. Axim. "How? On what lines? Surely we looked into everything?"

The sergeant withered him with a look of scorn. He produced from beneath his cloak a paper parcel and slowly unwrapped the paper.

"That was worth looking into," he said. "It's the first clue that would occur to a baby. That's a kettle, sir, an ordinary kettle. See it?"

He held it up so that all could see, while he glanced sideways at the unhappy master. Nor was the worthy sergeant disrespectful. There was merely mild indignation in his manner. But then he happened to have a lad of his own of Clive's age, and could thoroughly sympathise with that young fellow. His experience also of the law told him that Mr. Axim's deductions had been hasty and entirely misleading, for he had rushed to conclusions without searching for obvious clues and following those thoroughly. At arm's length overhead he now held a common kettle.

"That's a kettle, sir," he said again, "and that's paraffin."

Slowly he tipped it till a clear fluid trickled from the spout, and falling on the wooden boards of the dais began to spread into a dark, oily patch.

"And paraffin's what this incendiary was pouring along the passage," continued the sergeant. "That kettle was in the Headmaster's study. Were you in the habit, sir, of keeping an article like this in that part?"

It must be frankly admitted that the Head looked thoroughly startled.

"A kettle! Certainly not! Such articles are kept in the proper department. But I follow your reasoning, sergeant, we ought to have investigated this matter."

"And so you would, sir, if you hadn't been led off the path in the wrong direction. The detection of crime ain't only a matter of reasoning. It's a question of facts often enough, and this here kettle's a fact. Now, it don't belong to your people. I've asked the maids and the boy. They don't own to it. Then I searched elsewhere. It was about that time that I ran against Mr. Feofé and his friends. They'd been down to the station making enquiries."

The Head looked intensely surprised. Such an act was a direct breach of school rules and discipline. It amounted almost to a breaking out of the school, and was a crime he would, as a rule, punish severely. But, as a matter of fact, he had not even missed these boys from the collection of Ranleighans. He had no suspicion that they were not present, and the fact can be understood considering the nature of the business which had brought him to meet the assembled school. Nor was this the moment in which to discuss their breach of Ranleigh rules. He motioned to the sergeant to continue.

"They'd learned he was along at my cottage, fixed up in the station, and insisted I should fetch him so as to follow the clue I've put before you. Well, gentlemen, there wasn't a doubt as to the owner. We know him. He knows that we know him. He's here present. He's the guilty party."

No one stirred. If the Head expected that now one of the boys would stand forward he was much mistaken. Not one attempted to move. More than that, though he searched the lines of faces, there was not a boy present who looked conscious or guilty. Was the sergeant mistaken? Was it he who had gone astray from the path, and got upon a wrong line of reasoning and evidence? Mr. Axim started. He wanted to prove Clive innocent just as much as anyone else. He was honest enough not to care even if his own deduction proved childish. But, if clues were to be followed, they must be followed with intelligence.

"One moment, sergeant," he said. "This kettle."

"Yes, sir."

"You know the owner?"

"Without a shadow of doubt, sir."

"But do you know that it was the owner who made use of it last evening? Can you prove that fact? Can you show that Clive Darrell did not himself borrow it for this unfortunate business?"

Every eye turned upon the officer. He cleared his throat with a husky cough and returned the frank and anxious stare of Ranleigh with one of confidence.

"I can," he answered, with decision. "The dressing-gown belonging to the owner of that kettle has the tails of the skirt wet with paraffin."

"But—but——" began Mr. Axim.

"But you can say the same for the dressing-gown belonging to Mr. Darrell. It's saturated. You see, he was bowled over in the passage where the stuff had been laid; at least, sir, that's his story."

"Yes, his. He told me that at once."

"But you didn't believe him. I did," said the sergeant sharply, whereat there was a stir amongst the boys. They were on the point of bursting out. That sergeant had become wonderfully popular.

"One of the best!" Masters was observing to himself, while he scowled at Mr. Axim. Not that he meant much by that. Masters had changed his old ideas by now. The teaching staff at Ranleigh weren't such bad fellows, and decidedly not tyrants. But then the days of Masters' impots were long since finished. "One of the best!" he repeated, looking at the sergeant. "I've got a whole quid in my pocket. The Governor actually stumped up to that extent. Blessed if I don't tip the sergeant a sovereign."

"So we've got no further at the moment. Now, sir," went on the officer, addressing the Headmaster, "I'd been making enquiries round the village, and as a result I've learned that there was someone up here buying paraffin. You see, after that first fire, school stores were safely locked away, so that anyone who wanted the stuff had to look elsewhere for it. That paraffin was carried away by a gent who's the same as the one owning the kettle."

There was a deep hum in the Hall. And then a hush which was almost awe-inspiring.

"But that wasn't quite all I wanted. I looked for more. I looked where anyone else might have looked who'd followed the clue of that kettle. I searched the locker and boxes of that individual. I found there a diary, in which each fire is recorded, while the words make it clear that the writer was the man we're after. Now, sir, is there anyone here who doubts longer that Mr. Darrell can be innocent?"

Not one. Their faces showed it. But not a boy spoke, nor even a master. The moment was far too serious for that, for a tragedy lay still before them. Clive was cleared, even to the satisfaction of Mr. Axim. But there was still a guilty party. He was one of the Ranleigh boys, he was there, actually amongst them, and added to the enormity of his crime was the fact that he had failed to come forward. All eyes were on the sergeant. He was looking thoughtfully down the Hall, and seemed to glance at no one in particular. Then the boys turned their attention to the Headmaster, to Susanne, even to Masters and Trendall. Someone stirred. It was Clive. He stepped swiftly across to the sergeant, and then to the side of the Headmaster, whispering to both of them. The School was electrified a moment later when it received a sharp order.

"That will do," said the Headmaster. "Boys will at once go to their class-rooms. This matter is happily ended, and we rejoice that Clive Darrell is still amongst us, an honoured member of Ranleigh."

There was amazement on all faces. Obedient to the order the School at once filed out of the Hall, while questions shot from one boy to another. Susanne went off arm in arm with Masters. Trendall followed our hero, while the latter actually stepped up to Rawlings and took his arm.

"Come on, old chap," he said kindly. "Let's be going. The Head has dismissed the School."

The fellow was dazed. Anyone who had taken the trouble to watch him almost from the commencement of this business would have noticed that Rawlings stood as one in a dream. He seemed unable to follow the discussion taking place on the dais. His eyes were staring, his mouth half open, while his gaze was fixed on Clive Darrell, and now he was babbling and grinning in extraordinary fashion. They led him gently from the Hall to the sick-room, where the doctor was soon in attendance, and that afternoon the School had another sensation. Rawlings had lost his senses. He had become insane, and was no longer responsible for his actions. More than that, it was he who had set fire so often to the school premises, and with the cunning of one who is insane had managed so long to elude his comrades. And now his curious behaviour of late came to be understood. Fellows wondered why they had not noticed his strange ways, his taciturnity and silence. They were, in fact, the early symptoms of the misfortune which had attacked him. Clive, however, was destined to learn more of this extraordinary matter. It appeared, indeed, that for some while Rawlings had been troubled with home matters. Somehow he had discovered that his father was none too honest, and, in fact, had committed a forgery. That act had enabled him to become possessed of the estate which had once been Clive Darrell's father's. And the antipathy which Rawlings had from the first taken to our hero had persuaded him to put aside this most important discovery. But he was not all bad. The fear of a downfall, of loss of dignity, and of poverty had encouraged him to make the utmost of the benefits which his father's fraud had provided at the expense of Clive's people. And then his better nature and his conscience swayed him in an opposite direction. What was he to do? Expose his own father? Bring ruin on him and disgrace, with a long sentence of imprisonment? The responsibility of such a position can be well imagined. The youth was harassed. The matter preyed on his mind, and this breakdown was the result.

"It was rough on Rawlings," said Clive, when he talked the matter over with his old friends. "I'm sorry for him, awfully. And it's really lucky that the father died. Of course, we've come back to our own again. I'm glad for my mother's sake. But I'm sorry for Rawlings."

"And about that fire. You knew it was he?" asked Bert.

"Yes. I felt certain."

"And you wouldn't speak. Why?"

"Because I caught only a glimpse, and because I hated to be the one to ruin him."

That was the sort of spirit at Ranleigh. Perhaps not always employed wisely and in a right manner. But it did the School honour. At any rate, the boys were sufficiently satisfied with the honour and wisdom of Clive Darrell that they straightway elected him as King of Ranleigh.

The End